About the authors

Steve Biddle is a professional entertainer and Origami expert. He has been teaching Origami to children and adults since 1976. While he was in Japan studying under the top Japanese Origami Masters, he met and married his wife Megumi. Megumi is one of the foremost Japanese paper artists working in *Washi* hand-made Japanese paper, and her work has received many top awards in Japan and abroad. She has designed for some of Japan's top fashion designers, and has worked on many award-winning commercials for Japanese television. Since their return to England, Steve and Megumi have taken their craft all over the country to schools, festivals and arts centres, and have designed for television and feature films. They present Origami as entertainment, art and education to young and old alike.

Also available in Red Fox
by Steve and Megumi Biddle

Things to Make in the Holidays
Newspaper Magic
The Paint and Print Fun Book
Magical String
Amazing Flying Objects

AMAZING ORIGAMI FOR CHILDREN

Steve and Megumi Biddle

Illustrations by Megumi Biddle

RED FOX

A Red Fox Book
Published by Random House Children's Books
20 Vauxhall Bridge Road, London SW1V 2SA

A division of Random House UK Ltd
London Melbourne Sydney Auckland
Johannesburg and agencies throughout the world

Red Fox edition 1990
Reprinted in 1994

Set in Palatino
by JH Graphics Ltd, Reading

Printed in China

RANDOM HOUSE UK Limited Reg. No. 954009

ISBN 0 09 966180 2

Contents

Acknowledgements 6
Introduction 7

Paper sizes *Traditional* 8
Paper hat *Traditional* 10
Origami card *Traditional* 11
Envelope *Steve Biddle* 12
Butterfly *Traditional* 13
Flower and leaves *Traditional* 14
Crab *Toshio Chino* 16
Penguin *Steve Biddle* 18
Gift box *Traditional* 19
Fancy box *Traditional* 21
House with a chimney *Satoshi Takagi* 23
Heart *Hiroshi Kumasaka* 24
Candy stick *Megumi Biddle* 25
Two-piece star *Traditional* 26
Sailing boat *Traditional* 28
Yacht *Traditional* 30
Vehicles (Lorry, Jeep & Car) *Masao Mizuno* 31
Pencil *Takenao Handa* 33
Rose and leaf *Seiryo Takekawa* 34
Party decorations *Megumi Biddle* 36
Animal faces *Traditional* 38
Animal body *Traditional* 41
Santa Claus *Masao Mizuno* 44
Christmas wreath *Minako Ishibashi* 46
Balloon decoration *Traditional* 48
Goldfish *Traditional* 50
Rabbit *Traditional* 51
Blow top *Traditional* 53
Fruit *Toshie Takahama* 55
Bananas *Hiroshi Kumasaka* 56
Shirt *Toshie Takahama* 58
Napkin boot *Traditional* 60
Napkin bunny *Steve Biddle* 62
Sweet dish *Traditional* 63
Yakko san/crown *Traditional* 65
Jumping frog *Traditional* 66
Water lily *Traditional* 69
Water lily leaf *Megumi Biddle* 71
Talking crow *Makoto Yamaguchi* 72
Koron-koron *Isamu Asahi* 74
Rolling ball *Isamu Asahi* 77
Skittles *Isamu Asahi* 79
Flapping bird *Traditional* 80
Crane *Traditional* 83
Pop-up star *Traditional* 85
Cat *Toshie Takahama* 87
Jewel unit fold *Toshie Takahama* 90
Coaster *Traditional* 91
Decorative cube *Traditional* 92
Pop-up jewel *Toshie Takahama* 93
Multiplex challenge *Traditional* 95

Acknowledgements

We would lilke to thank the following members of the Nippon Origami Association for sharing their ideas with us: Isamu Asahi, Toshio Chino, Takenao Handa, Minako Ishibashi, Hiroshi Kumasaka, Masao Mizuno, Satoshi Takagi, Toshie Takahama, Seiryo Takekawa and Makoto Yamaguchi.

Also our deepest thanks go to Takuma Kuroiwa, Manager of the Nippon Origami Association.

Introduction

Welcome to the amazing world of Origami – the art of paper folding. If you have been watching our television series called *Origami with Steve and Megumi* then you already know how fascinating origami can be, and how with just a few pieces of paper you can fold many wonderful items. This book will teach you some of the traditional folds as well as many new ones. Do not panic if you have problems with your first few attempts. Check the illustration to see what has to be done. Look at the next illustration to see what shape your paper should make as the result of the step you are following. Also remember that the arrows show the direction in which the paper has to be folded. So look very carefully at the illustrations to see which way the arrows go over, through, and under, and fold your paper accordingly. To help you become accomplished at paper folding, here are some very helpful tips:

- Fold on a flat surface, such as a table or a book
- Make your folds straight and accurate
- Crease your folds by running your thumb nail along them
- Find a piece of paper that will be ideal for the particular model you are going to fold
- The shading represents the coloured side of the paper

We would very much like to hear from you concerning your interest in origami, or if you have any problems obtaining origami materials. So please write to us, care of our publishers, enclosing a stamped addressed envelope.

We do hope that you have a great deal of fun and enjoyment with *Amazing Origami for Children*.

Steve and Megumi

Paper sizes

Traditional

Many of the items to be found in *Amazing Origami for Children* start with a square of paper. So here is a quick and easy way to make one.

You will need:

Rectangle of paper, coloured on one side and white on the other
Scissors

1 Place the rectangle sideways on, with the coloured side on top. Fold the left-hand side up to meet the top, so making a triangle.

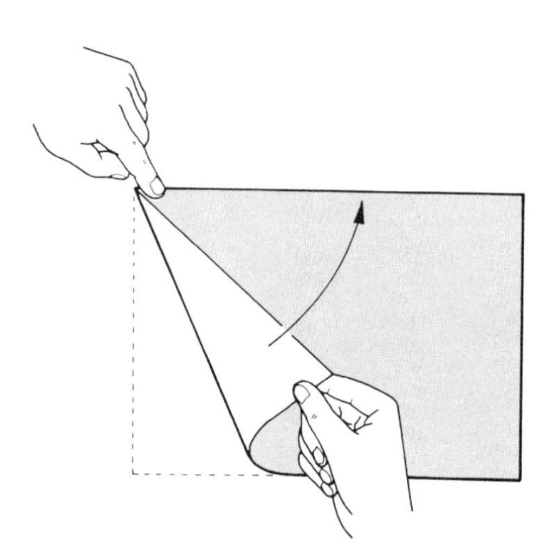

2 Cut along the side of the triangle. Discard the rectangular piece of paper.

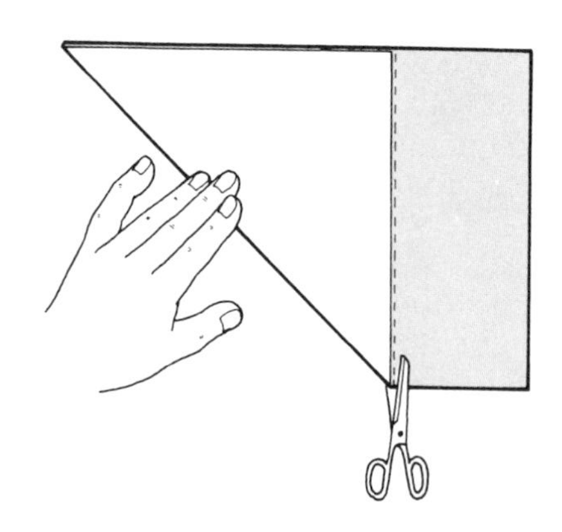

3 To complete, open out the triangle into a square.

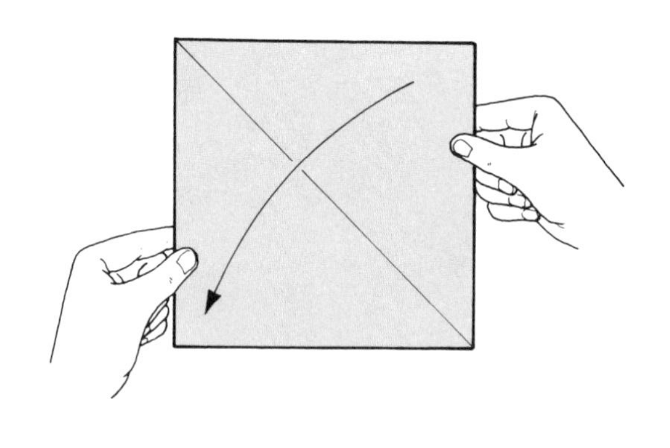

Sometimes it is very difficult to find a rectangular piece of paper that has straight and parallel sides, so making it very hard to fold a perfect square. Here is an ideal way to make a perfect square from such a piece of paper.

You will need:
Irregular-shaped piece of paper, coloured on one side and white on the other
Scissors

1 Place the irregular piece of paper on a flat surface, with the coloured side on top. Fold it in half from side to side.

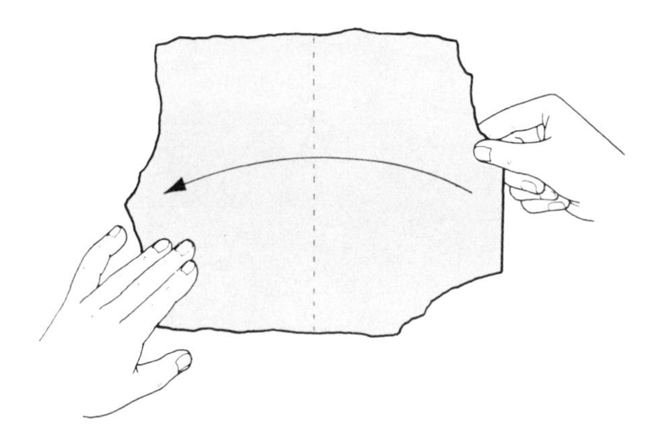

2 Fold it in half from bottom to top.

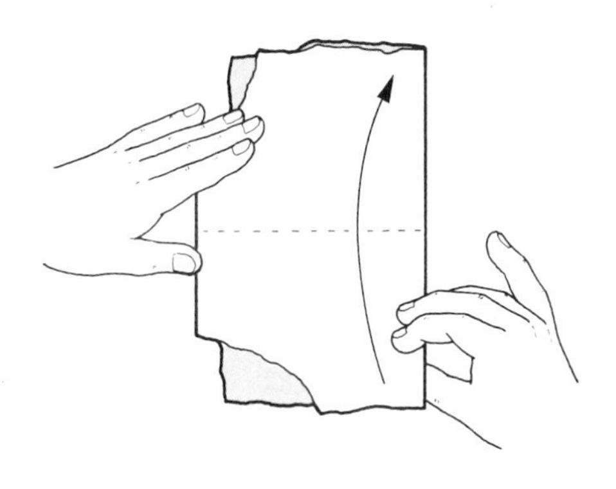

3 Fold the right-hand side down to meet the bottom. Press the paper flat and unfold it.

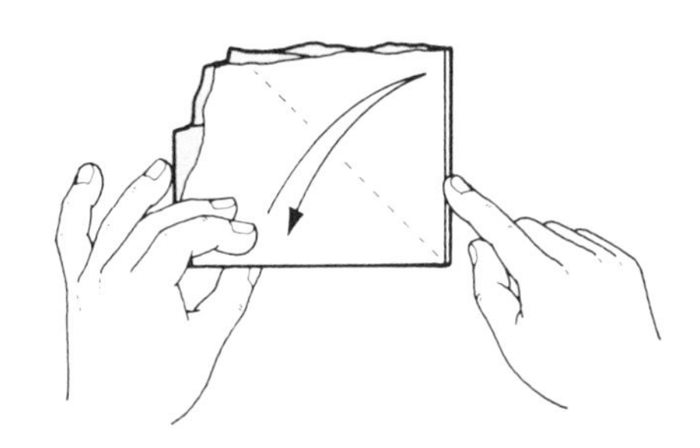

4 Fold the bottom right-hand point up to lie anywhere along the fold-line made in step 3 (how far you fold this point up will determine the final size of your square), so making a triangle. Cut along the sides of the triangle, being careful not to cut through the triangle's folded sides. Discard the remaining pieces of paper.

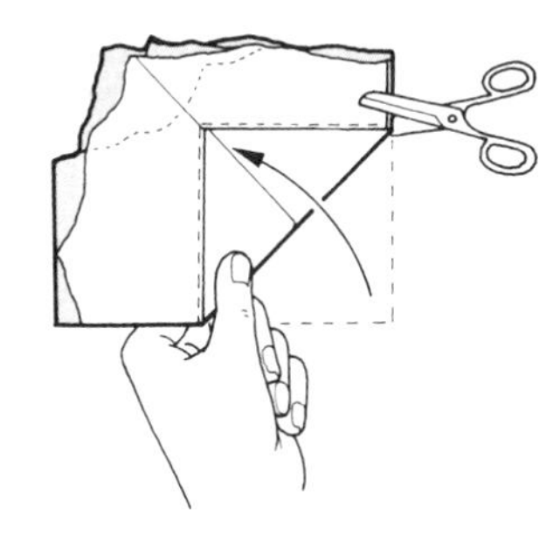

5 To complete, open out the triangle into a square. You will see many fold-lines in the square that will be useful later on.

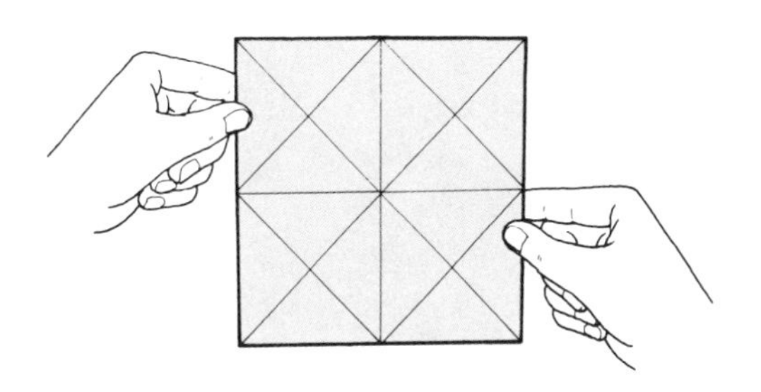

Paper hat

Traditional

Here is a very simple way to make a super hat. If made from a sheet of colourful gift paper it will become a great hat to wear at a party.

You will need:
Rectangle of paper, coloured on one side and white on the other
Scissors
Small rectangle of paper
Glue
Cocktail stick

1 Place the rectangle lengthways on, with the white side on top. Fold it in half from top to bottom.

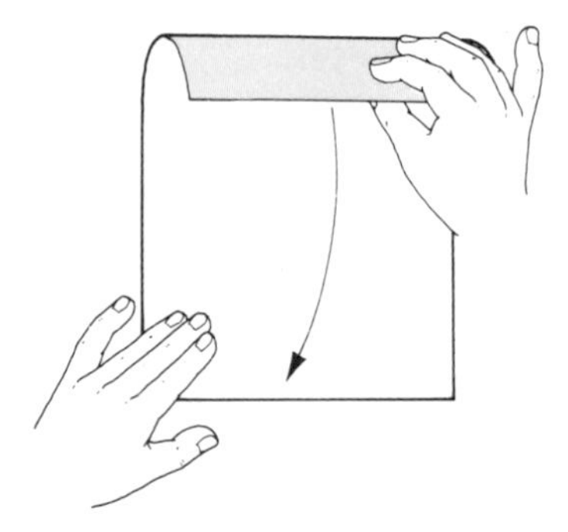

2 Fold and unfold it in half from side to side.

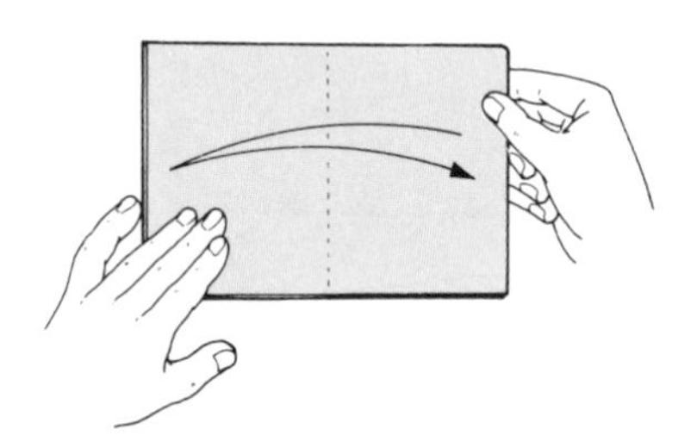

3 Fold the top corners down to meet the middle fold-line.

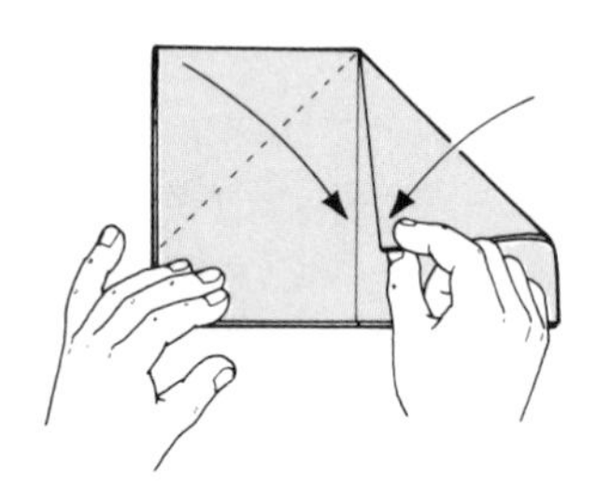

4 From the bottom, fold up the topmost layer of paper.

5 Turn the paper over. Repeat step 4.

6 Press the paper flat.

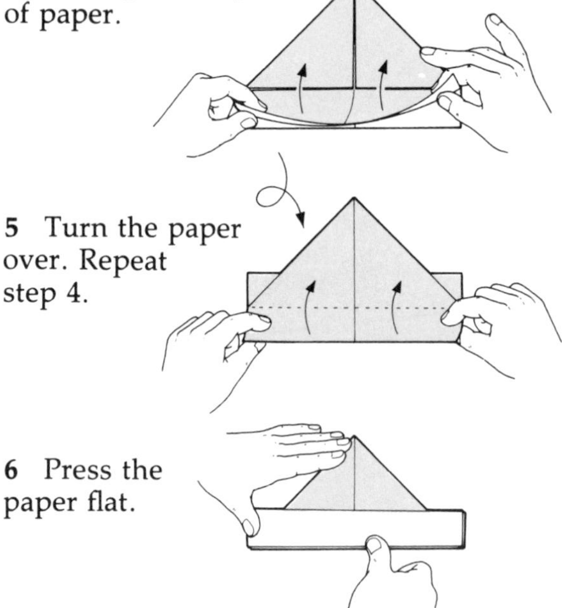

7 To make the plume decoration, roll the small rectangle of paper up into a tube. Cut slits into one end of the tube. Fluff out the ends of the strips. Glue the opposite end on to the hat.

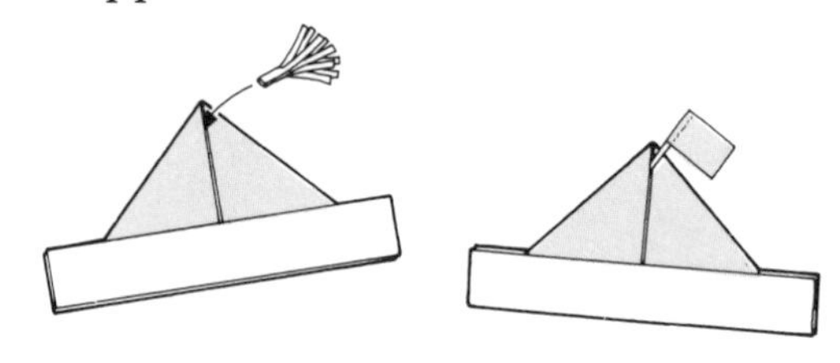

8 To make the flag decoration, cut out a flag from the small rectangle of paper, and glue it on to one end of a cocktail stick. Glue the opposite end on to the hat.

Origami card

Traditional

One of the many things that you can do with origami is to decorate your own stationery.

You will need: Rectangle of paper, about A4 in size, coloured on one side and white on the other Glue Miniature pieces of origami

1 Place the rectangle sideways on, with the white side on top. Fold it in half from top to bottom.

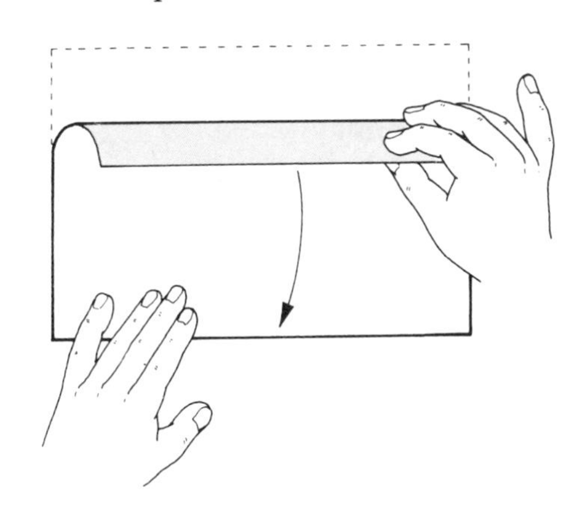

2 Fold it in half from side to side.

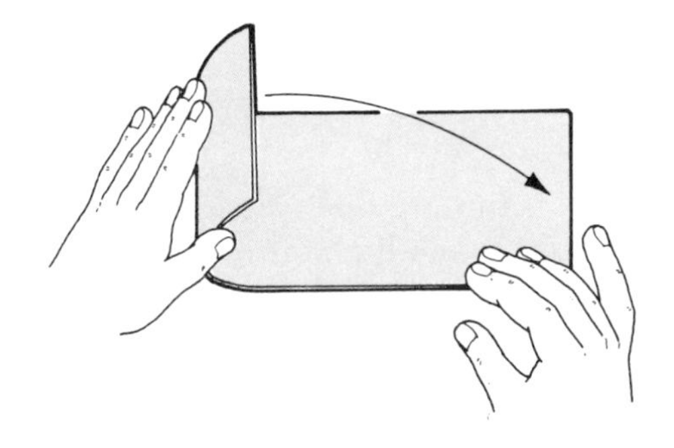

3 Press the paper flat.

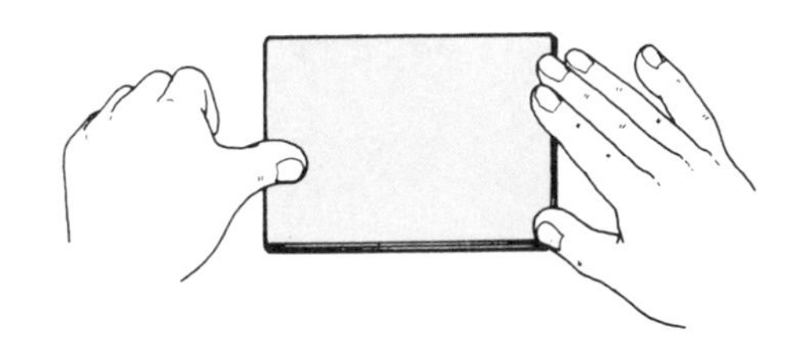

4 Decorate the front of the card by gluing on miniature pieces of origami.

Envelope

Steve Biddle

Here is a quick and easy way of making an envelope to match the origami card on page 11.

You will need:
Rectangle of paper, about A4 in size, coloured on one side and white on the other
Origami card (see page 11)
Glue

1 Place the rectangle lengthways on, with the white side on top. Fold in half from side to side. Press the paper flat and unfold it.

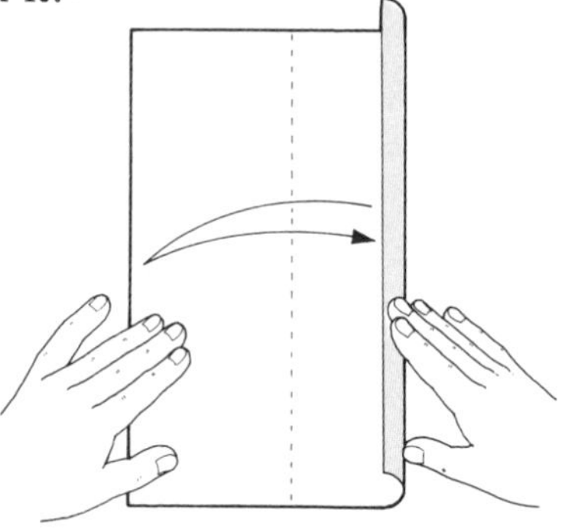

2 Fold the top corners down to meet the middle fold-line, so making a shape that looks like the roof of a house.

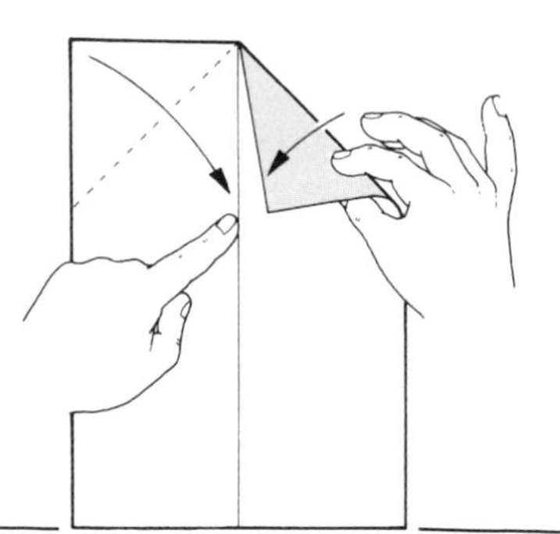

3 Lay the origami card centrally on the paper, underneath the roof. Fold the sides in and over the card.

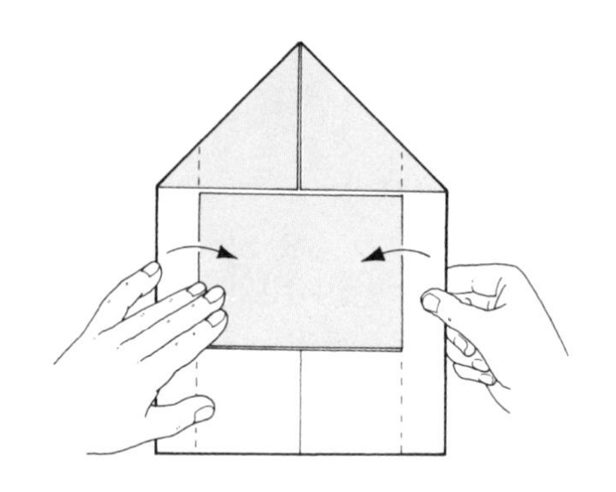

4 Fold the bottom up and over the card.

5 Fold the top point down and over the card.

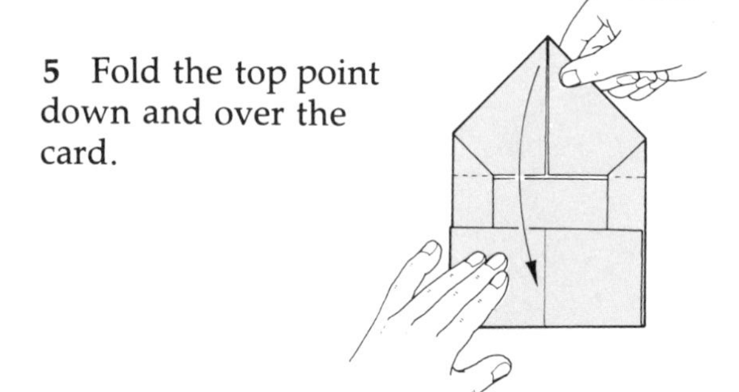

6 To send the envelope through the post, glue the top point down. Do not forget to address it and to stick on the stamp.

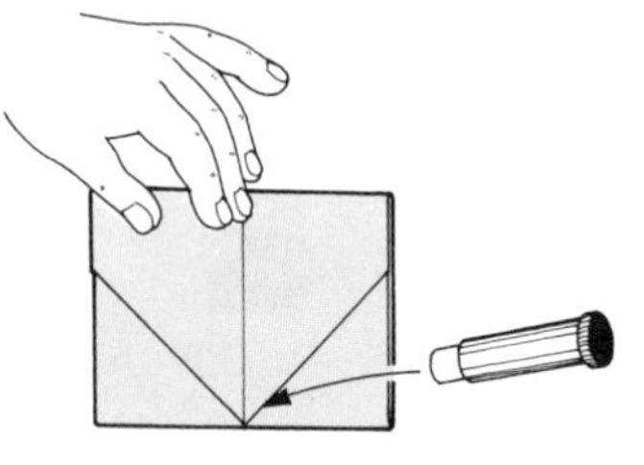

Butterfly

Traditional

With just three folds you can make a lovely simple butterfly.

You will need: Square of paper, coloured on one side and white on the other

1 Turn the square around to look like a diamond, with the white side on top. Fold it in half from side to side.

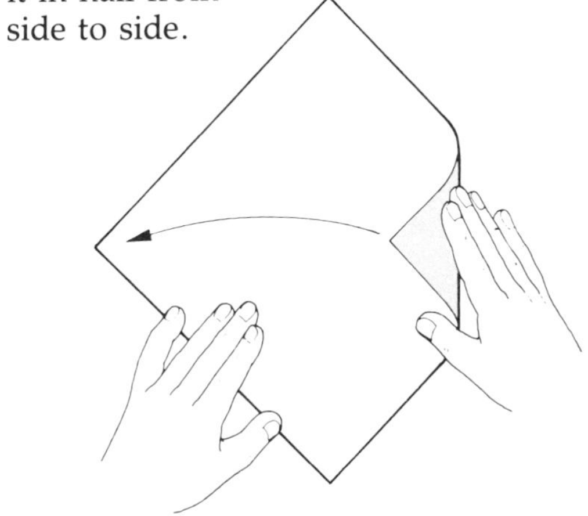

2 Fold the bottom point up to lie over the opposite sloping side.

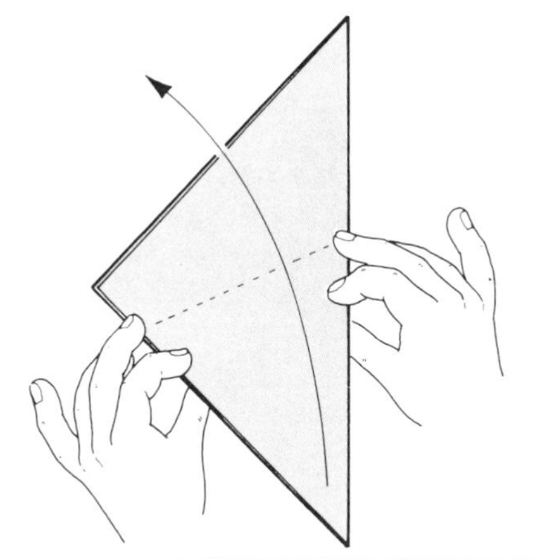

3 To complete, press the paper flat.

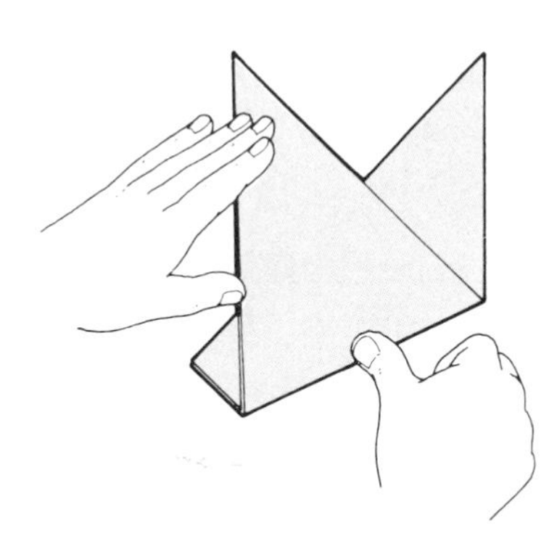

4 When made in miniature the butterfly is ideal for gluing on to an origami card. Try adding a few imaginative details with a felt-tip pen.

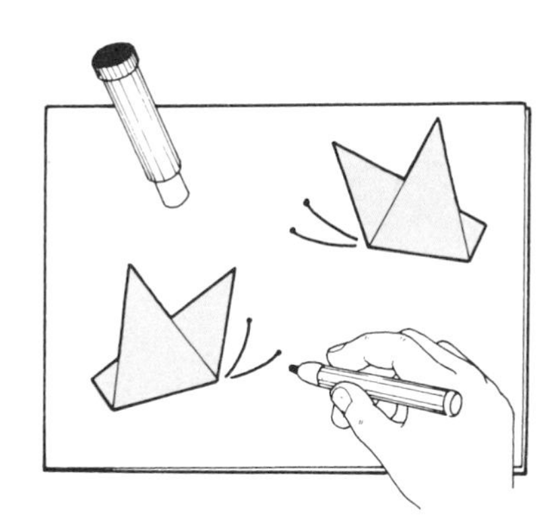

Flower and leaves

Traditional

Origami flowers and leaves look most beautiful when they are arranged in a vase or basket. They also make ideal gifts to give on special occasions.

You will need:
3 squares of paper all the same size, coloured on one side and white on the other (try using a colourful one for the flower and two green ones for the leaves)
Glue

1 *Flower:* Turn the colourful square around to look like a diamond, with the white side on top. Fold it in half from bottom to top, so making a triangle.

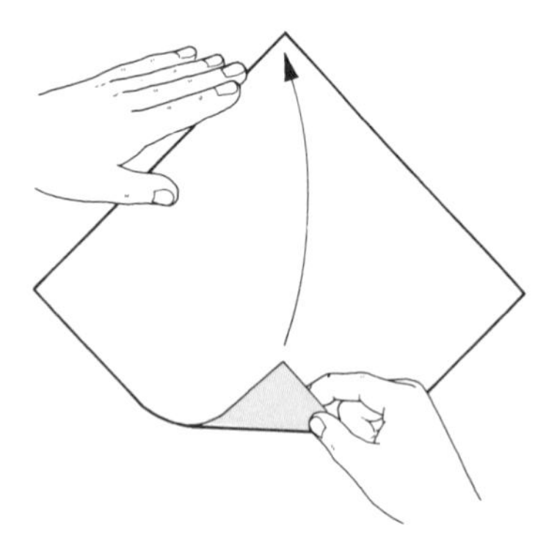

2 Fold and unfold the triangle in half from side to side, being careful to press the paper only a little at this bottom point.

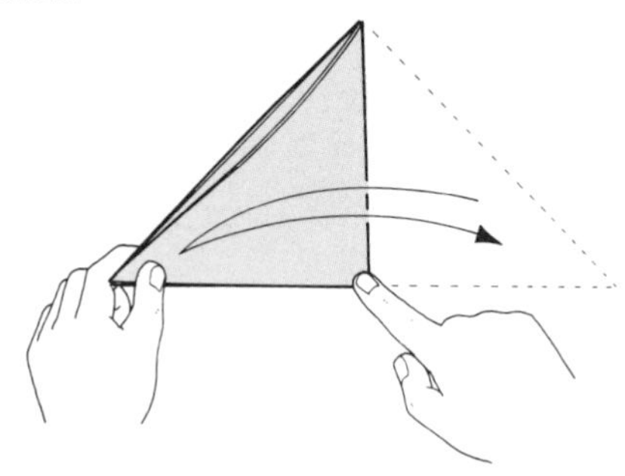

3 From the fold mark that you made in step 2, fold up one bottom point, so that it lies over the sloping side next to it.

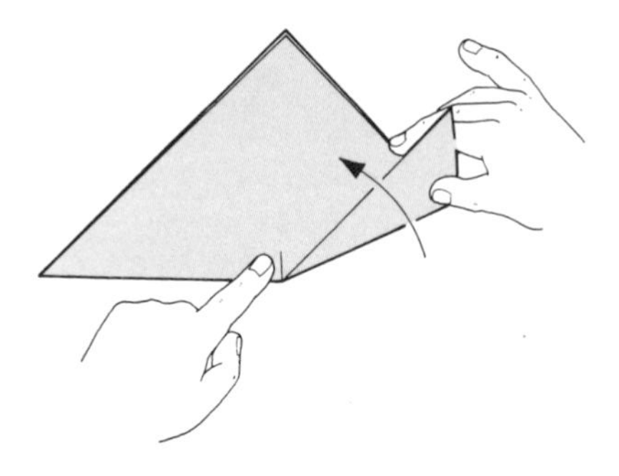

4 To complete the flower, repeat step 3 with the remaining bottom point.

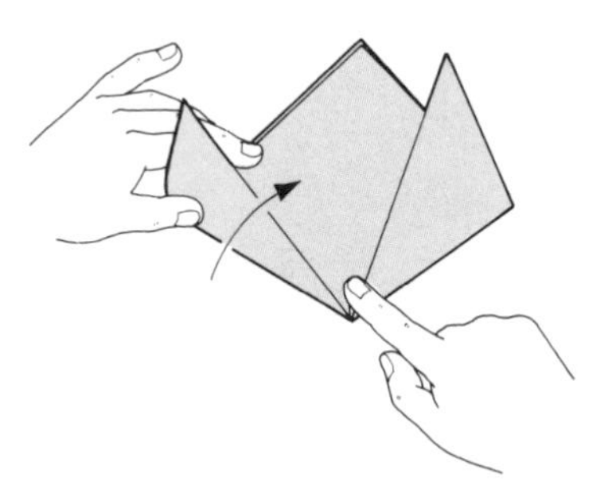

5 *Leaf:* Turn one green square around to look like a diamond, with the white side on top. Fold and unfold it in half from side to side.

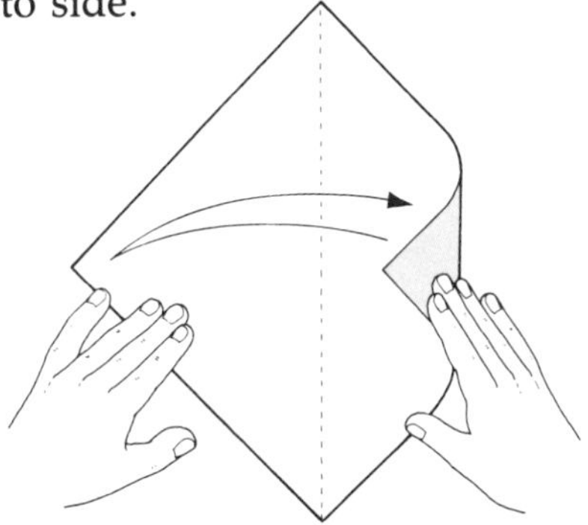

6 From the top point, fold the sloping sides in to meet the middle fold-line, so making a shape that in origami is called the kite base.

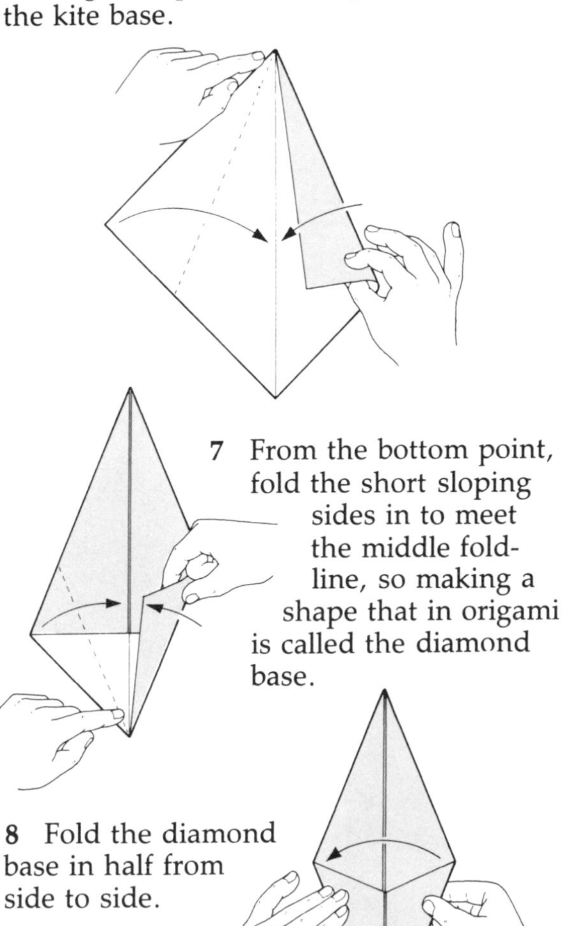

7 From the bottom point, fold the short sloping sides in to meet the middle fold-line, so making a shape that in origami is called the diamond base.

8 Fold the diamond base in half from side to side.

9 Repeat steps 5 to 8 with the remaining square, so making a second leaf. Tuck one leaf inside the other.

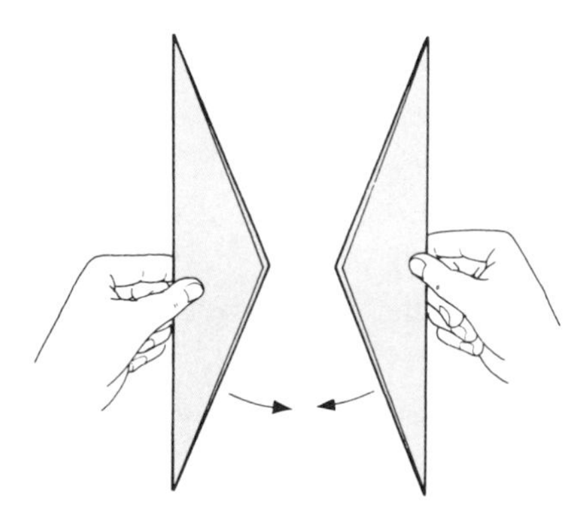

10 Glue the leaves together. To complete, glue on the flower.

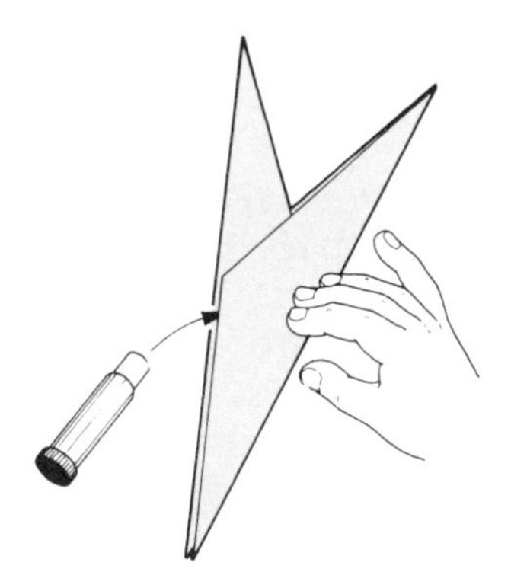

11 When made in miniature the flower and leaves are ideal for gluing on to an origami card.

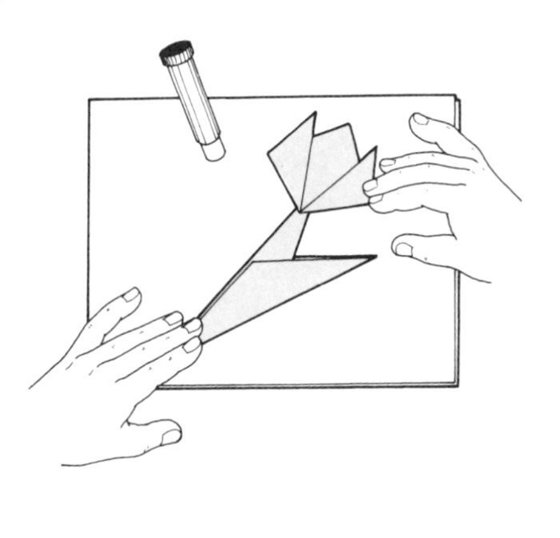

Crab

Toshio Chino

This figure is a perfect example of how, with just a few folds, you can make a complex looking piece of origami.

You will need:
2 squares of paper the same size, coloured on one side and white on the other
Glue

1 Fold each square into a diamond base (see steps 5 to 7 on page 15).

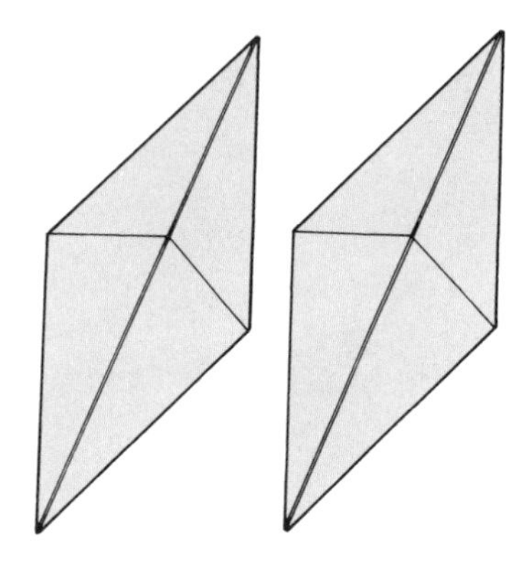

2 To make the legs, place one diamond base sideways on. Fold and unfold it in half from point to point.

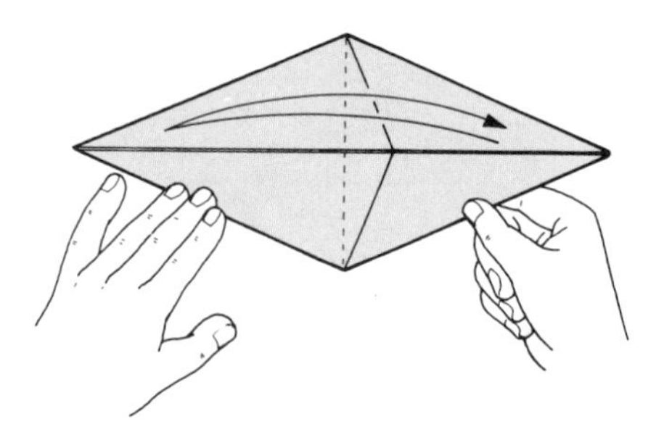

3 Fold the points in to meet the middle.

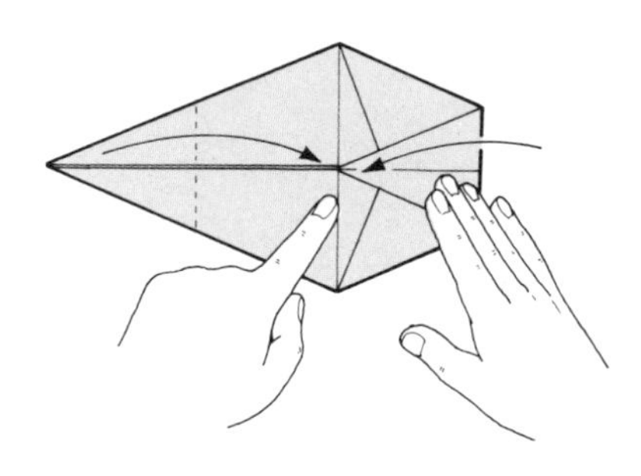

4 Fold it in half from top to bottom.

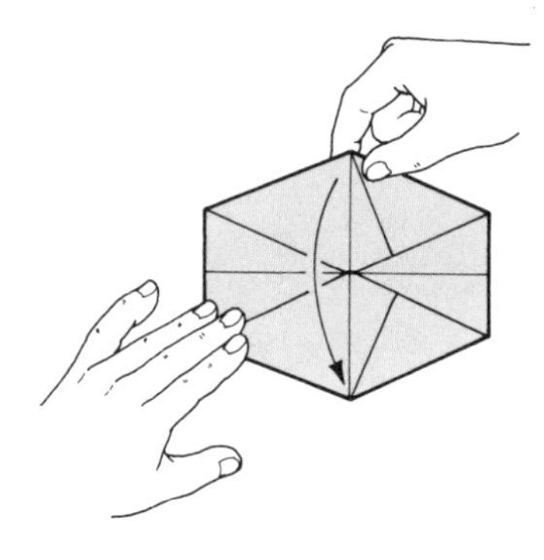

5 Pull the points out from the inside and press them flat . . .

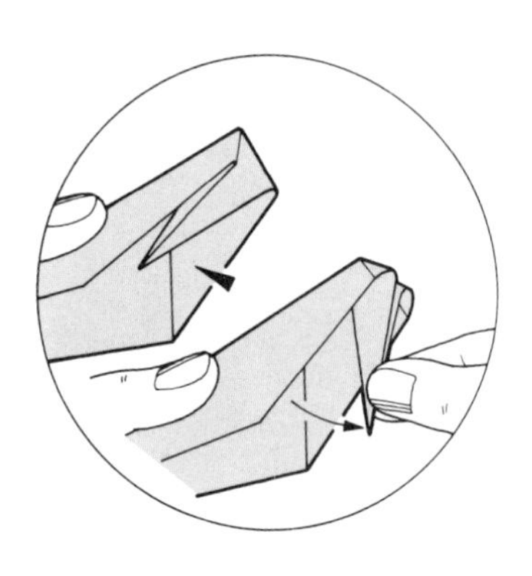

6 into this position, so completing the crab's legs.

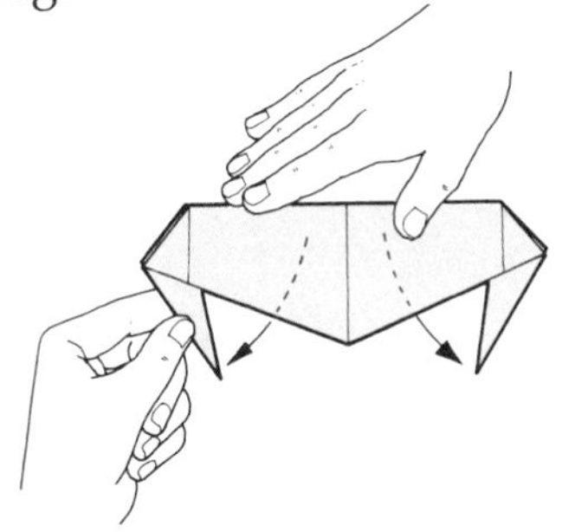

7 To make the body, turn the remaining diamond base over and place it sideways on. Fold the right-hand point over one-third of the way.

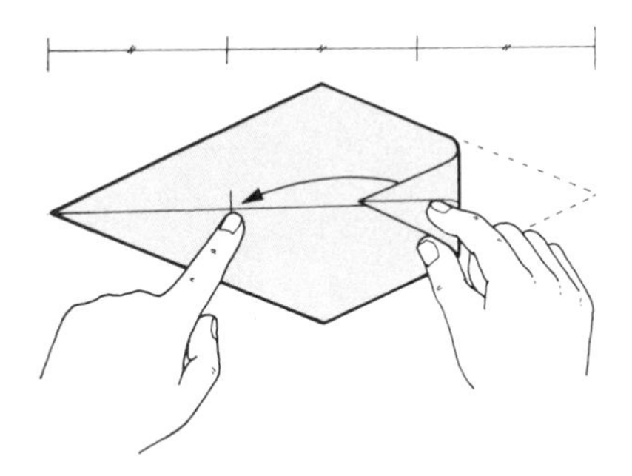

8 Repeat step 7 with the left-hand point.

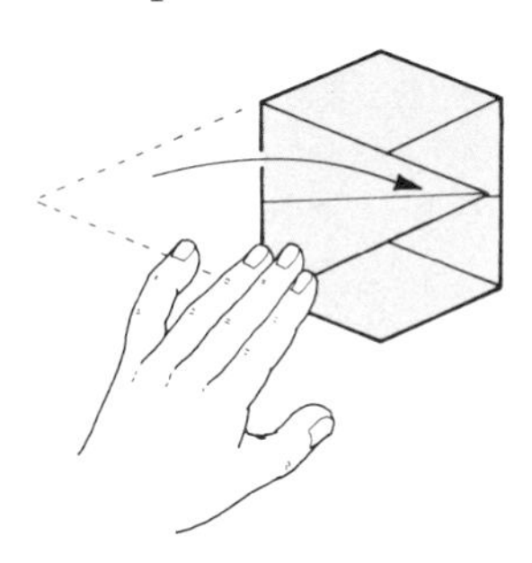

9 Turn the paper over. Fold it in half from top to bottom.

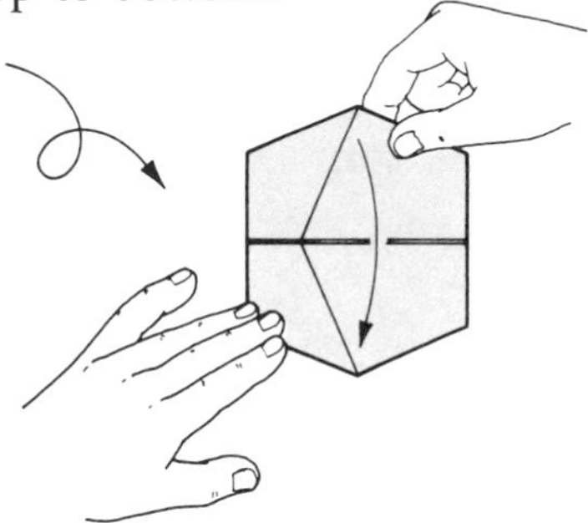

10 Pull the topmost point upwards and press it flat into the position as shown by the dotted lines.

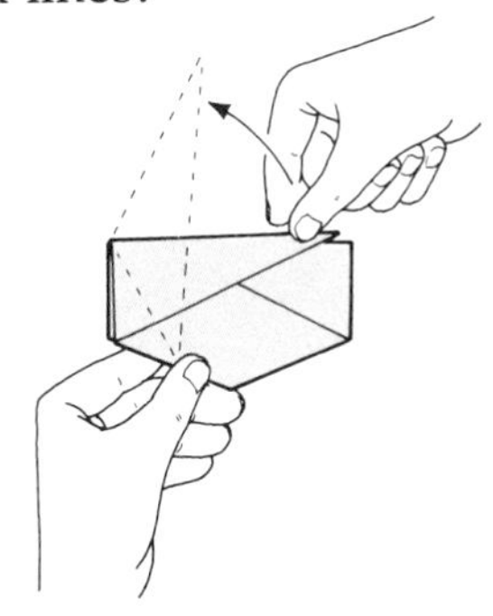

11 Repeat step 10 with the remaining point, so completing the crab's body.

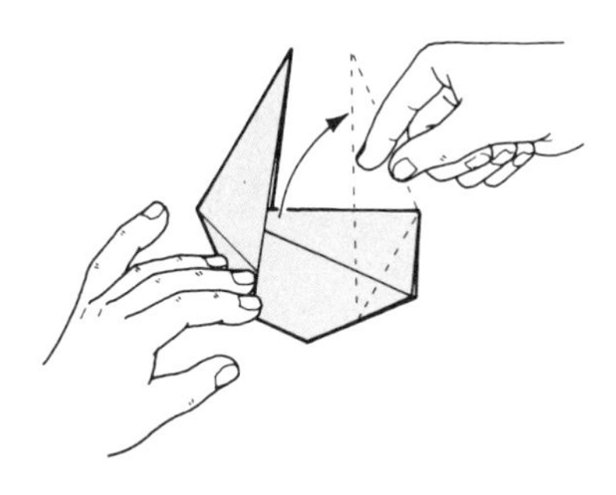

12 To complete, tuck the legs inside the body. Glue them both together. When made in miniature the crab looks very lifelike and is ideal for gluing on to an origami card. Try adding a few details, such as its eyes, with a felt-tip pen.

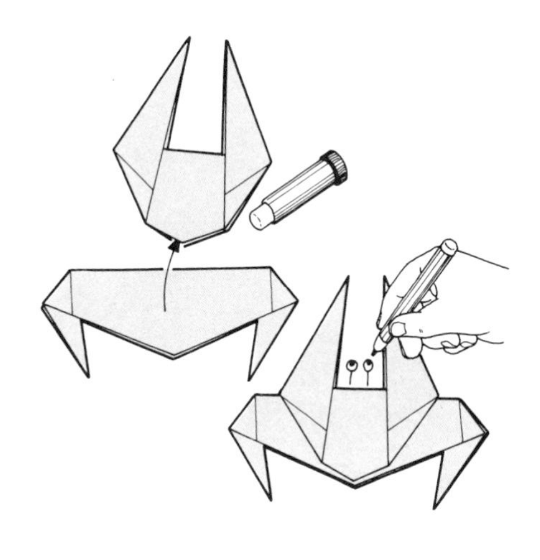

Penguin

Steve Biddle

Origami folds look most effective when they are displayed together. So why not try making a display of penguins.

You will need:
Square of paper, black on one side and white on the other

1 Turn the square around to look like a diamond, with the coloured side on top. Fold it in half from side to side.

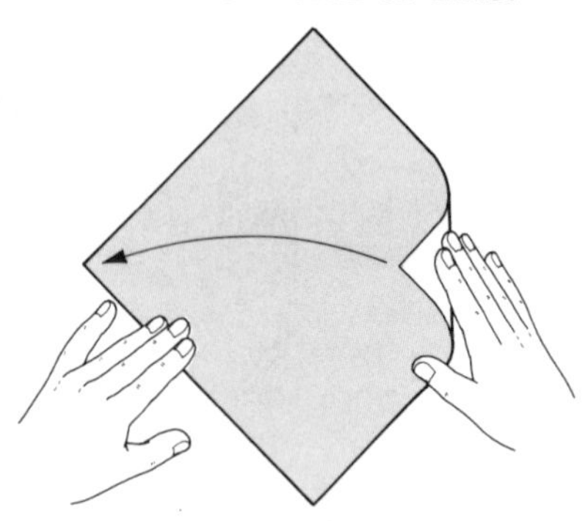

2 From the top point, fold the topmost layer of paper over towards, but *not* to meet, the folded side.

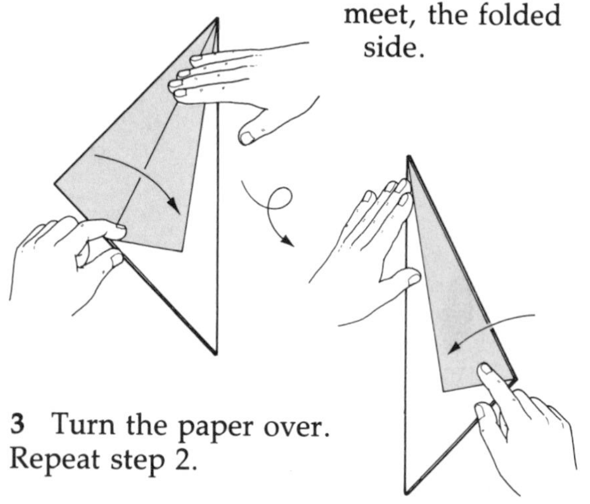

3 Turn the paper over. Repeat step 2.

4 Unfold the paper into this position. Fold the top point down into the position as shown by the dotted lines, so making the penguin's head.

5 Turn the paper over. Fold the bottom point up as shown.

6 Fold it in half from side to side.

7 Holding the penguin as shown, pull its head upwards, so it becomes free and sticks out from the folded side.

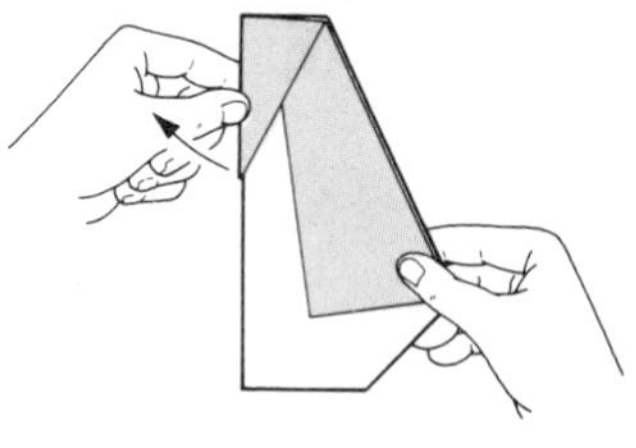

8 To complete, press the top of the penguin's head flat. Try folding a baby penguin from a small square of paper, or a larger penguin from a bigger piece of paper.

Gift box

Traditional

The following origami fold can be made from any rectangle of paper, whatever its size. Made out of fancy gift paper it makes an ideal gift box for a very special present.

You will need:
Rectangle of paper, coloured on one side and white on the other

1 Place the rectangle sideways on, with the white side on top. Fold it in half from side to side.

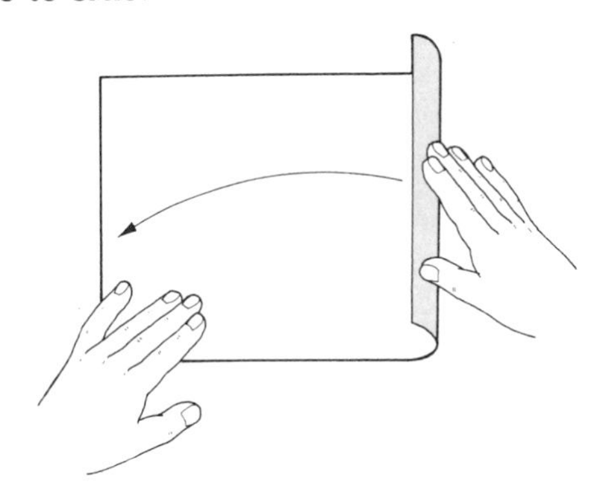

2 Fold and unfold it in half from bottom to top.

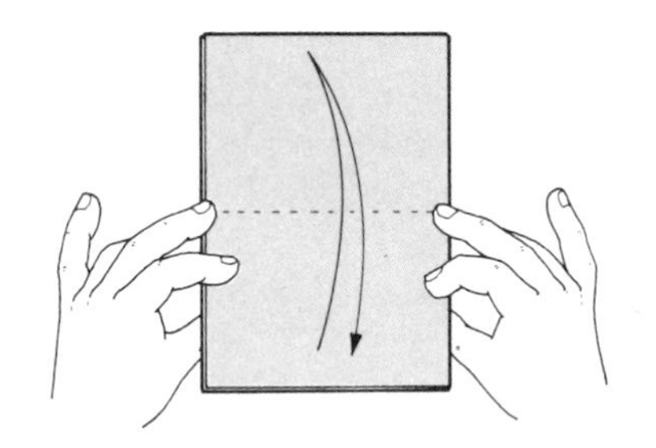

3 Fold the bottom and top in to meet the middle fold-line.

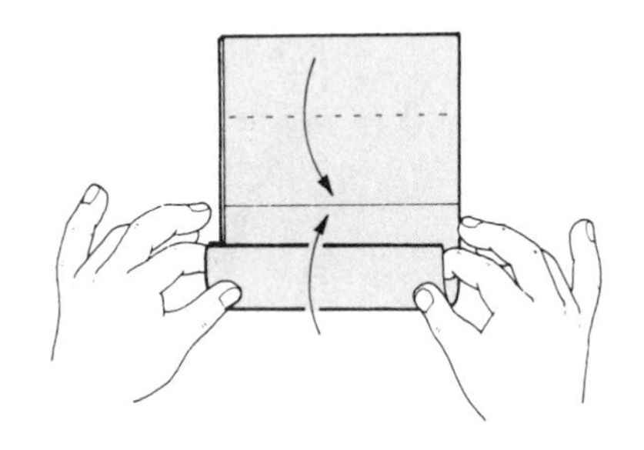

4 Open out the paper completely, back to step 1.

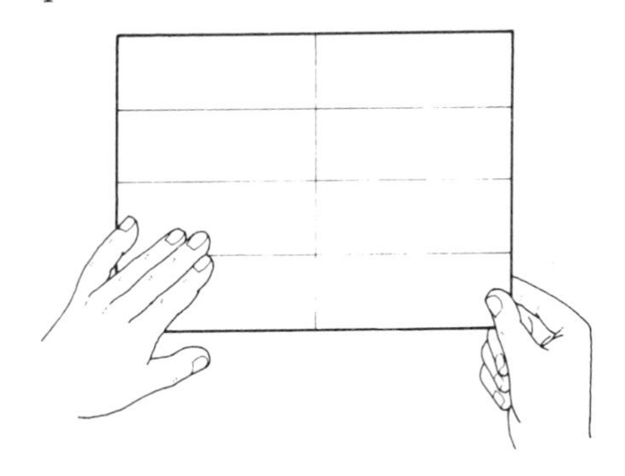

5 Fold the sides in to meet the middle fold-line.

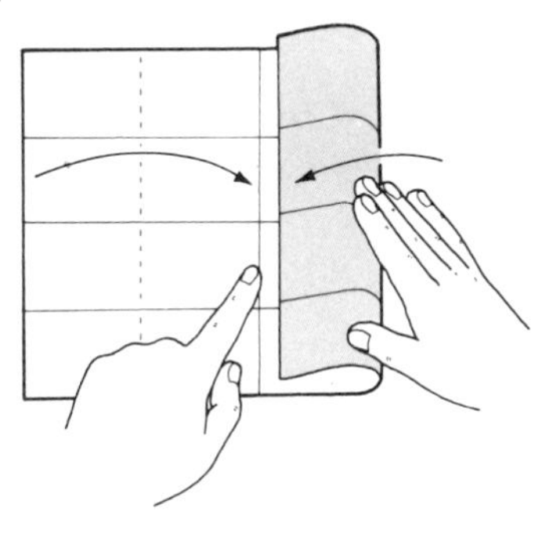

6 Fold one corner in to meet the fold-line nearest to it.

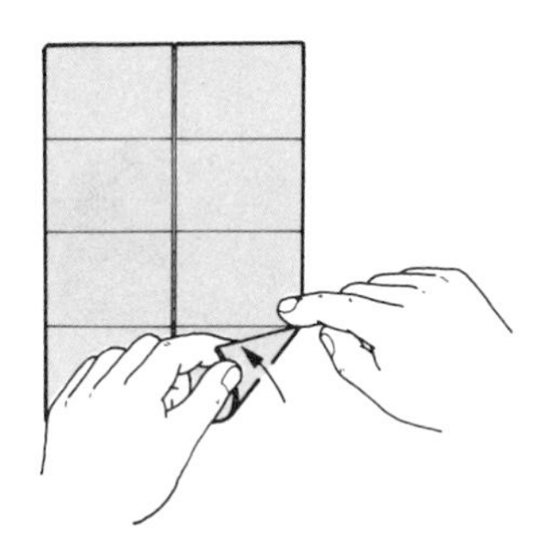

7 Repeat step 6 with the remaining corners.

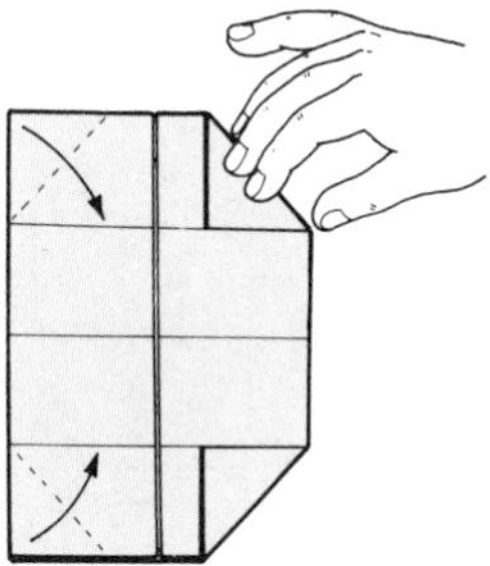

8 This should be your finished result.

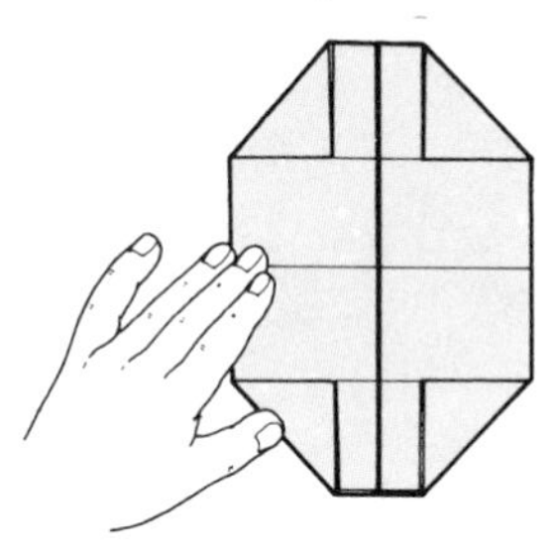

9 From the middle, fold over as far as possible one single layer of paper.

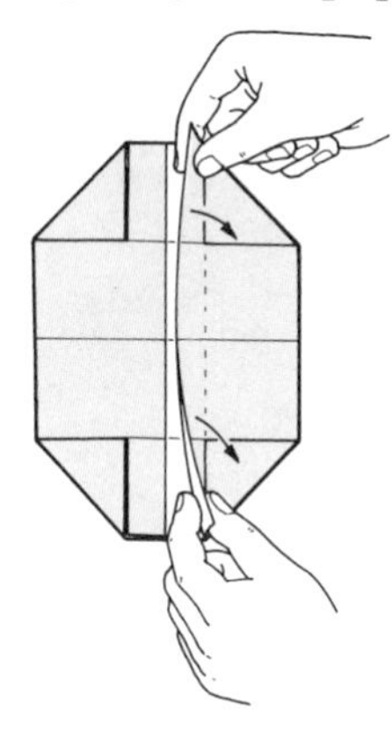

10 Repeat step 9 with the remaining single layer of paper.

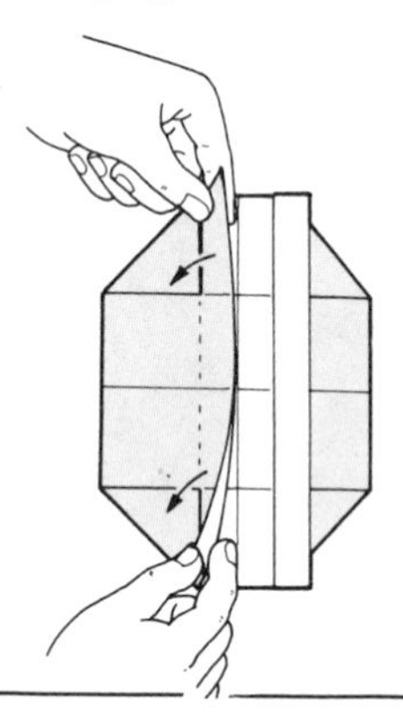

11 Put your fingers inside the paper.

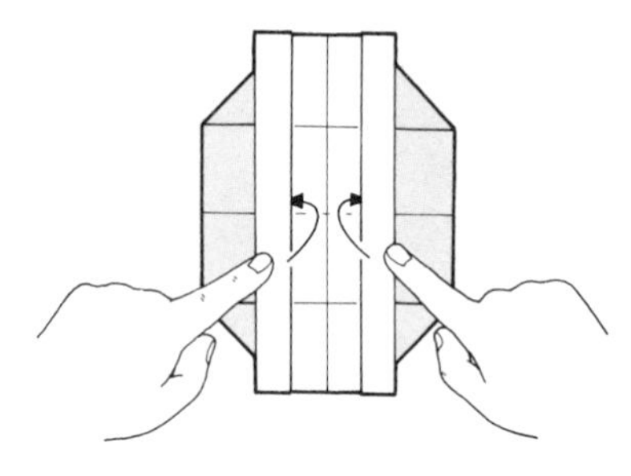

12 Gently pull your hands apart.

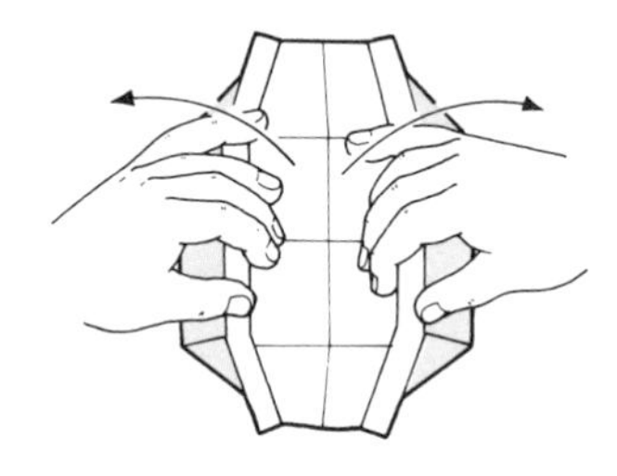

13 The paper will start to open out into a box.

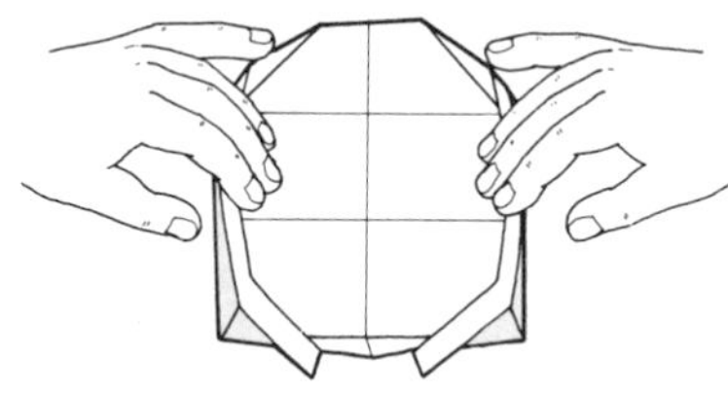

14 Pinch the corners and sides of the box together, so making it firm and strong.

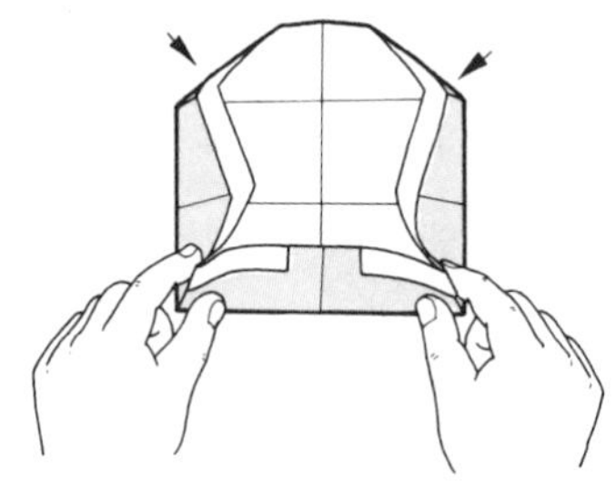

15 Now you have the completed gift box. By starting with a slightly larger rectangle of paper and following the folding steps from 1 to 14, you will be able to make a lid.

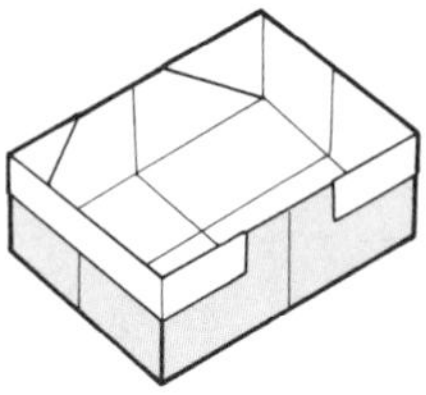

Fancy box

Traditional

This origami fold is ideal as a desk tidy container, as it can hold all those drawing pins, paper clips and rubber bands that you might just have lying around.

You will need:
Rectangle of paper, about A4 in size, coloured on one side and white on the other

1 Place the rectangle lengthways on, with the white side on top. Fold and unfold it in half from side to side.

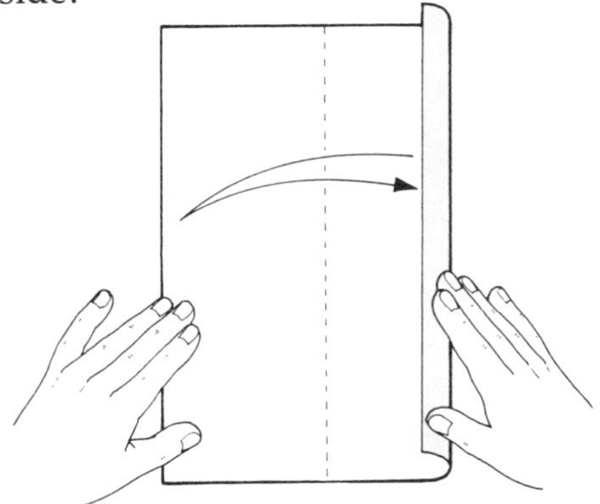

2 Fold the corners in to meet the middle fold-line.

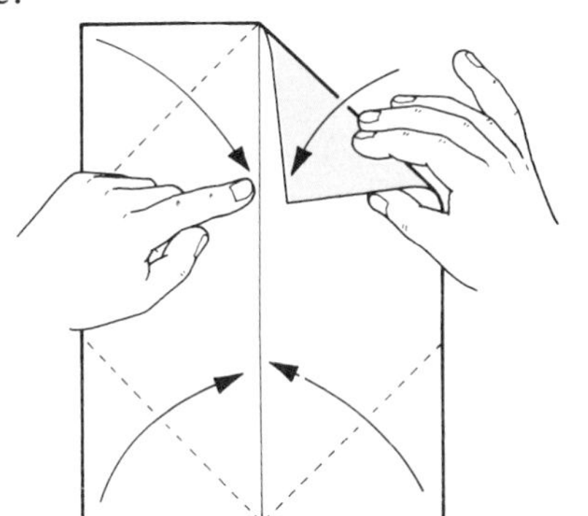

3 Fold it in half from bottom to top.

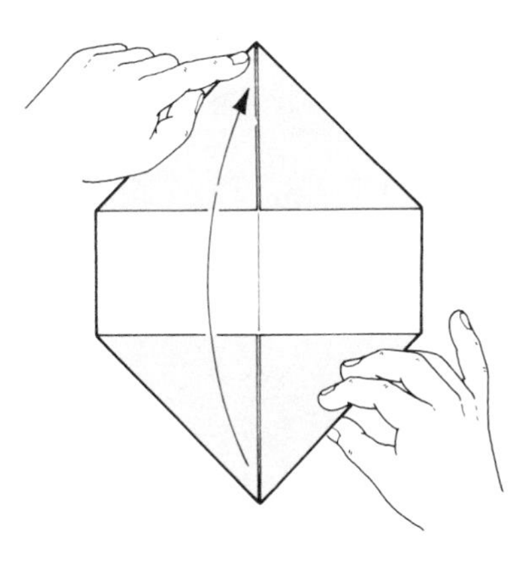

4 Fold the topmost point down to meet the bottom.

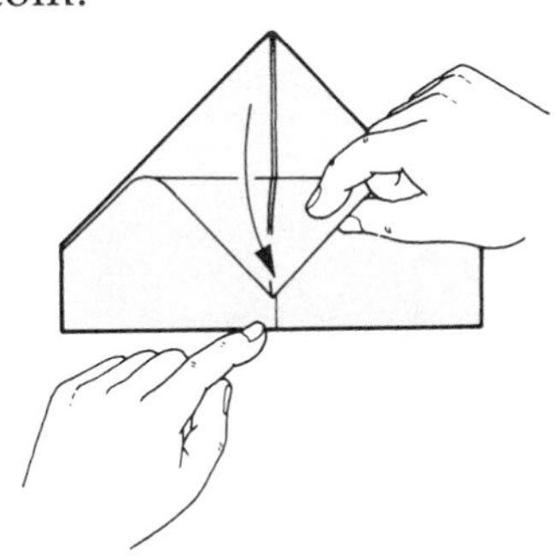

5 Turn the paper over. Fold the bottom points up as shown, so making two small triangles.

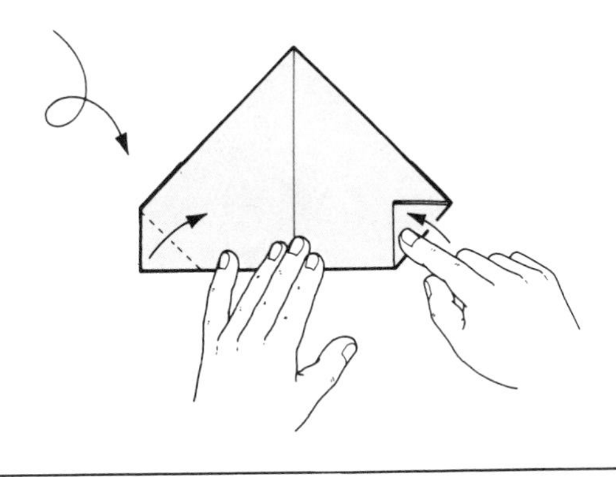

6 Fold the side points in.

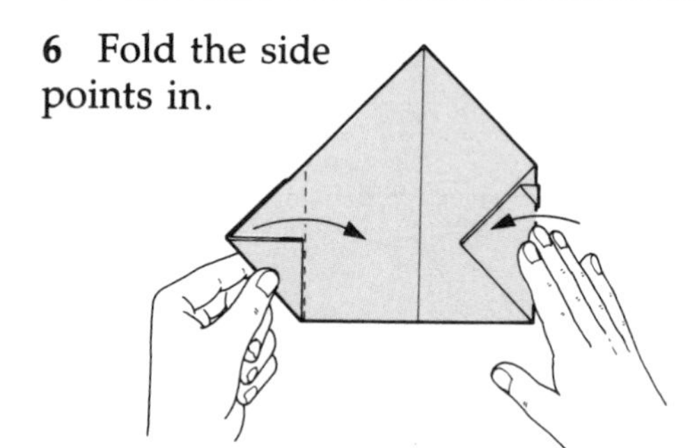

7 Repeat step 4.

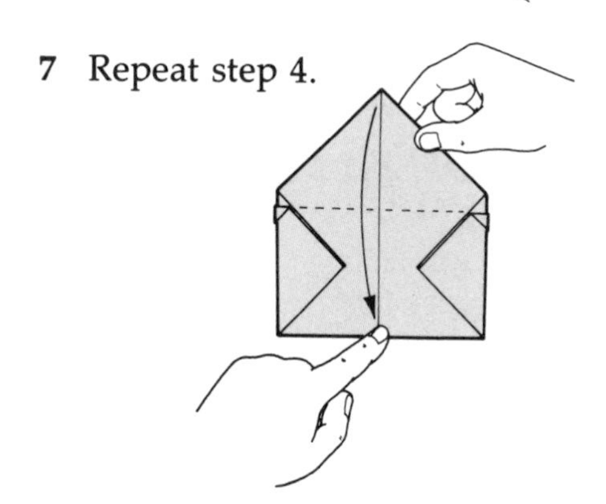

8 From the top, put your fingers in between the layers of paper. From the inside, begin to open out the fancy box.

9 With your free hand, push the bottom of the box upwards, so that on the inside you make a diagonal centre division.

10 Here is the completed fancy box.

11 If you make a fancy box out of a rectangle of white paper, and turn it upside down . . .

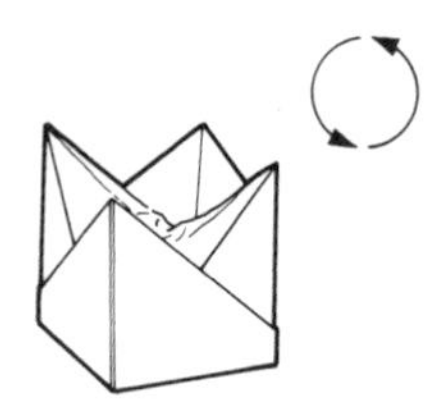

12 you will have a perfect iceberg for the penguin display. The other iceberg is an upside-down gift box (see page 19).

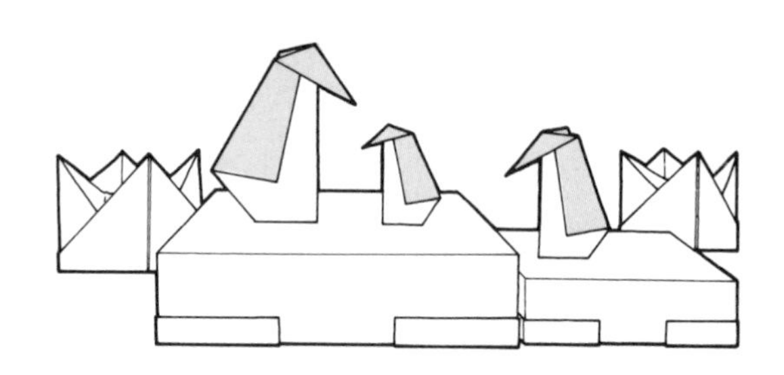

House with a chimney

Satoshi Takagi

Once you have learned how to make a few origami folds, why not share them with your friends, teaching them how to fold origami.

You will need:
Square of paper, coloured on one side and white on the other

1 Fold and unfold the square in half from side to side, with the white side on top.

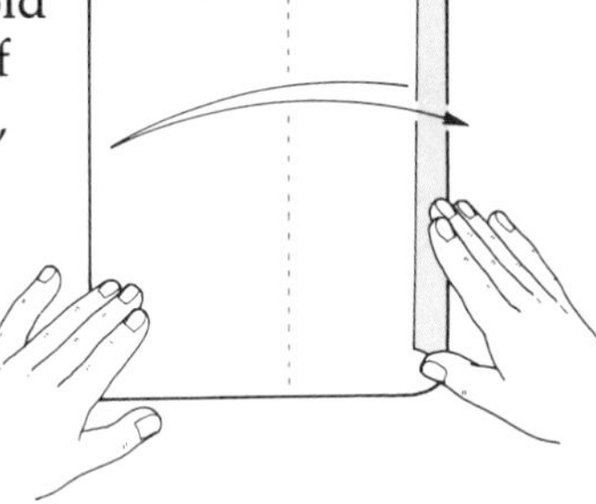

2 Fold the top corners down to meet the middle fold-line.

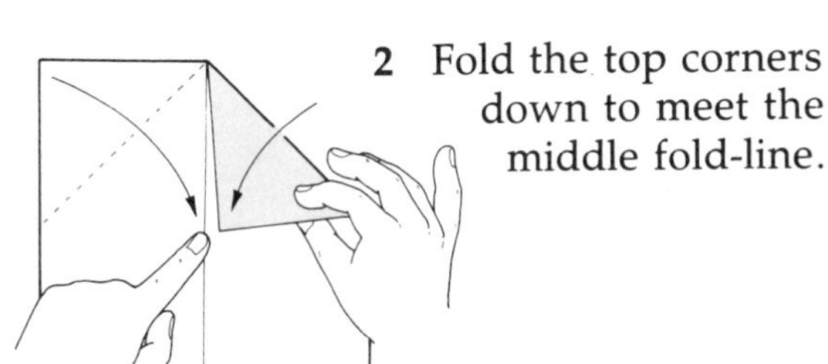

3 To give the impression of a chimney, fold a corner out from the middle into the position as shown by the dotted lines.

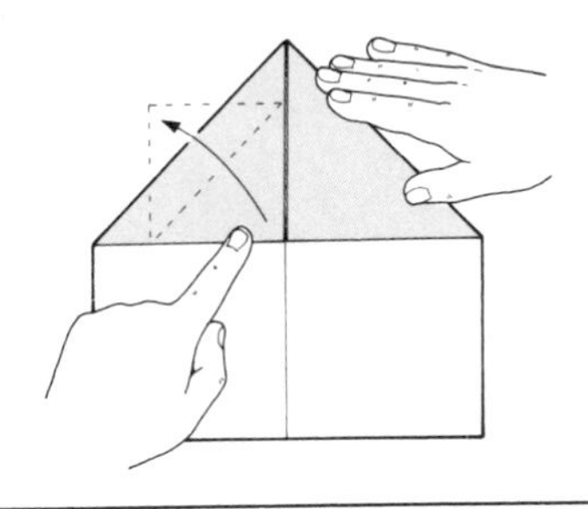

4 Fold the paper in half from bottom to top.

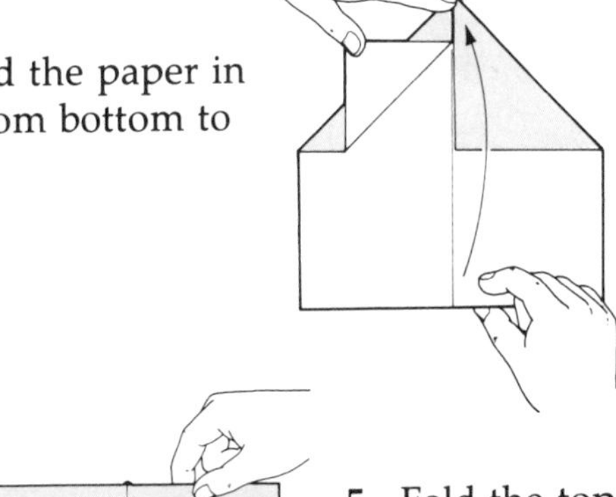

5 Fold the top layer of paper down, so making a small pleat.

6 Fold the sides in. At the same time press the triangular side pockets down neatly.

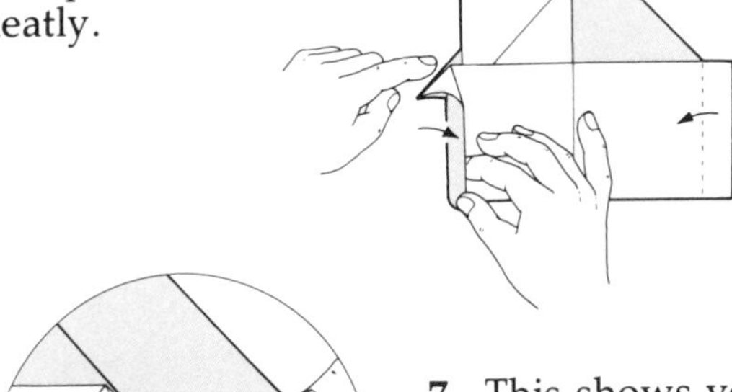

7 This shows you step 6 in more detail.

8 To complete the house, turn the paper over from side to side.

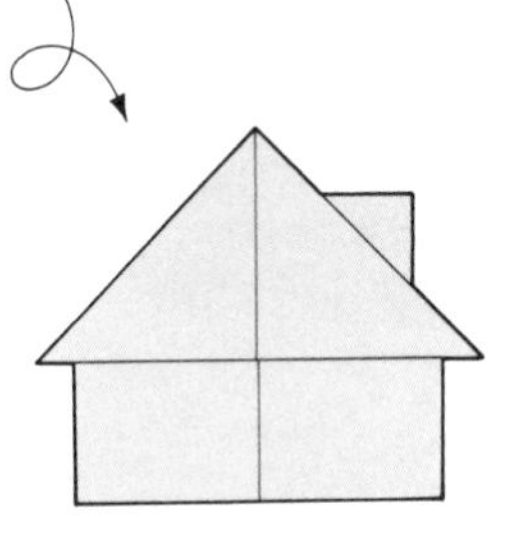

Heart

Hiroshi Kumasaka

The folding of origami is a great way to spend a rainy afternoon or to keep you occupied on a long train or plane journey. This fold makes an ideal table place card or name card if tucked into a top pocket.

You will need:
Square of paper, red on one side and white on the other

1 Fold and unfold the square in half from side to side, with the white side on top.

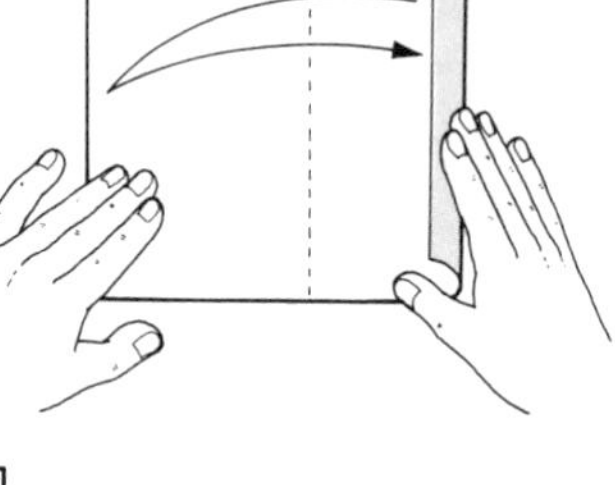

2 Fold over a little of each bottom corner.

3 Now fold what is left of each bottom corner up to meet the middle fold-line.

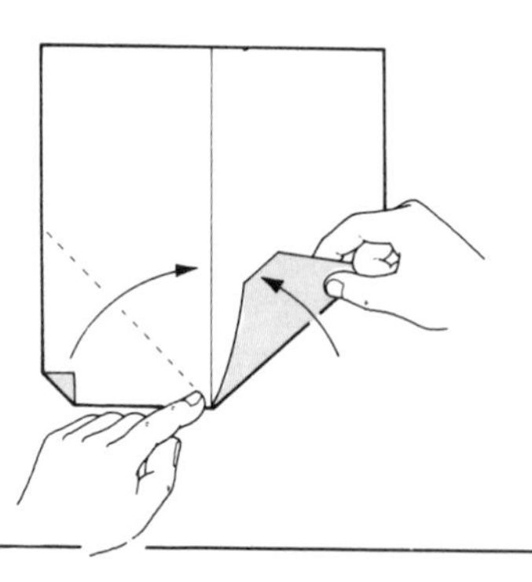

4 Turn the paper over. Fold the sides in to meet the middle fold-line.

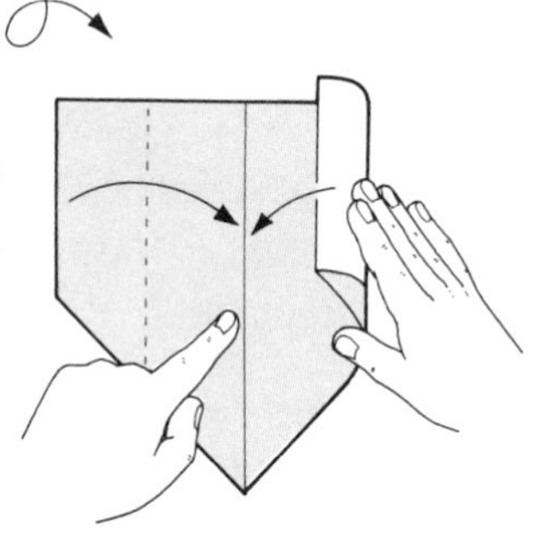

5 Fold the paper in half from top to bottom.

6 Fold down a little of each top corner. Press them flat and unfold.

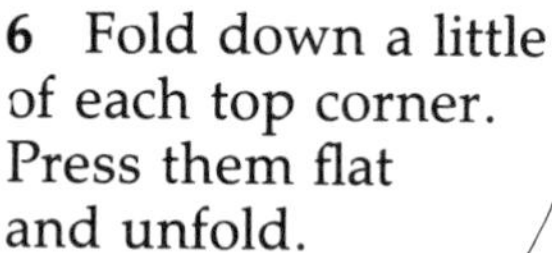

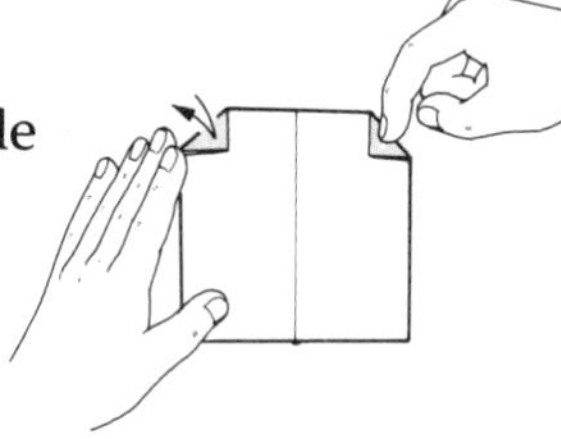

7 Push the top corners down inside the heart along the fold-lines made in step 6.

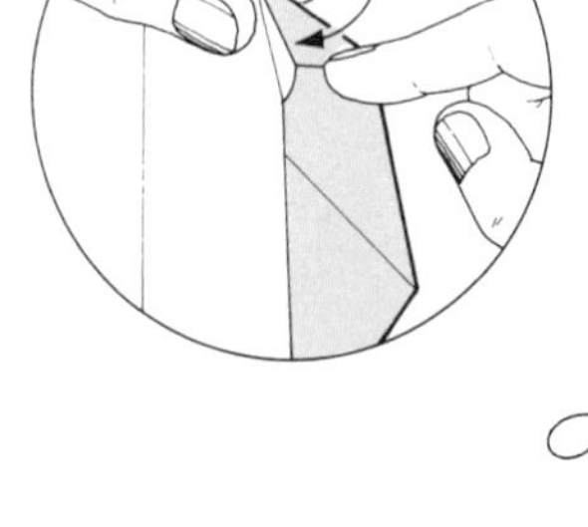

8 To complete the heart, turn the paper over from side to side.

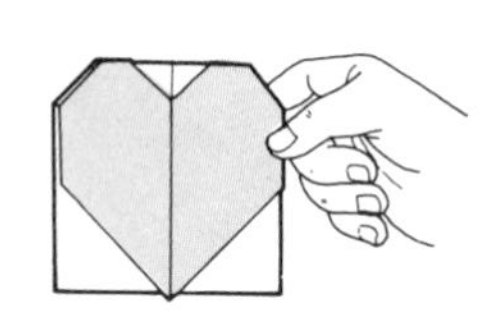

Candy Stick

Megumi Biddle

Origami folds make ideal Christmas tree decorations. But to look really beautiful your origami has to be neatly folded.

You will need: Rectangle of paper, coloured on one side and white on the other Glue

1 Place the rectangle sideways on, with the coloured side on top. Fold down a little of the top.

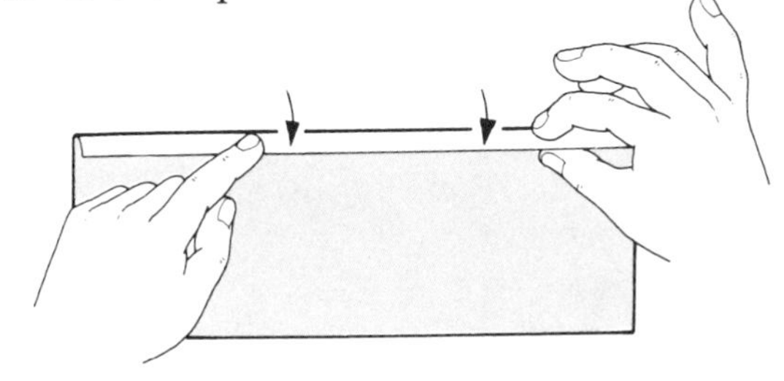

2 Turn the paper over. From the bottom right-hand corner, roll the paper tightly into a pencil-like shape.

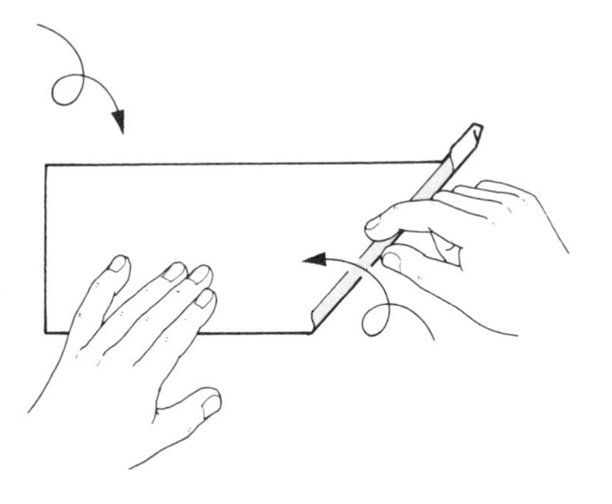

3 Near the end, glue the loose corner of paper to the 'pencil', to prevent it from unravelling.

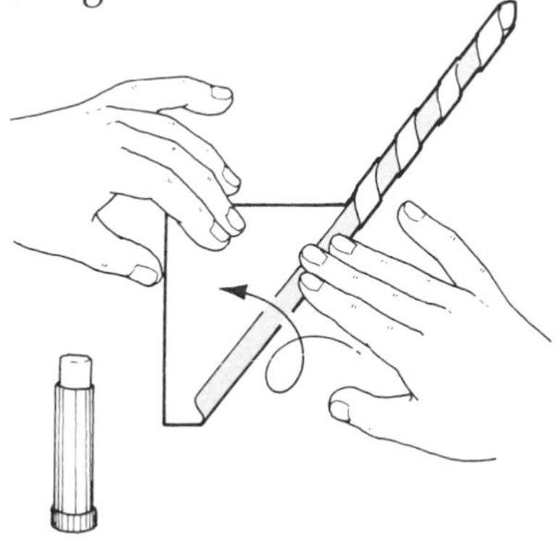

4 To complete the candy stick, flatten one end and bend it over into a crook.

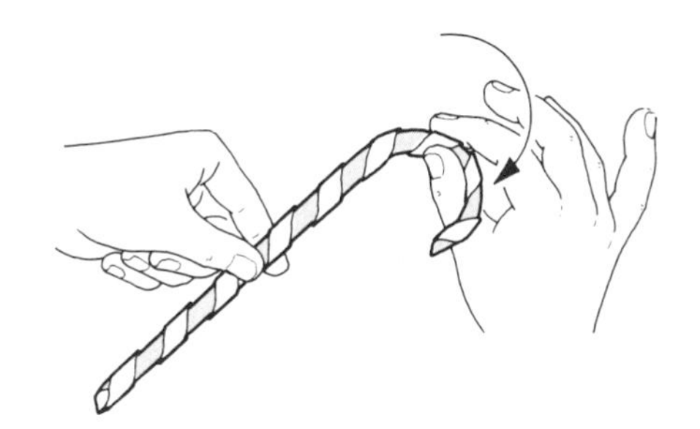

Two-piece star

Traditional

A useful tip to remember when folding origami decorations such as this star, is that they look most beautiful when made out of shining metallic foil (the kind that is used for gift wrapping).

You will need:
2 squares of paper the same size, coloured on one side and white on the other Glue Needle and cotton

1 Turn one square around to look like a diamond, with the coloured side on top. Fold it in half from side to side.

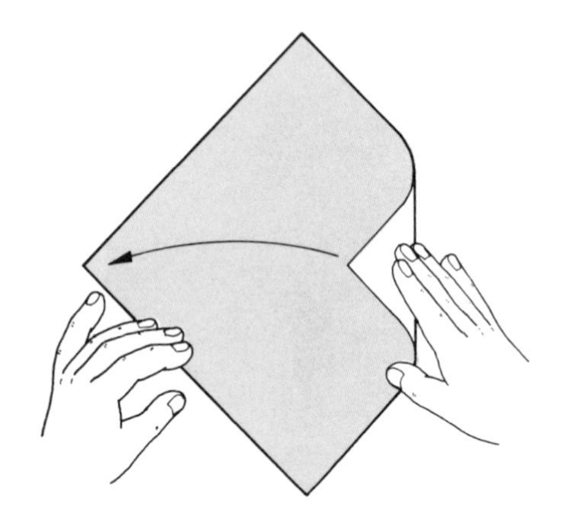

2 From the top point, fold the topmost layer of paper over to meet the folded side.

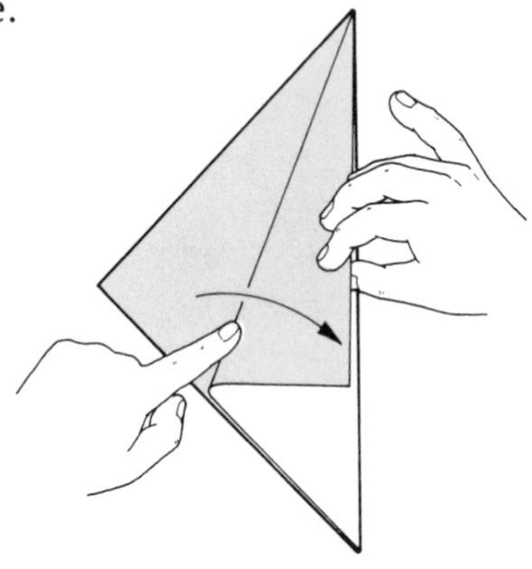

3 Turn the paper over. Fold it in half from bottom to top.

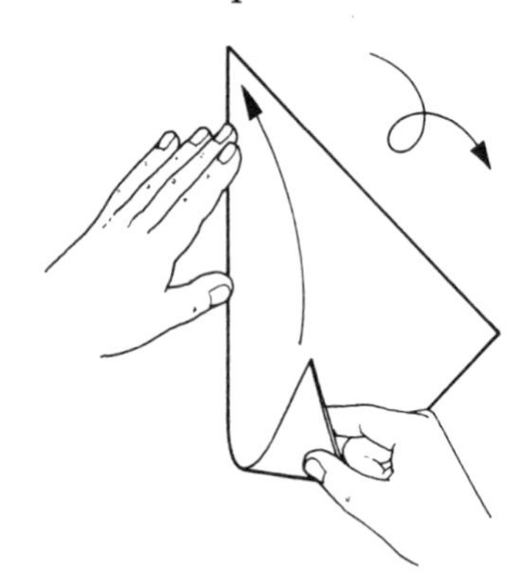

4 Put a finger under the topmost layer of paper. Pull the layer of paper down towards you . . .

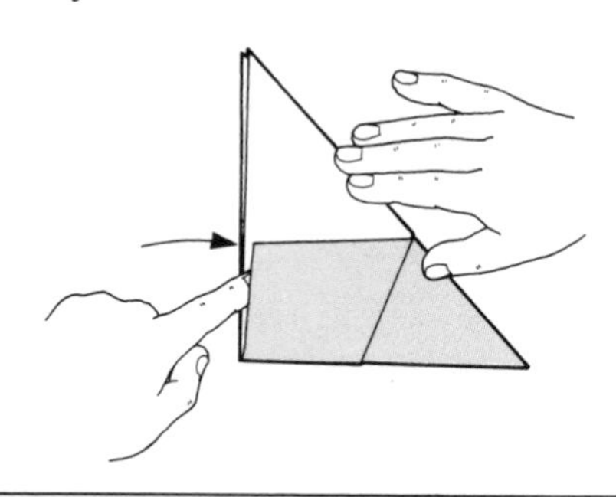

5 and press it down neatly.

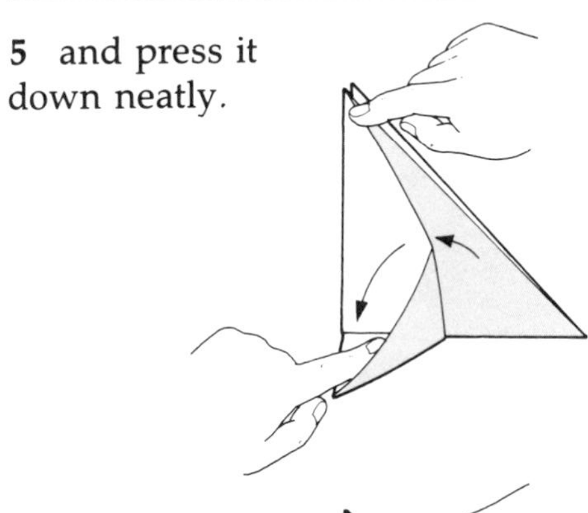

6 This should be your finished result.

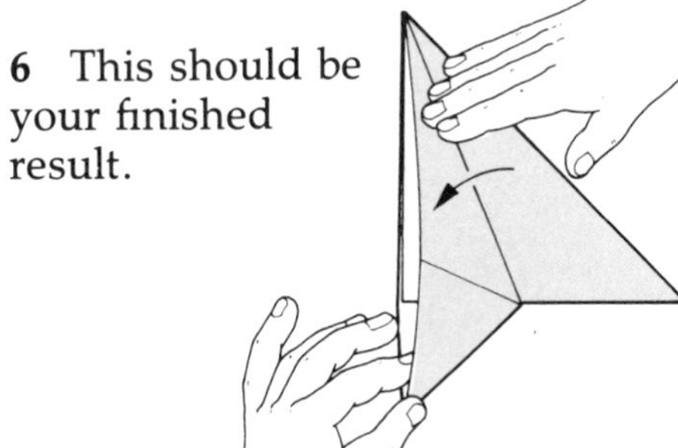

7 Turn the remaining square around to look like a diamond, with the white side on top. Fold it in half from bottom to top, so making a triangle.

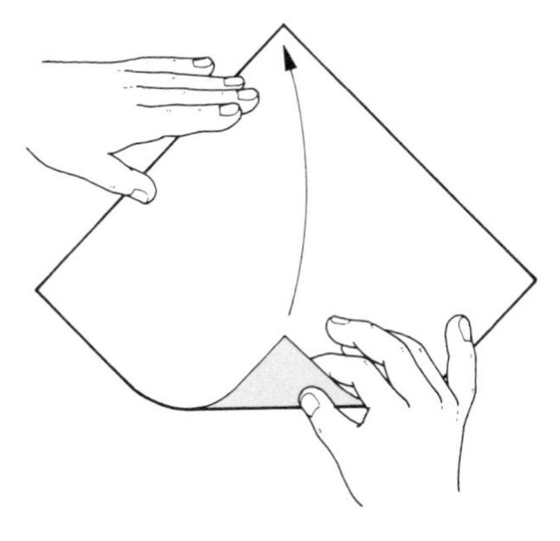

8 Fold the triangle in half from side to side.

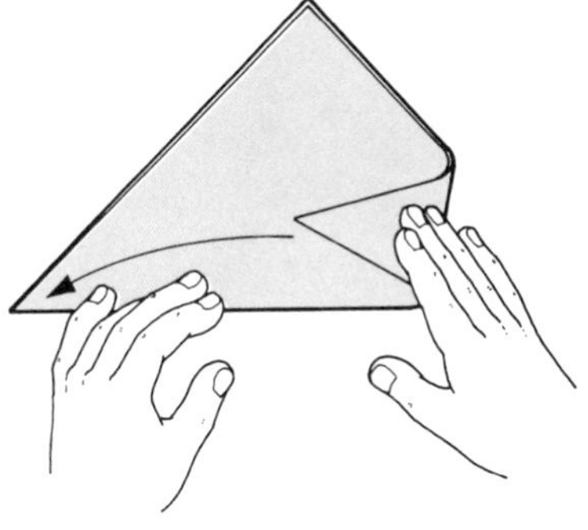

9 Press the triangle flat.

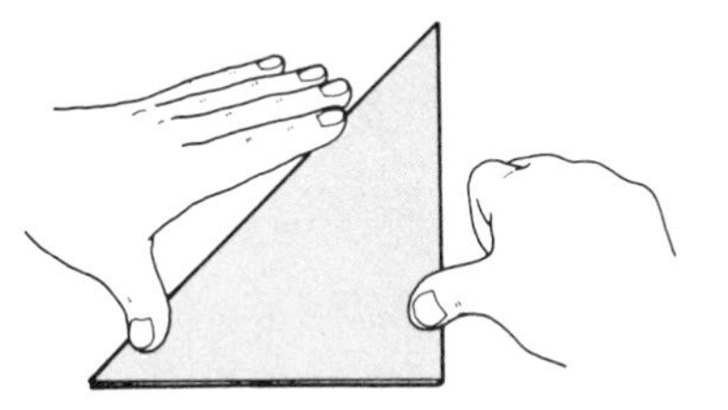

10 Tuck the triangle inside the first piece of the star.

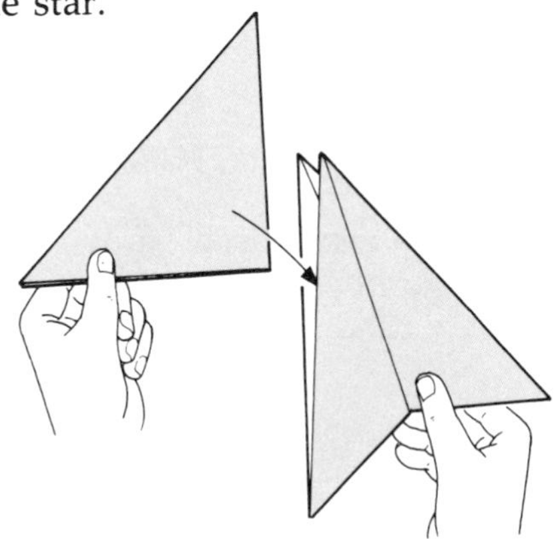

11 Glue them together.

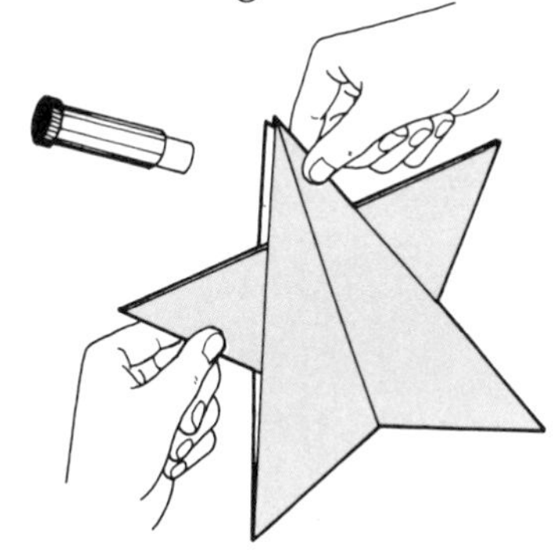

12 To complete the star, attach a loop of cotton to the top of it, so that you can hang it from the Christmas tree.

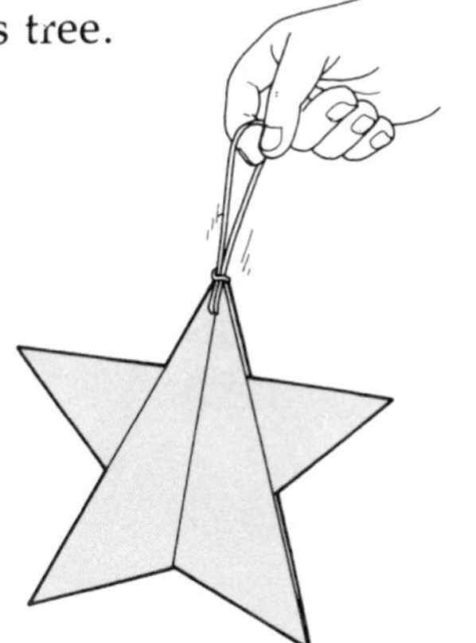

Sailing boat

Traditional

This delightful traditional origami fold makes an ideal place card for a party.

You will need:
Square of paper, coloured on one side and white on the other

1 Turn the square around to look like a diamond, with the white side on top. Fold it in half from bottom to top, so making a triangle.

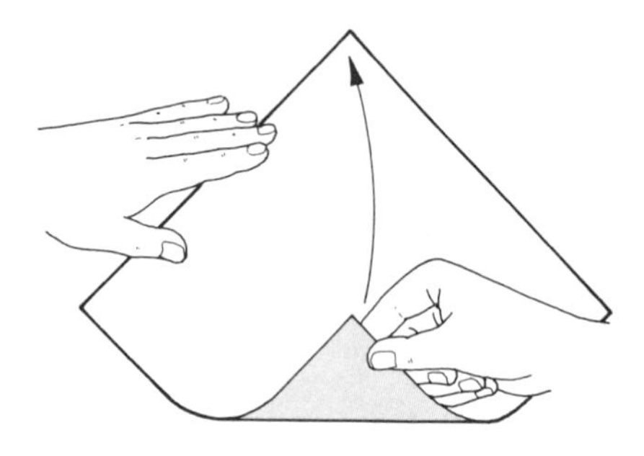

2 Fold the triangle in half from side to side. Press the paper flat. Open out the paper completely, back to step 1.

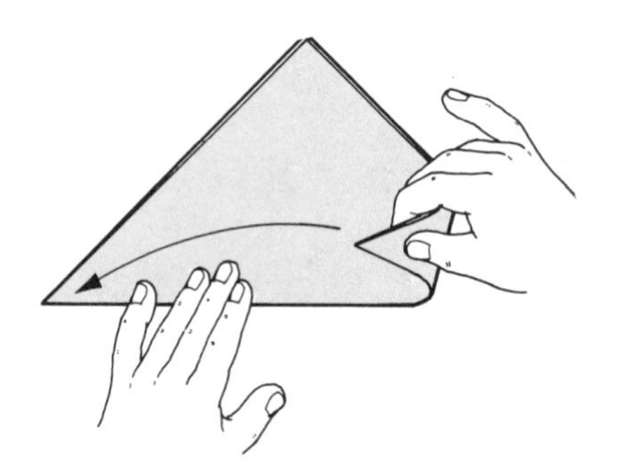

3 Fold two opposite corners in to meet the middle.

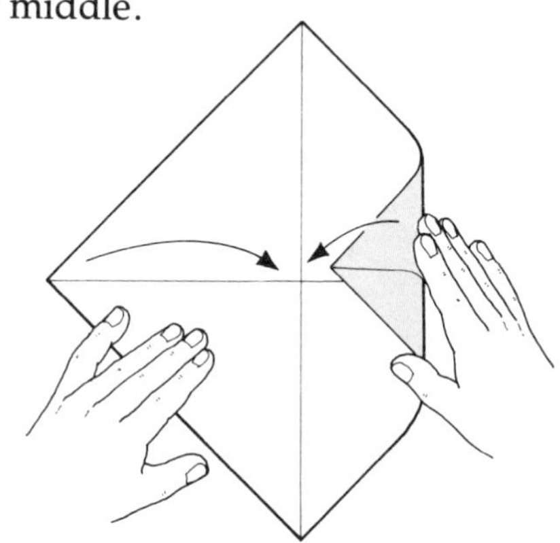

4 Fold the paper in half from top to bottom.

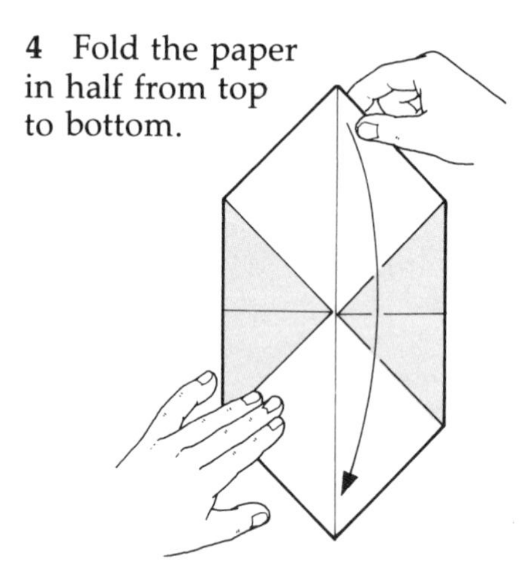

5 Fold the paper in half from side to side. Lift the top half up along the middle fold-line. Start to open the paper out and with your free hand . . .

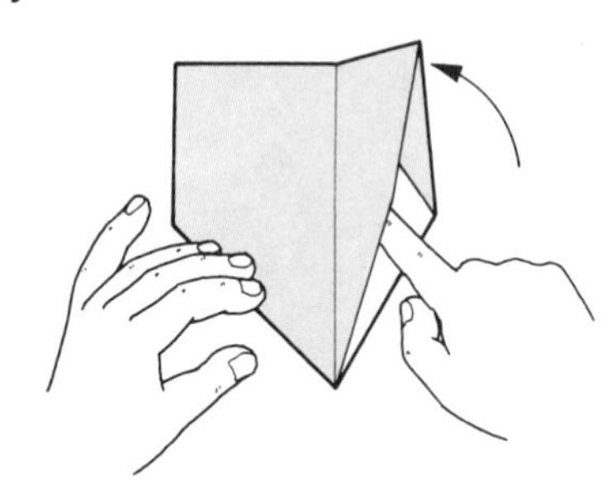

6 press it down neatly into a coloured triangle.

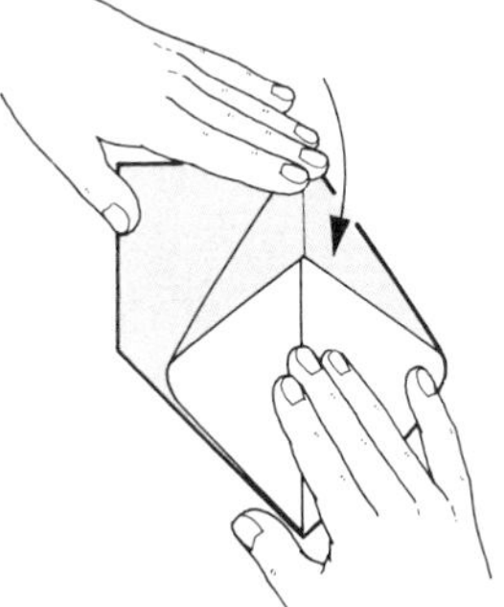

7 Turn the paper over. Repeat step 5.

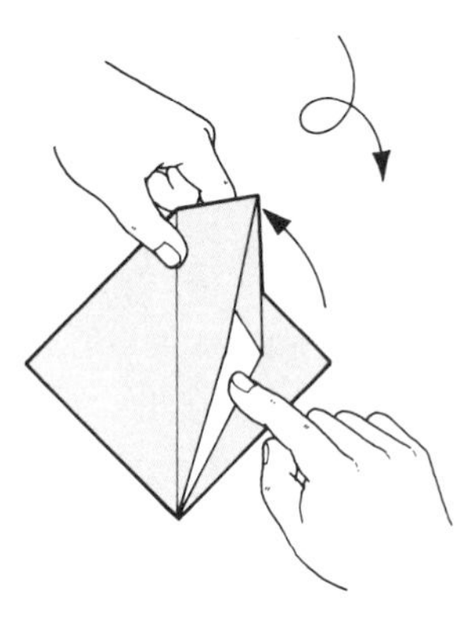

8 Repeat step 6.

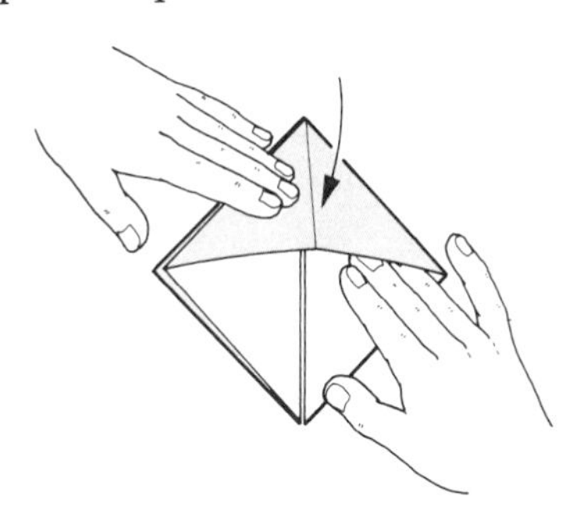

9 Turn the paper around. Fold the right-hand point down to meet the bottom point.

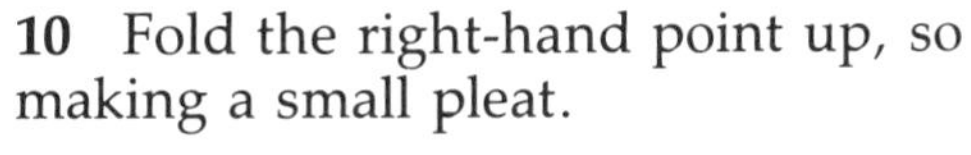

10 Fold the right-hand point up, so making a small pleat.

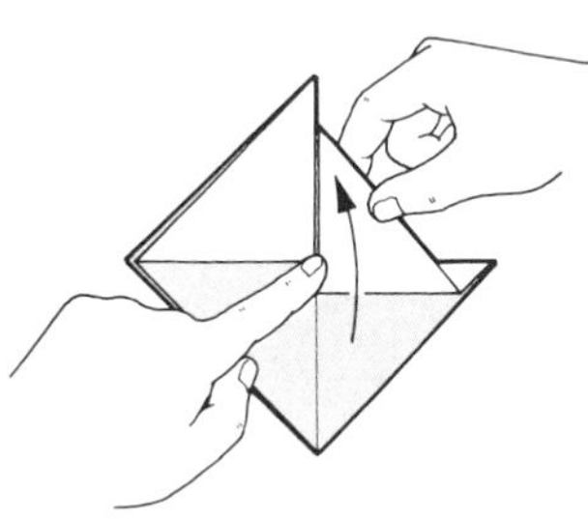

11 Tuck the pleat inside the sailing boat. Fold the bottom point up to meet the middle.

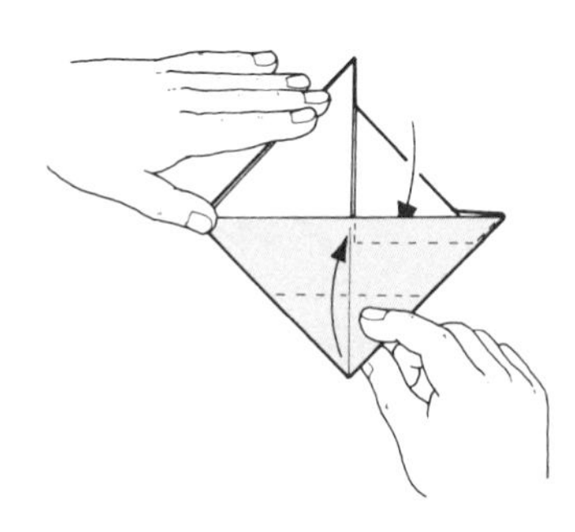

12 To complete, fold the bottom point outwards, so that the sailing boat will sit up straight when placed on a flat surface.

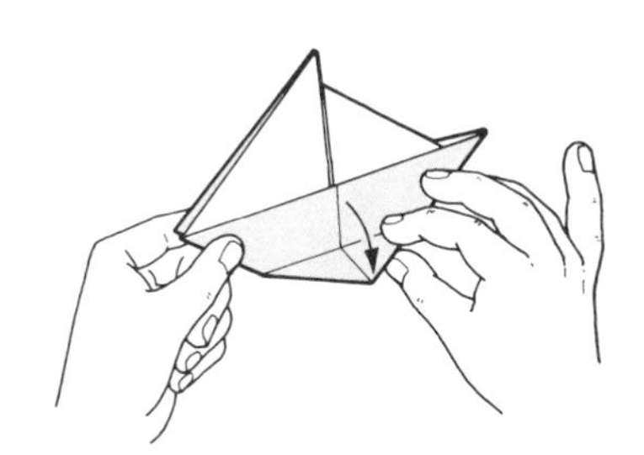

Yacht

Traditional

Action origami folds are very popular. With this particular action fold you should have a lot of fun and enjoyment.

You will need:
Square of paper, coloured on one side and white on the other

1 Turn the square around to look like a diamond, with the white side on top. Fold and unfold it in half from side to side.

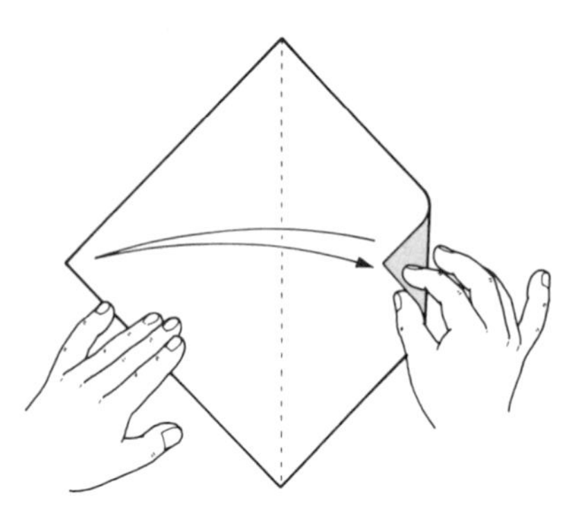

2 From the top point, fold the sloping sides in to meet the middle fold-line, so making the kite base.

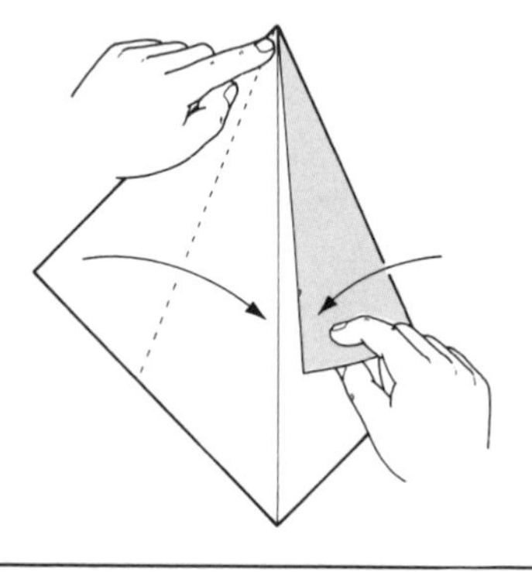

3 Fold the kite base in half from bottom to top.

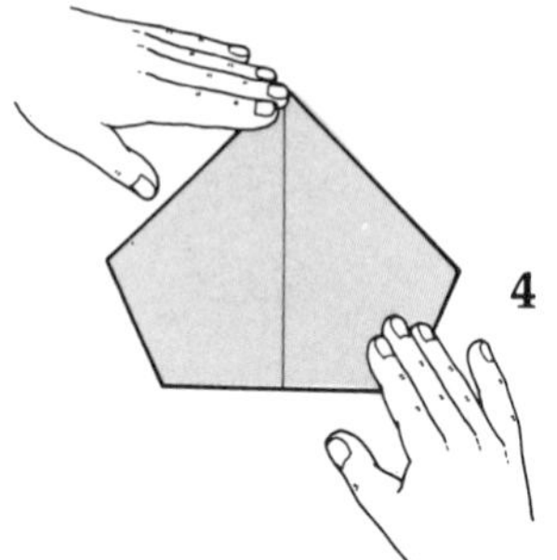

4 This should be your finished result.

5 Fold the short sloping sides in to meet the middle fold-line.

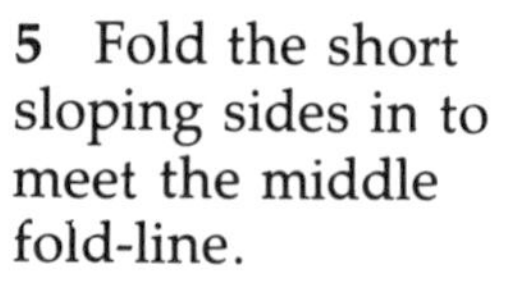

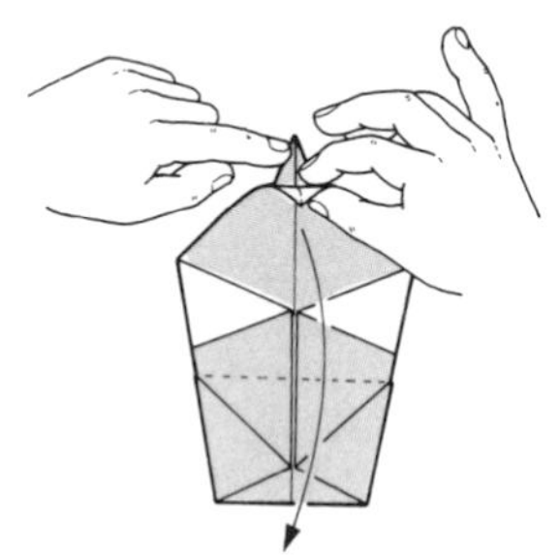

6 Fold the topmost layer of paper down as far as it will go.

7 Give the top point a gentle curve. Fold the top layer of paper up straight, so making the yacht's sail.

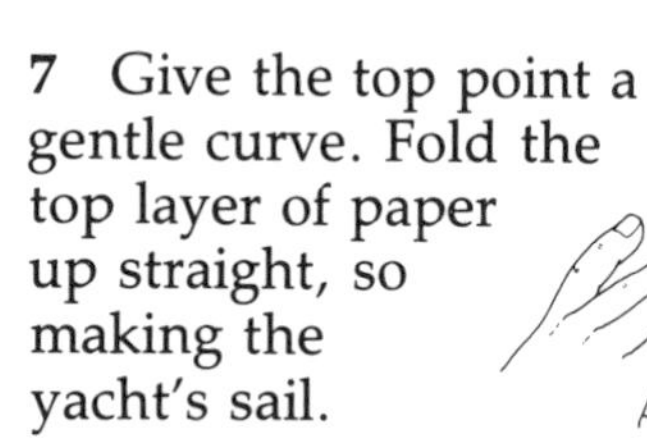

8 To complete, turn the yacht around. If you now place the yacht upon a flat surface and gently blow where indicated, it will happily sail away. Why not make some more yachts and have sailing races with a few friends?

Vehicles (Lorry, Jeep & Car)

Masao Mizuno

Here, from just one basic shape you can make many unique folds. Why not see what other 'new' folds you can invent.

You will need:
For each vehicle, a different square of paper, coloured on one side and white on the other

1 *Lorry:* Fold one square in half from bottom to top, with the white side on top.

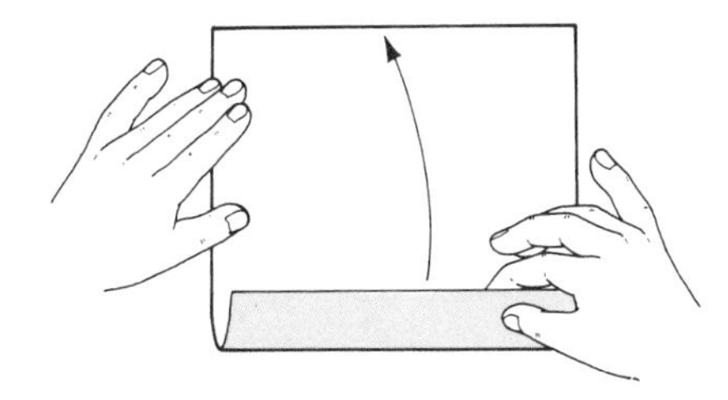

2 Fold it in half from side to side.

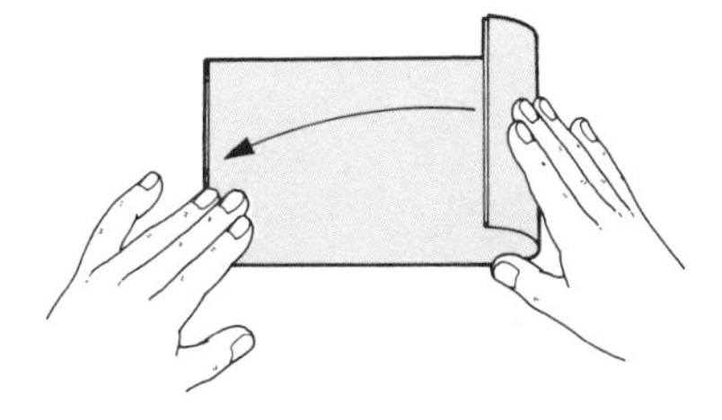

3 Open out the paper completely, back to step 1. Fold the bottom up to meet the middle fold-line.

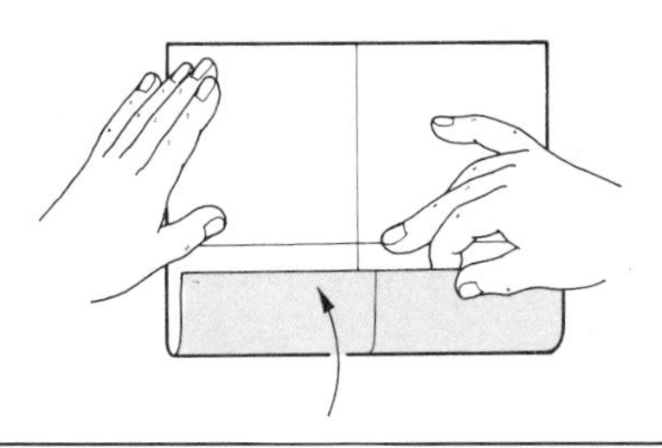

4 Fold the right-hand layer of paper down from the middle, as shown by the dotted lines.

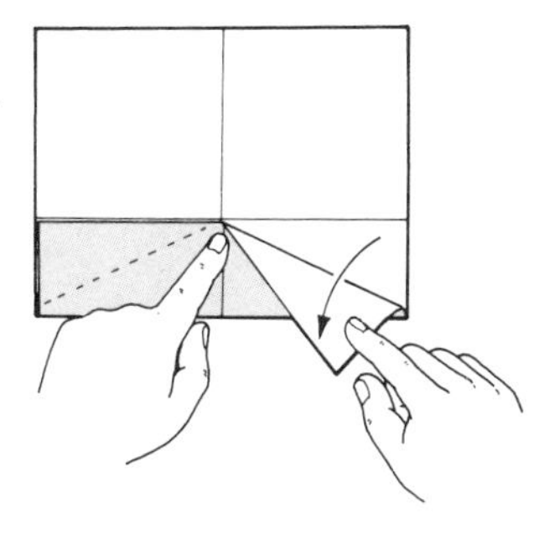

5 Repeat step 4 with the left-hand layer of paper.

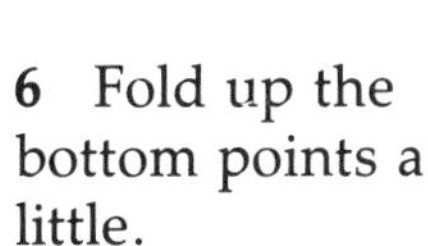

6 Fold up the bottom points a little.

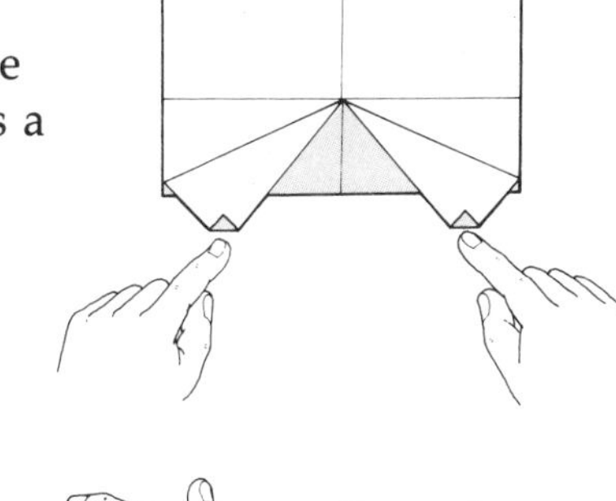

7 Turn the paper over. Fold the top down to meet the middle fold-line.

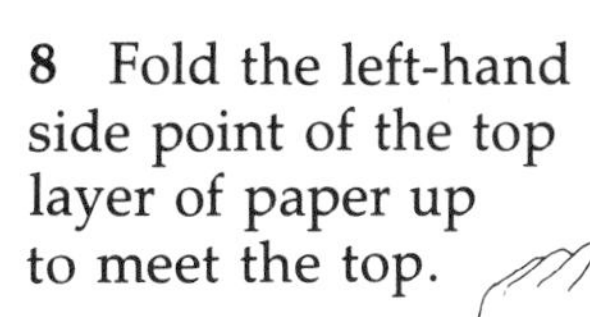

8 Fold the left-hand side point of the top layer of paper up to meet the top.

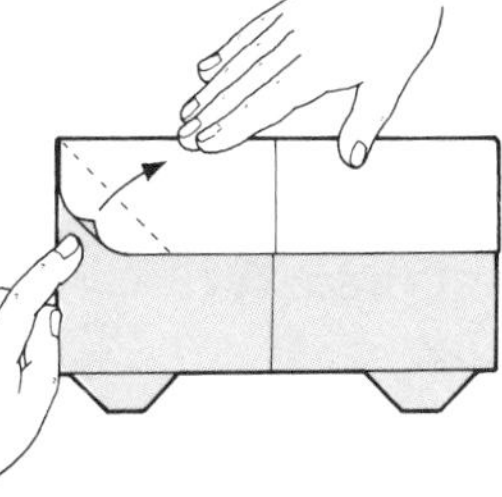

9 To complete the lorry, fold behind a little of the top left-hand point.

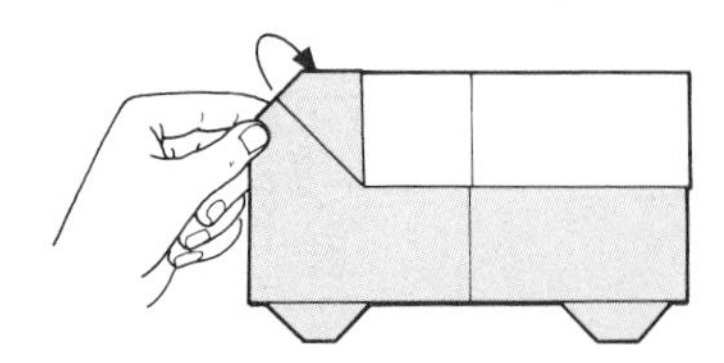

10 *Jeep:* Start with step 7 of the lorry on page 31. But do *not* fold the top down. Instead, fold the top left-hand corner in to meet the middle.

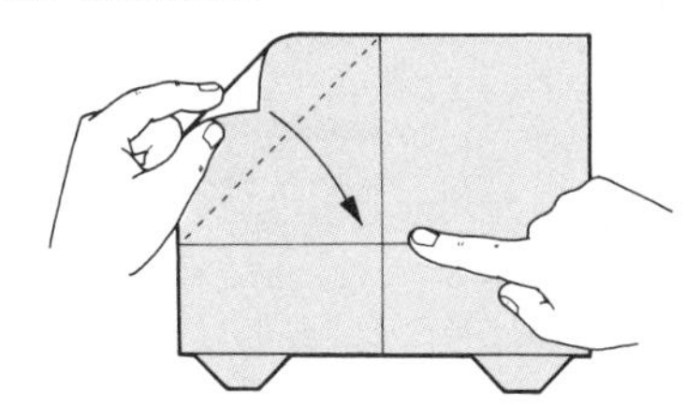

11 Turn the paper over. Fold the top down along the middle fold-line, into the position as shown by the dotted lines.

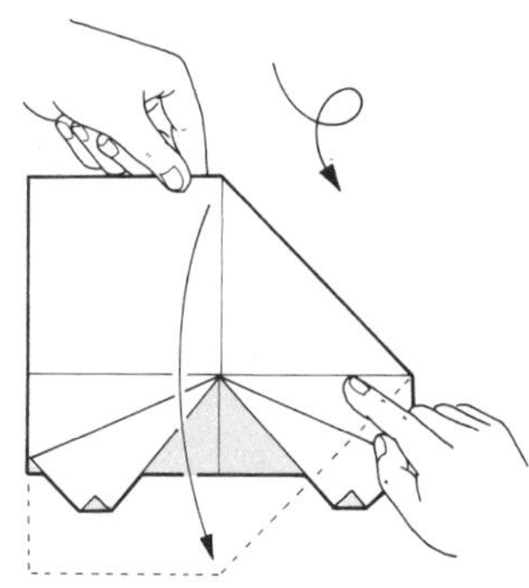

12 Fold the top up, into the position as shown by the dotted lines, so making a small pleat.

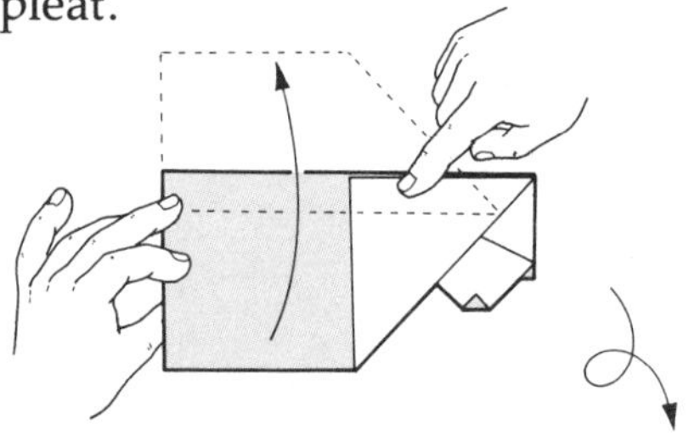

13 To complete the jeep, turn the paper over.

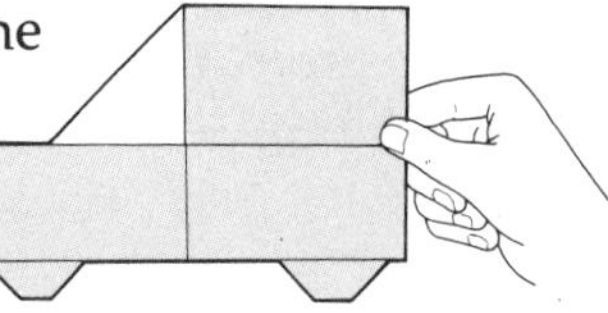

14 *Car:* Start with step 7 of the lorry on page 31. But do *not* fold the top down. Instead, fold the top corners in to meet the middle.

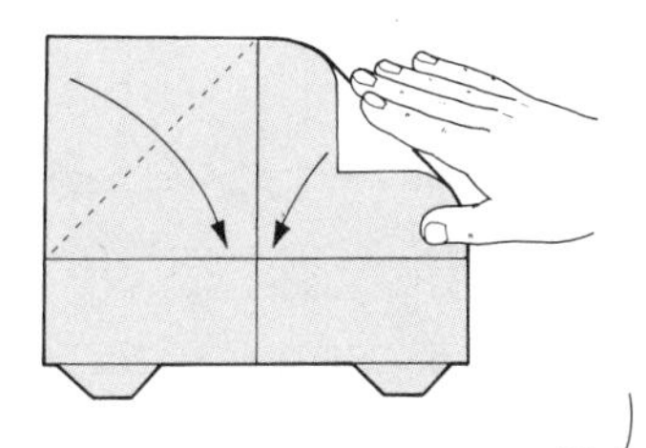

15 Repeat step 11.

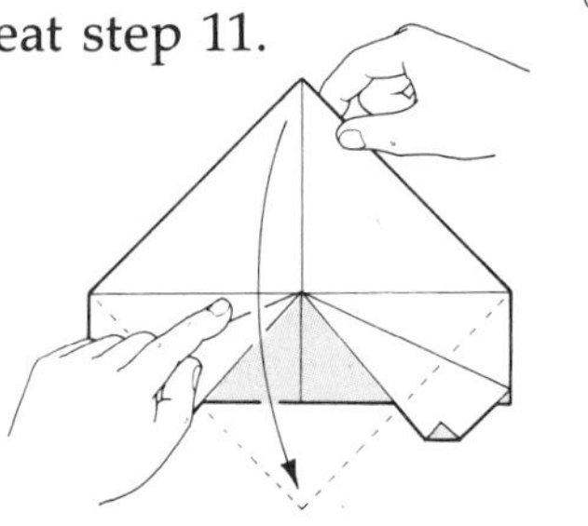

16 Repeat step 12.

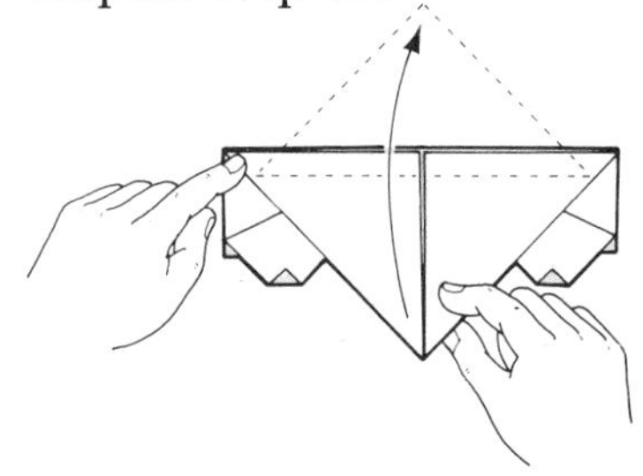

17 Fold down the top point a little.

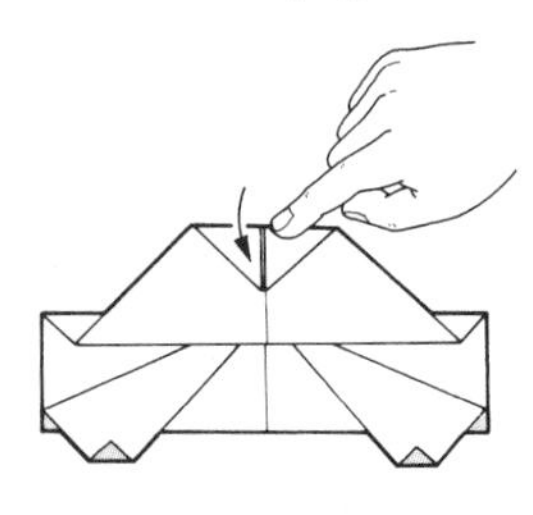

18 Turn the paper over. To complete the car, fold over the left-hand side point a little, so suggesting a headlight.

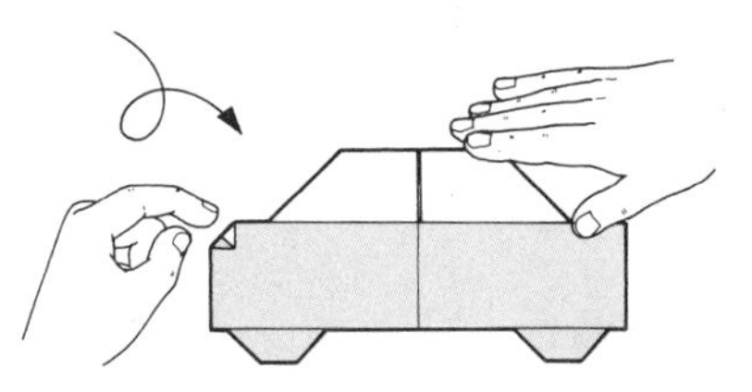

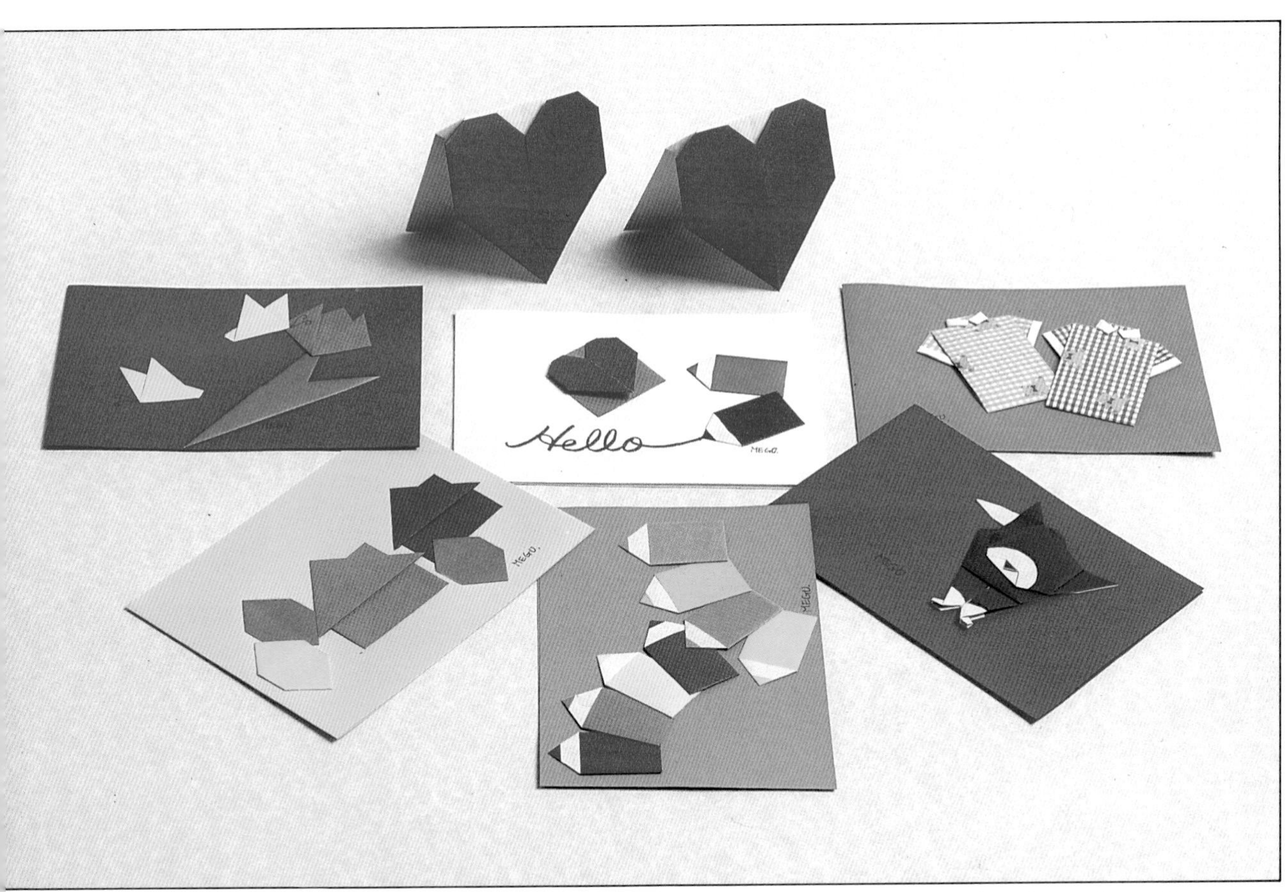

ift Cards Butterfly p13, Cat p87, Flower p14, Heart p24, House with a chimney p23, Pencil p33 and Shirt p58

ntarctic Fancy box p21, Gift box p19 and Penguin p18

Town scene Cat p87 Flower and leaves p14, House with a Chimney p23, Rose and leaf p34 and Vehicles (Lorry, Jeep and Car) p31

Christmas tree decorations Balloon decoration p48, Blow top p53, Candy stick p25, Pop up star p85 and Santa Claus p44

Show time Animal faces p38, Animal puppets p41, Butterfly p13 and Flower and leaves p14

Origami fun
Koron-Koron p74, Sailing boat p28 and Yacht p30

Christmas decorations Christmas bauble (sweet dish) p64, Christmas wreath p46, Party decoration (chain) p36 and Two piece star p26

Action Origami Flapping bird p80, Rabbit p51 and Talking crow p72

Fruit bowl Apple, Banana, Cherry, Grape and Orange p55-56

Party time Sweet dish p63, Coaster p91, Fancy box p21, Napkin boot and Napkin bunny p60-62

Lily pond
Goldfish p50, Jumping frog p66, Water lily and Water lily leaf p69-71

Masquerade
Gift box p19, Paper hat p10, Party decoration (mask) p36 and Yakko san/ crown p65

rigami ame Rolling all and Skittles 77-79

enbazuru housand anes) Crane nd a thousand anes p83

Origami Stationery Card p11, Cat p87, Crab p16, Envelope p12, Rose and Leaf p34 and Shirt p58

Modular Origami Multiplex challenge p95, Pop up jewel p93, Decorative cube p92

Pencil

Takenao Handa

This fold is ideal as a decoration on a piece of note paper or personal stationery.

You will need:
Square of paper, coloured on one side and white on the other
Scissors

1 Fold and unfold the square in half from side to side, with the white side on top. Cut along the middle fold-line, so making two rectangles.

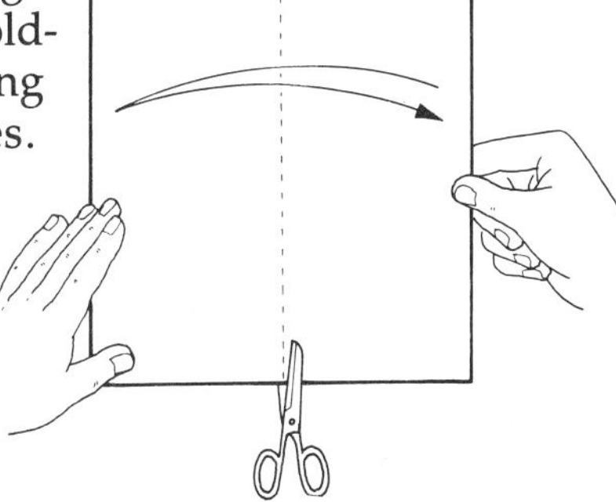

2 Place one rectangle lengthways on, with the white side on top. Fold down a little of the top.

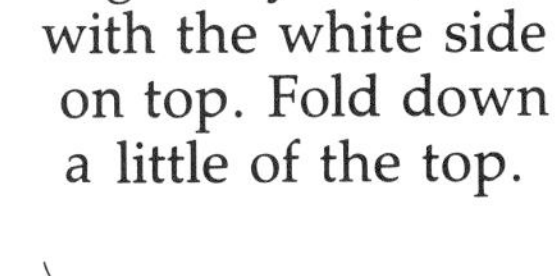

3 Turn the paper over. Fold and unfold it in half from side to side.

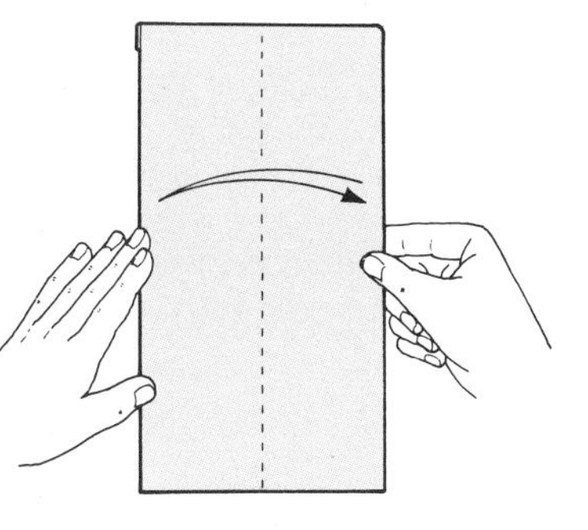

4 Fold the top corners down to meet the middle fold-line.

5 Turn the paper over. Fold the bottom up as far as shown.

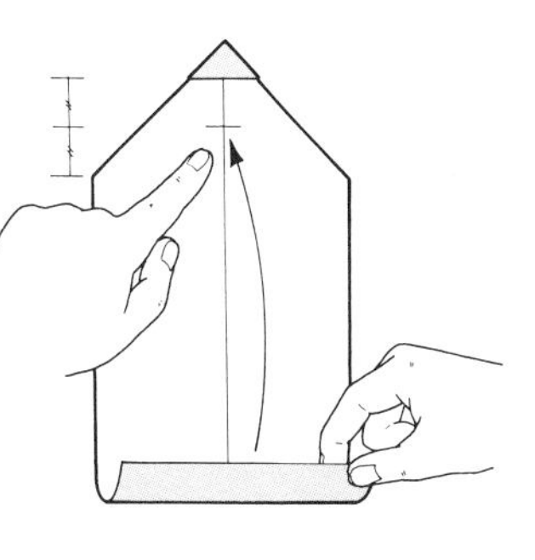

6 This should be your finished result.

7 Turn the paper over. Fold the sides in.

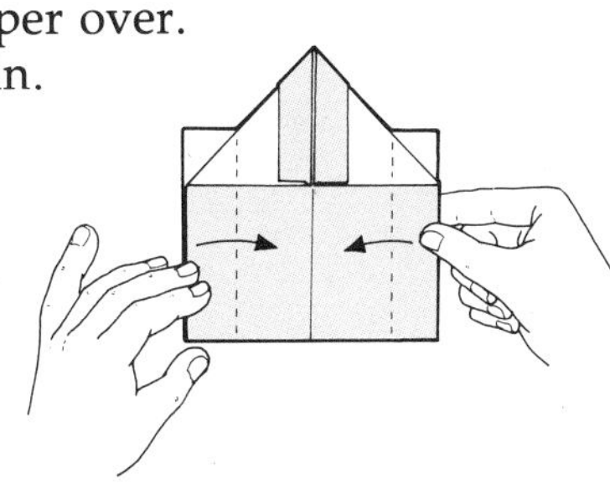

8 To complete the pencil, turn the paper over. Why not make another pencil with the remaining rectangle?

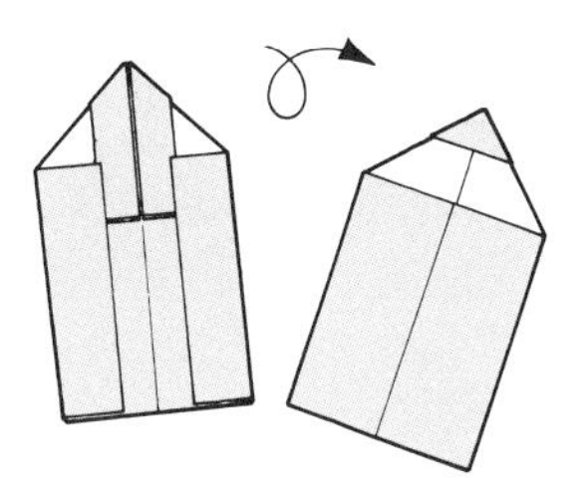

Rose and leaf

Seiryo Takekawa

The following folds look very pretty when they are fixed on to a gift.

You will need:
2 squares of paper the same size, coloured on one side and white on the other (try using a red one for the rose and a green one for the leaf)
Scissors

1 *Rose:* Fold the red square in half from bottom to top, with the white side on top.

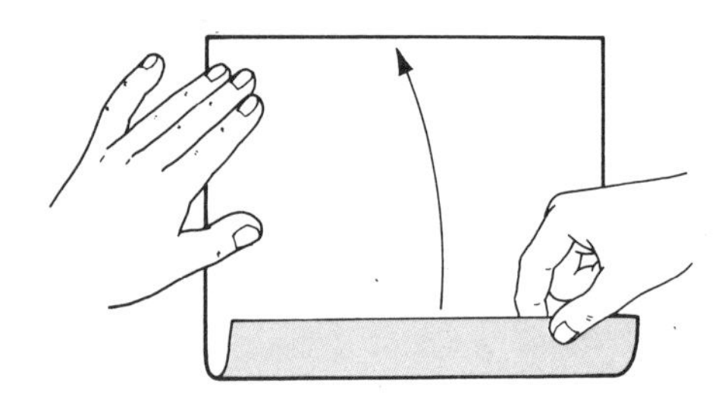

2 Fold it in half from side to side.

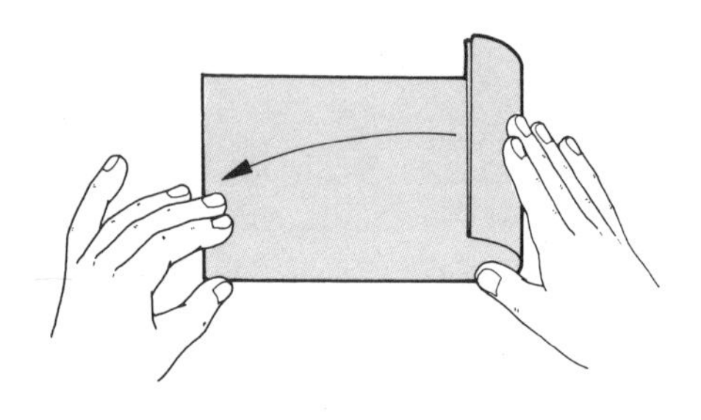

3 Open out the paper completely, back to step 1. Fold the corners in to meet the middle.

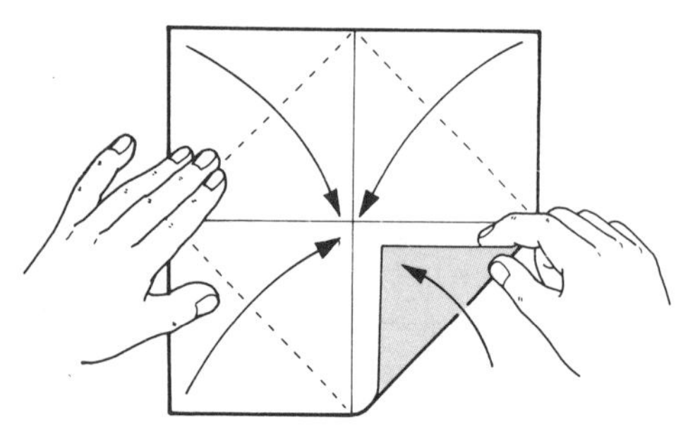

4 This should be your finished result, which in origami is called the blintz base.

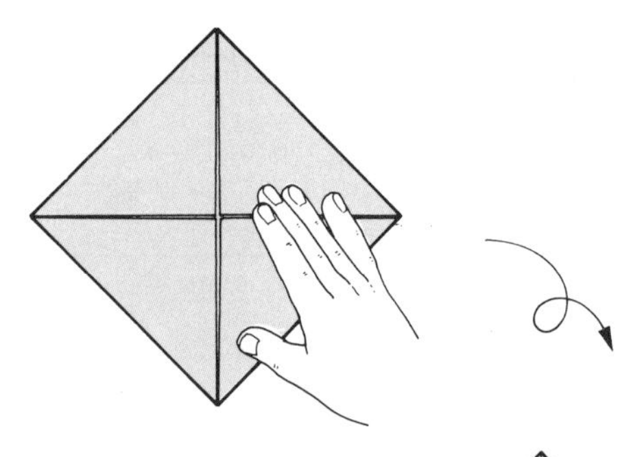

5 Turn the paper over. Once again fold the corners in to meet the middle. Press them flat and unfold.

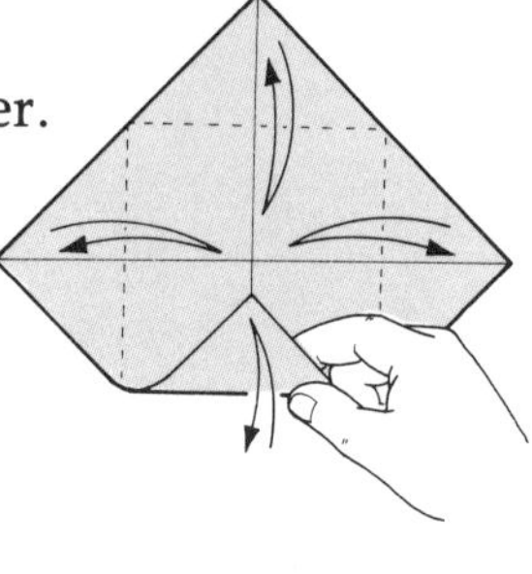

6 Fold the corners over to lie along the fold-lines made in step 5.

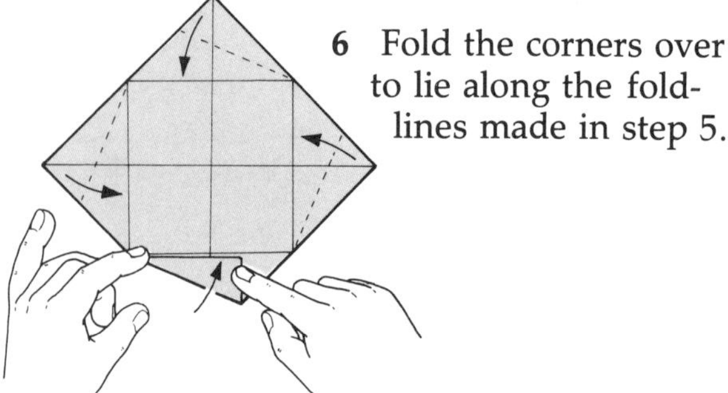

7 Turn the paper over. Fold each of the middle points out, so revealing a little of the rose's centre.

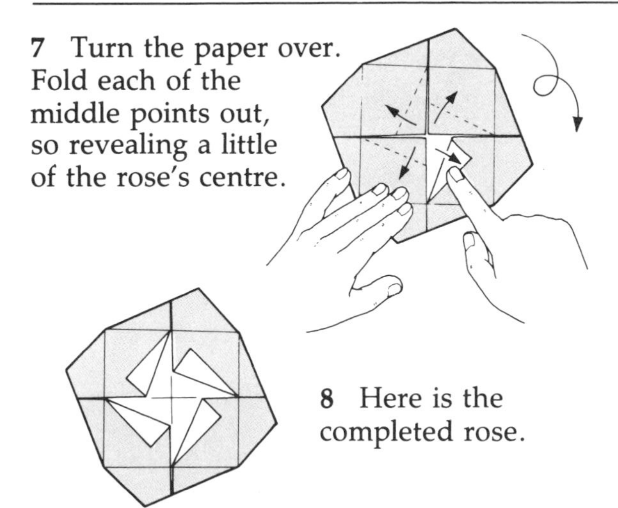

8 Here is the completed rose.

9 *Leaf:* Fold the green square in half from bottom to top, with the white side on top.

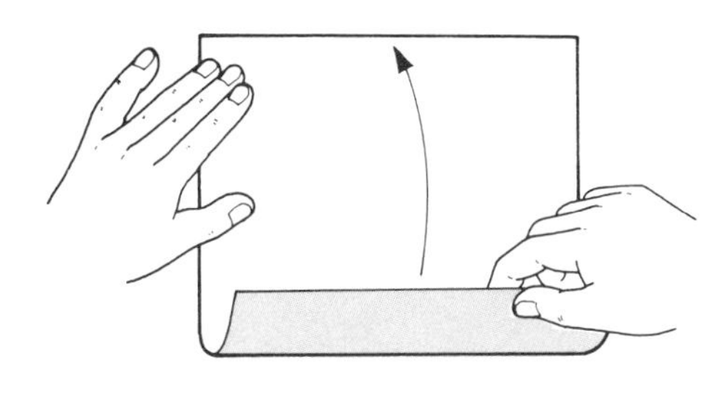

10 Fold the sides in one-third of the way. Press the paper flat. Open it out completely.

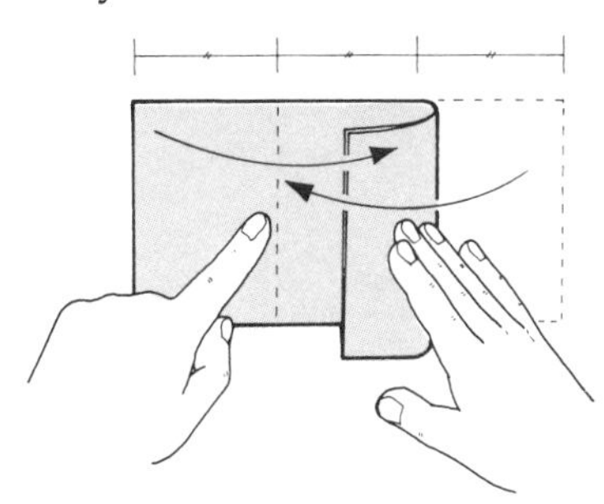

11 Using the fold-lines as a guide, cut the square into six rectangles.

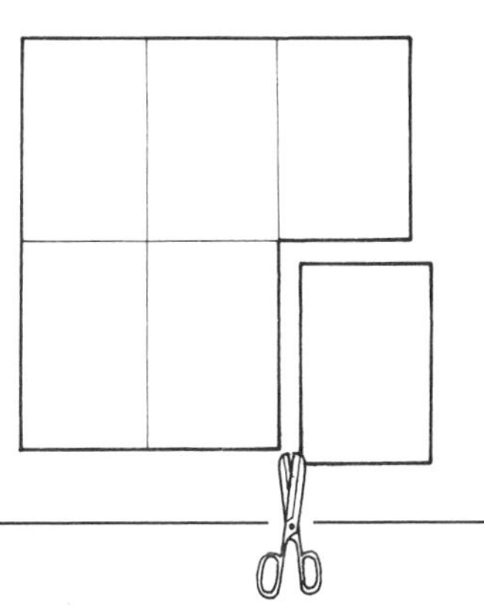

12 Turn one rectangle around, with the white side on top. Fold and unfold it in half from bottom to top.

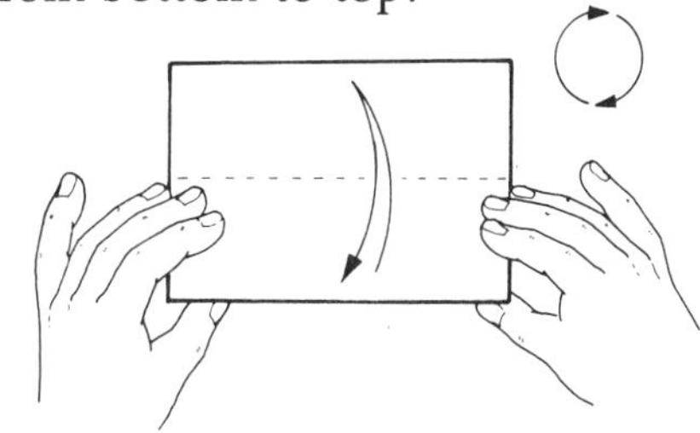

13 Fold the corners in to meet the middle fold-line.

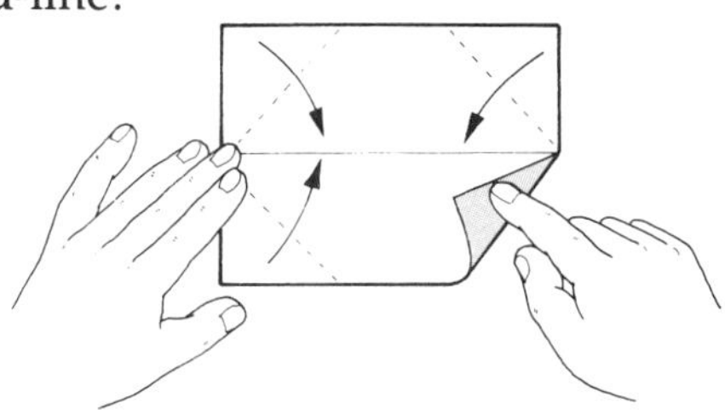

14 This should be your finished result.

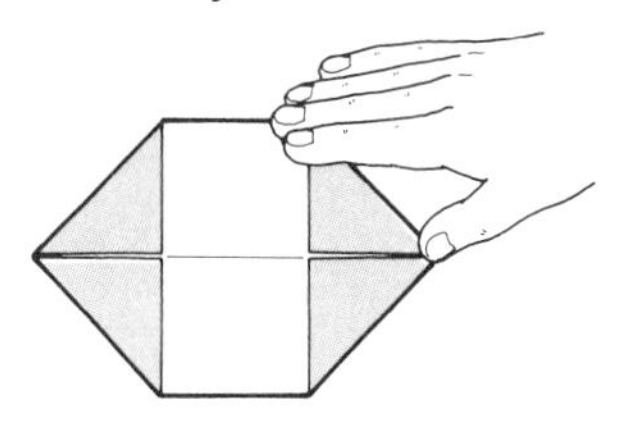

15 To complete the leaf, turn the paper over.

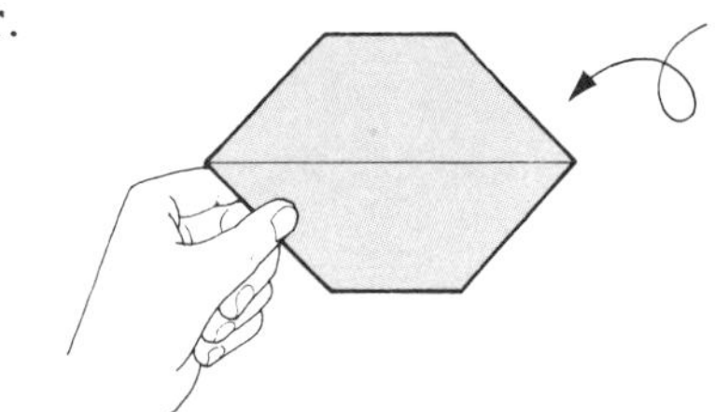

16 Now make two more leaves and display them along with the rose in a nice arrangement.

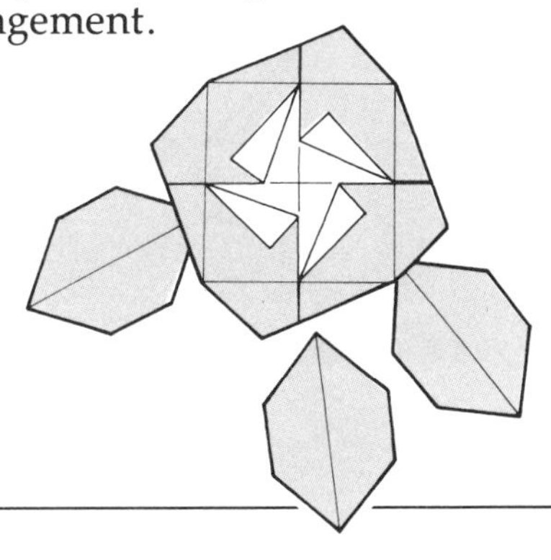

Party decorations

Megumi Biddle

All of the following folds are based around a very easy basic unit. Make them in a variety of different colours for the best effect.

You will need:
Few squares of paper all the same size, coloured on one side and white on the other
Glue
Elastic bands

1 Turn one square around to look like a diamond, with the white side on top. Fold it in half from bottom to top, so making a triangle.

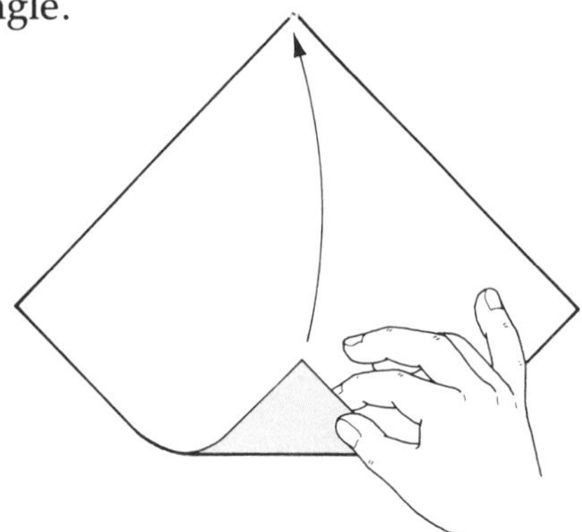

2 Fold the triangle in half from side to side. Press the paper flat. Open out the paper completely, back to step 1.

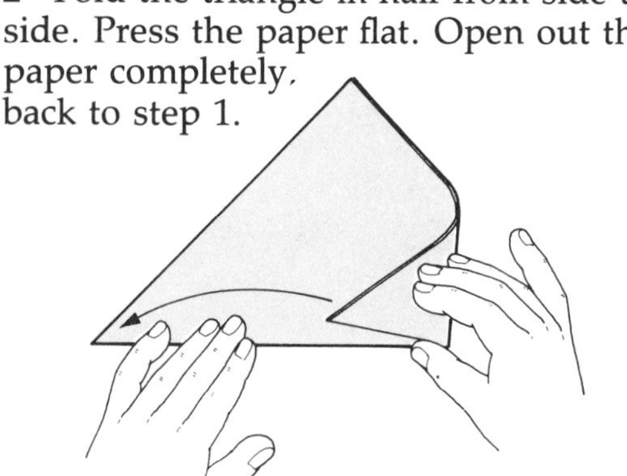

3 Fold the corners in to meet the middle, so making a shape that in origami is called the blintz base.

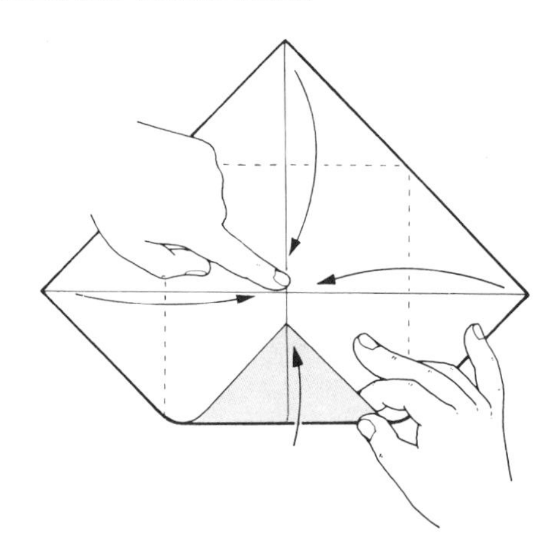

4 Once again, fold the corners in to meet the middle.

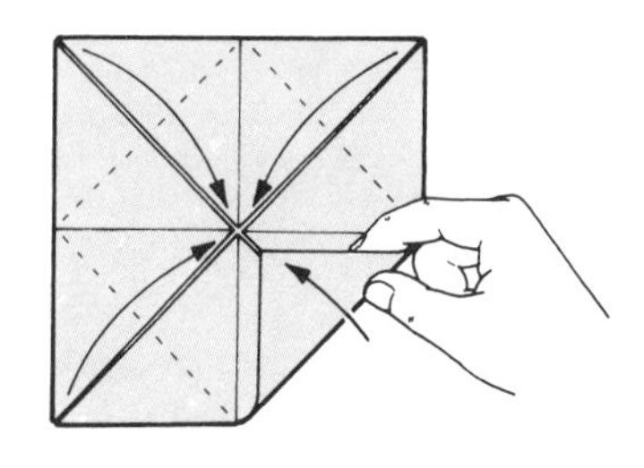

5 Unfold step 4.

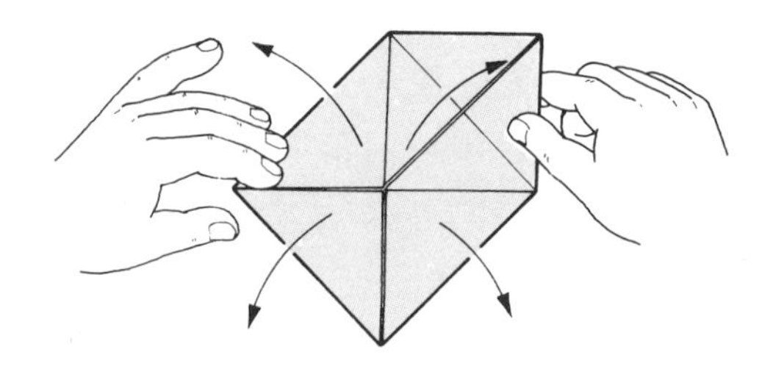

6 Turn the paper over. Fold it in half from side to side.

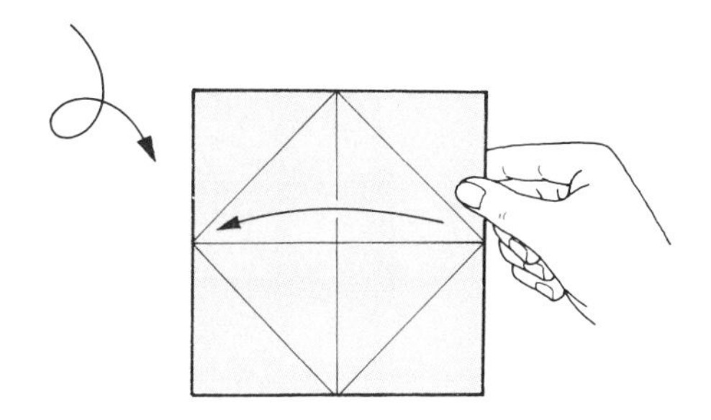

7 Hold the sides together. From the folded side, pull the top section of paper outwards, into the position as shown by the dotted lines.

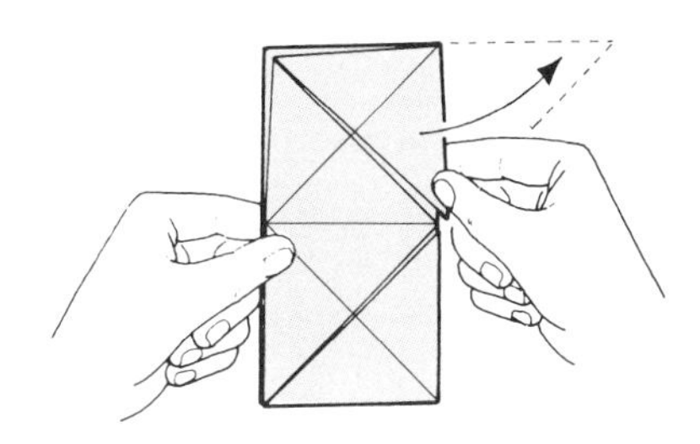

8 Repeat step 7 with the bottom section of paper.

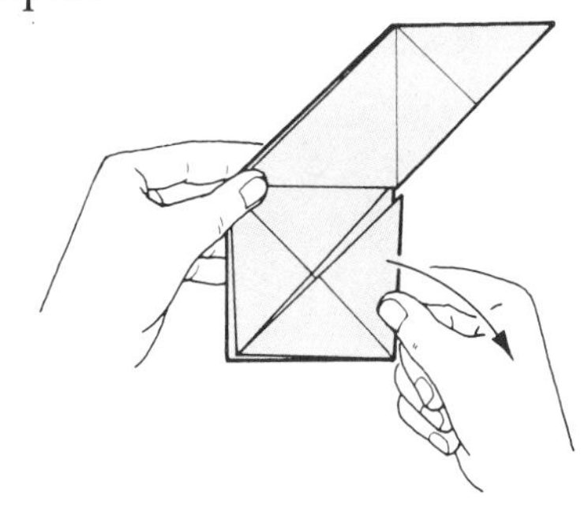

9 Here is the completed basic unit. Now fold a few more!

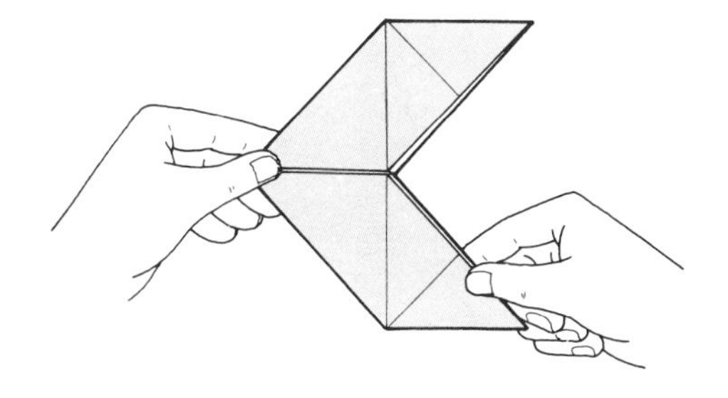

10 All the party decorations are built up around a 'link'. To make such a link, tuck one basic unit inside another and glue them together.

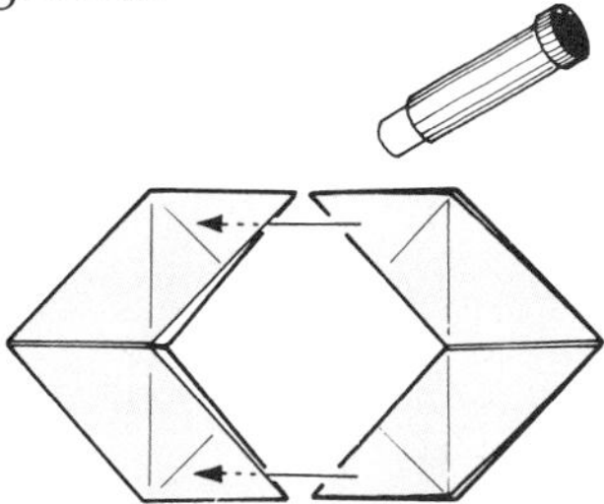

11 To create a wonderful party mask, glue two sets of links together and attach an elastic band to each side point.

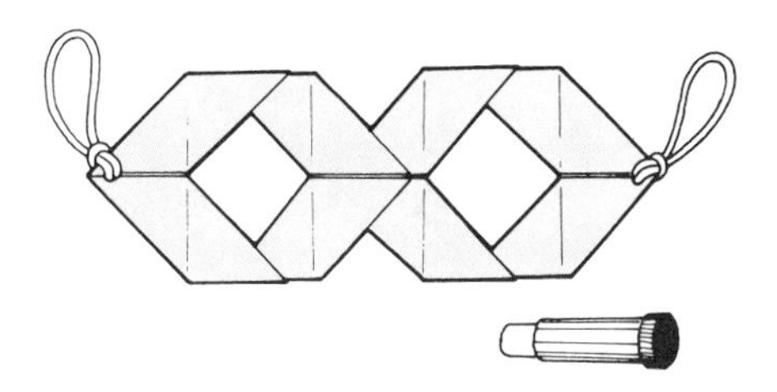

12 For a very colourful party chain, carefully tuck and glue together lots of basic units and links. When hanging your chain, make sure that you suspend it at frequent intervals, so that it will not fall apart and cause any damage.

Animal faces

Traditional

With just a few small changes in the folding, you will be able to create many different animals. Maybe you could try using them to illustrate a story.

You will need:
Square of paper for each animal face, coloured on one side and white on the other
Felt-tip pen

1 Turn one square around to look like a diamond, with the white side on top. Fold and unfold it in half from bottom to top.

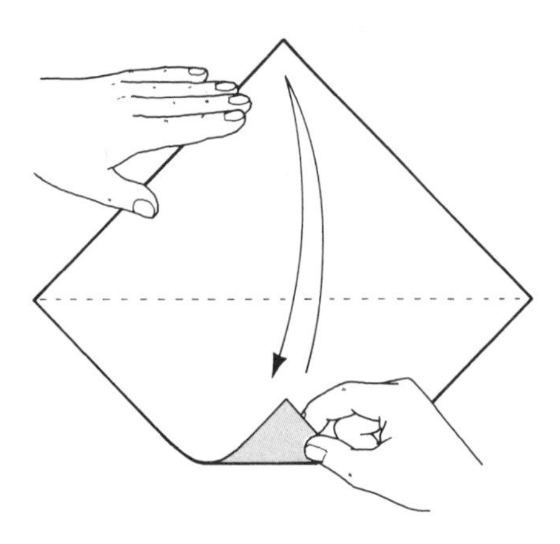

2 Fold and unfold it in half from side to side.

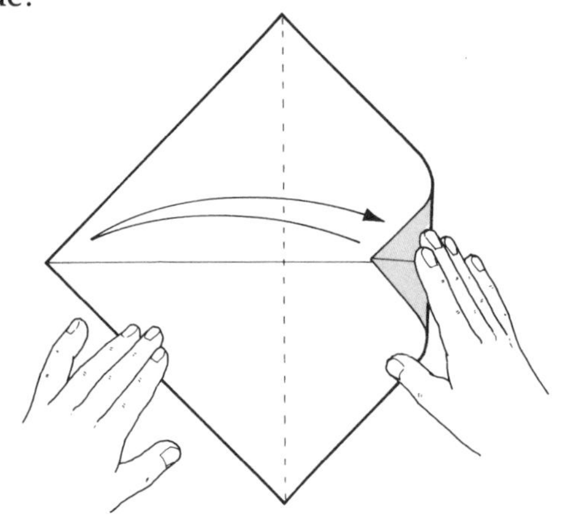

3 Fold the bottom corner up to meet the middle.

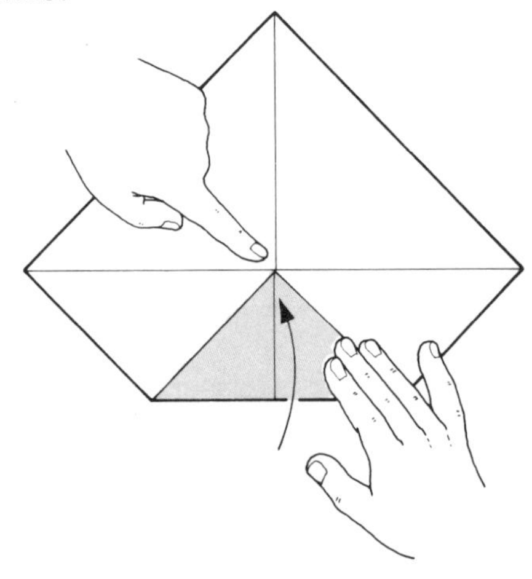

4 Fold the top down along the middle fold-line.

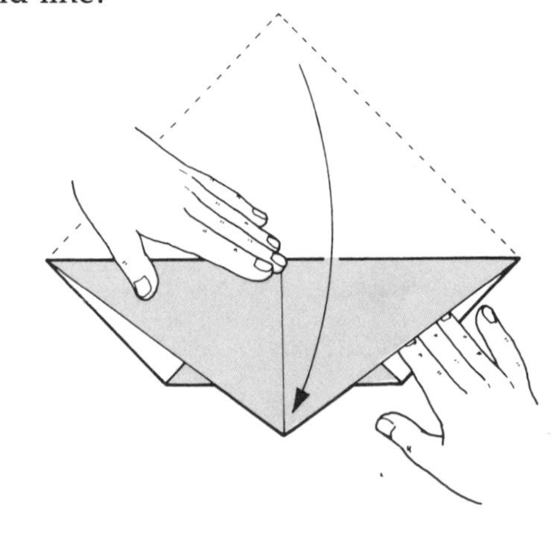

5 Fold the top side points down to meet the bottom point.

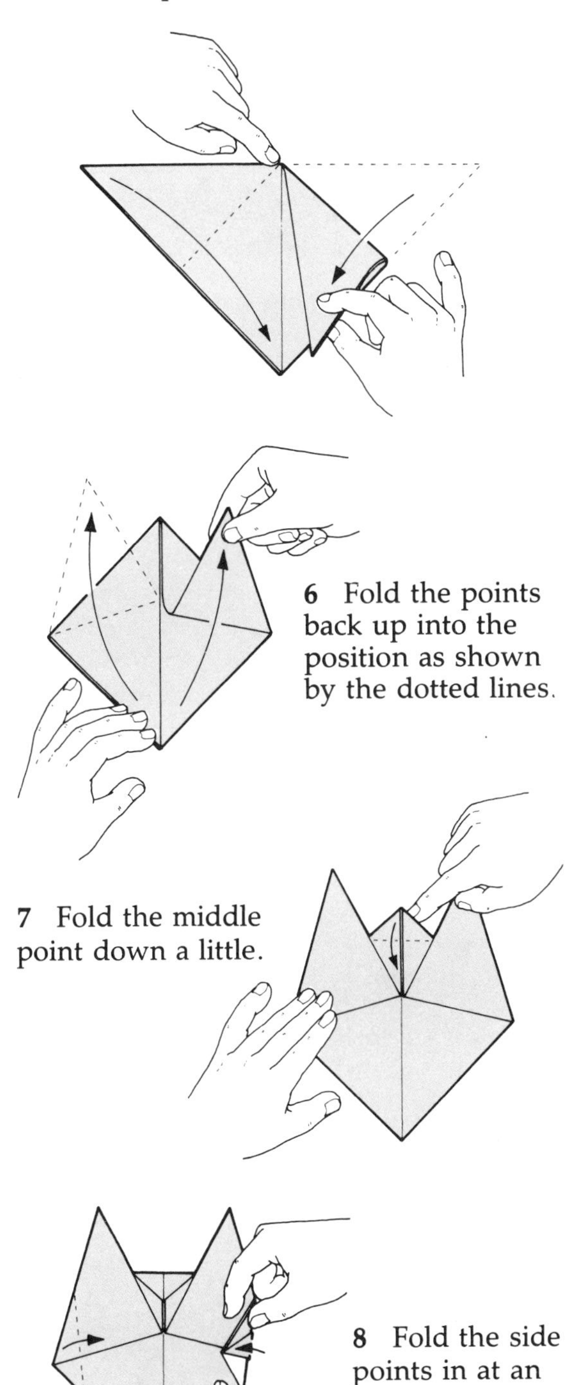

6 Fold the points back up into the position as shown by the dotted lines.

7 Fold the middle point down a little.

8 Fold the side points in at an angle.

9 Fold the bottom point up as far as possible.

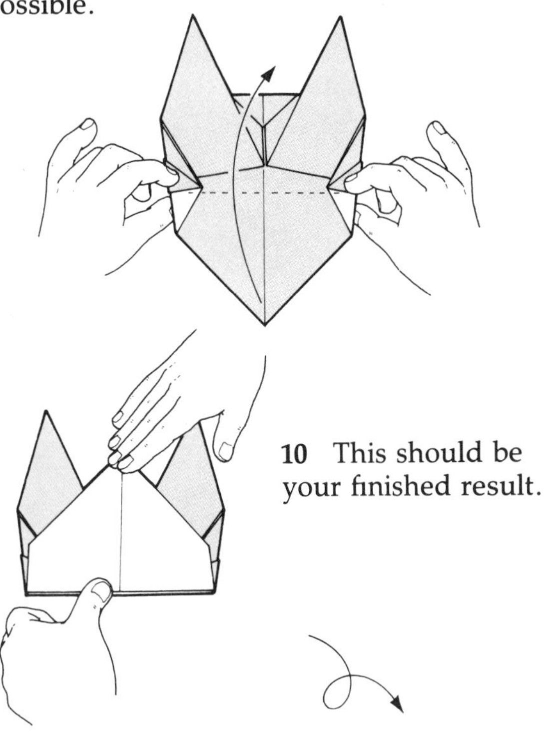

10 This should be your finished result.

11 Turn the paper over. Fold the middle point down, tucking it in between the front and back layers of paper.

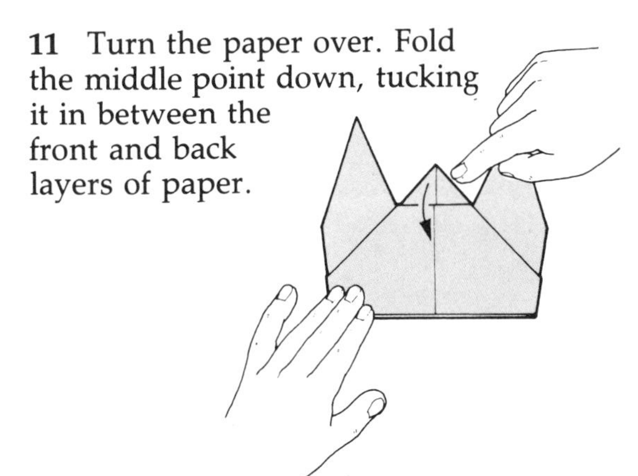

12 Carefully glue the front and back layers together, so making the basic animal face.

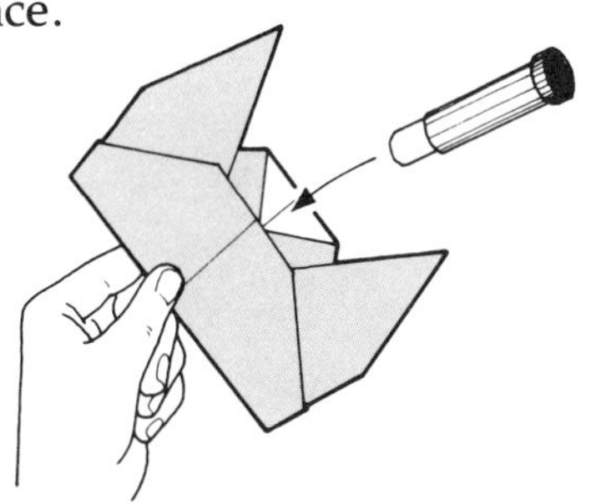

Here are just a few of the many animal faces that you can make:

13 *Fox or Cat:* Draw on facial details such as eyes, mouth and whiskers with a felt-tip pen.

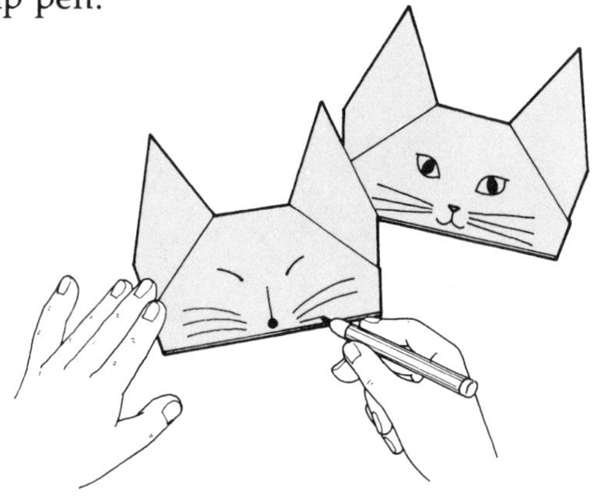

14 *Dog:* Fold the top points down and outwards as shown. Draw on facial details with a felt-tip pen.

15 *Pig:* Fold the top points down and inwards. Draw on facial details with a felt tip-pen.

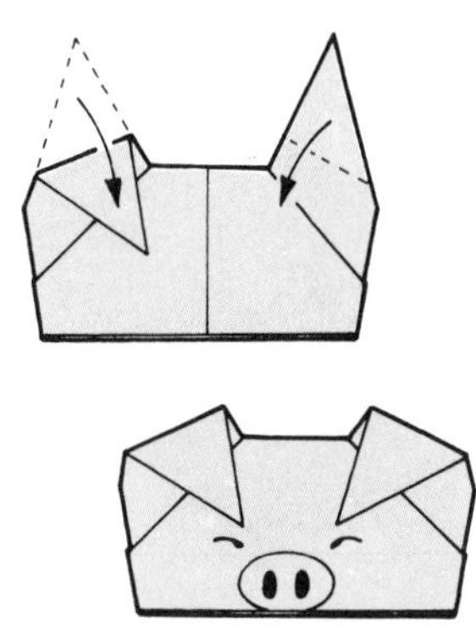

16 *Rabbit:* Start with step 8. Fold the side points in at a steep angle. Repeat steps 9 to 12. Draw on facial details with a felt-tip pen.

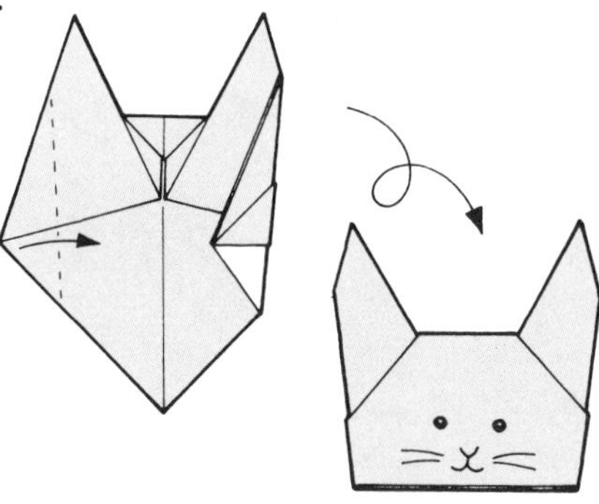

17 *Frog:* Start with step 15 (the pig's face). Lift the pig's ears upwards. Open out each ear and press it down neatly into a diamond shape. Draw on facial details with a felt-tip pen.

18 *Bear* (brown, koala or panda): Start with step 17 (the frog's face). Fold the frog's eyes up in half. Draw on facial details with a felt-tip pen.

Animal body

Traditional

You could use these origami puppets to give a show of a well-known folk tale to your younger brother or sister.

You will need:
2 squares of paper the same size, coloured on one side and white on the other
Animal face (see page 38)
Glue
Piece of thin strong card, about 20cm long and 3cm wide

1 The two squares for the body and arms should be two-thirds the size of the square used for the animal face.

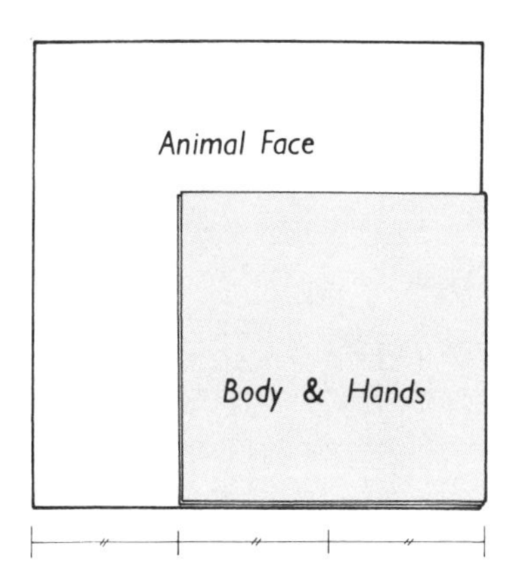

2 *Body:* Turn one square around to look like a diamond, with the white side on top. Fold and unfold it in half from side to side.

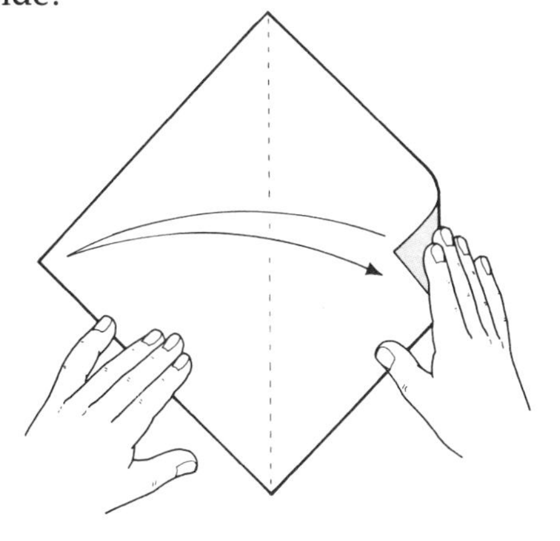

3 From the top point, fold the sloping sides in to meet the middle fold-line, so making the kite base.

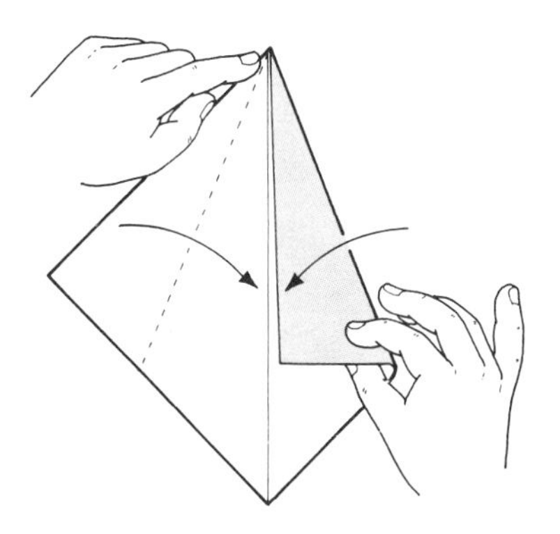

4 Fold the white triangle up along the base of the coloured triangle.

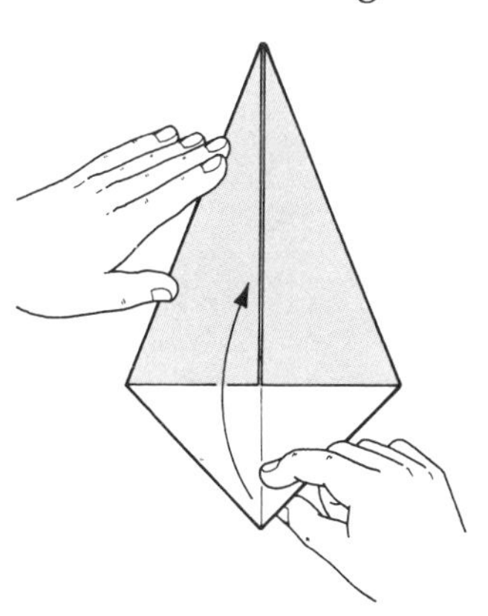

Animal body

5 Here is the completed animal boay.

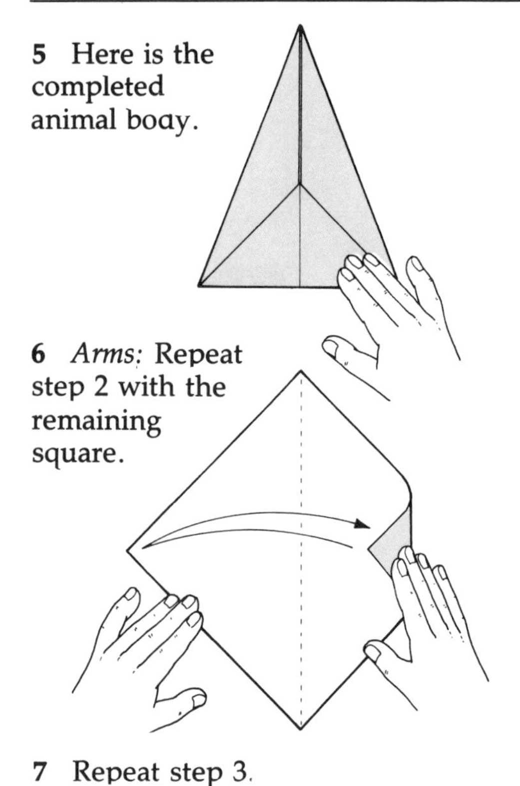

6 *Arms:* Repeat step 2 with the remaining square.

7 Repeat step 3.

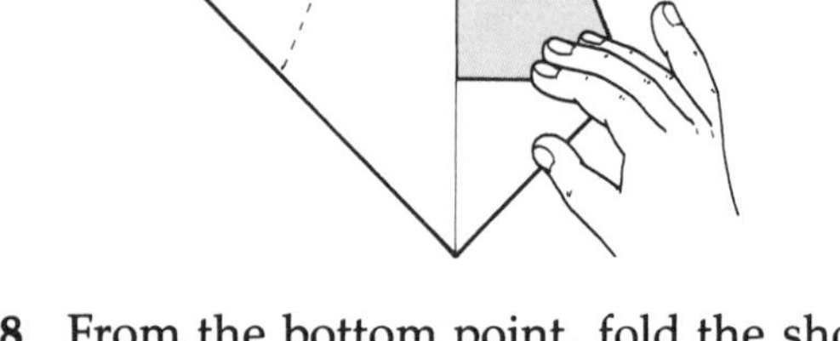

8 From the bottom point, fold the short sloping sides in to meet the middle fold-line, so making . . .

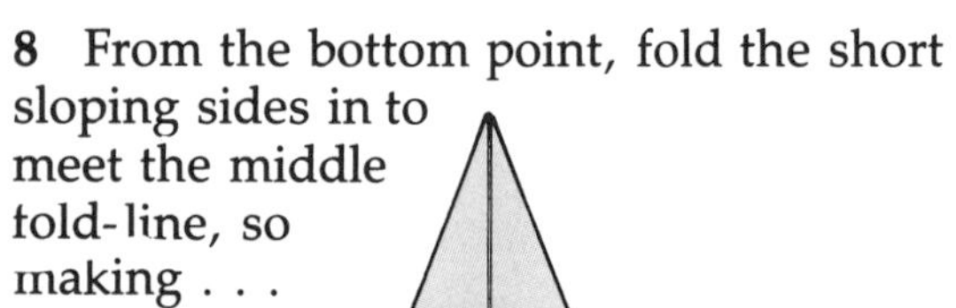

9 the diamond base.

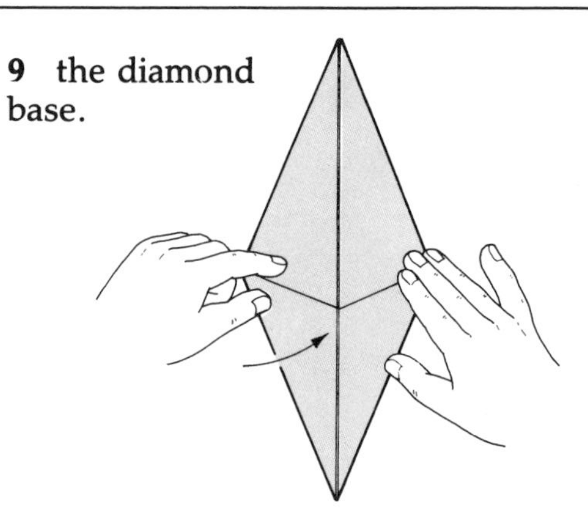

10 Turn the diamond base sideways on. Fold it in half from top to bottom.

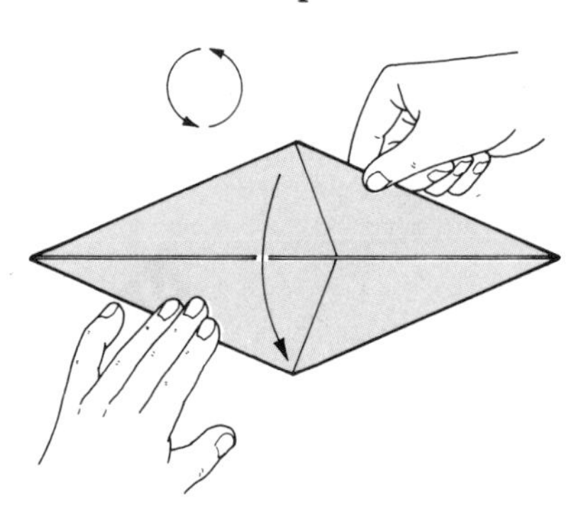

11 Fold the side points over into the position as shown by the dotted lines.

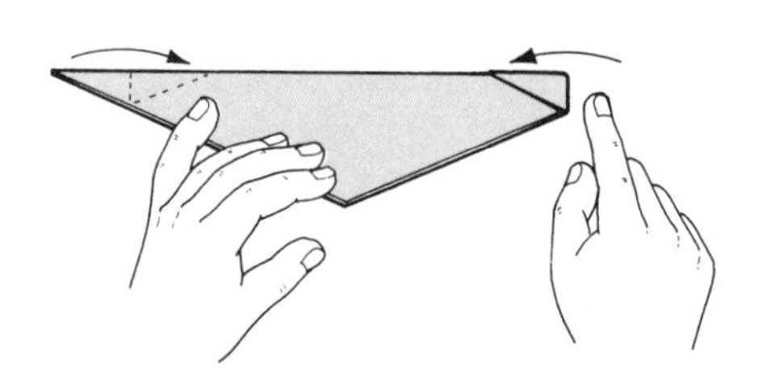

12 Lift the right-hand point upwards. Open it out and with your free hand . . .

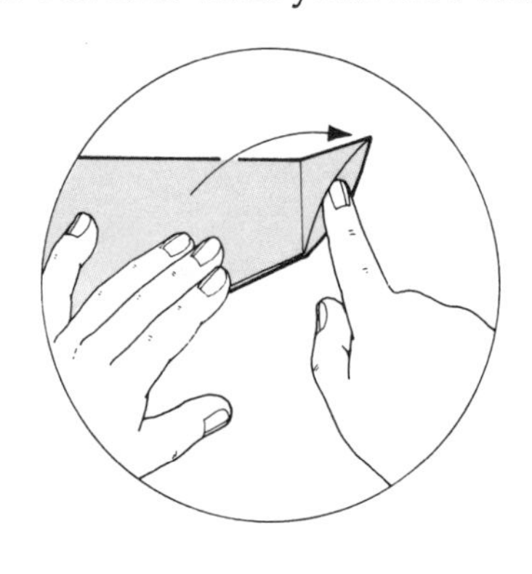

13 press it down neatly.

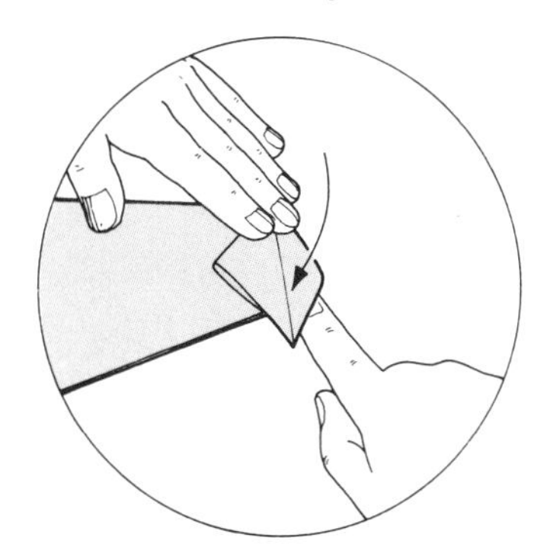

14 Fold the point up into the position as shown by the dotted lines.

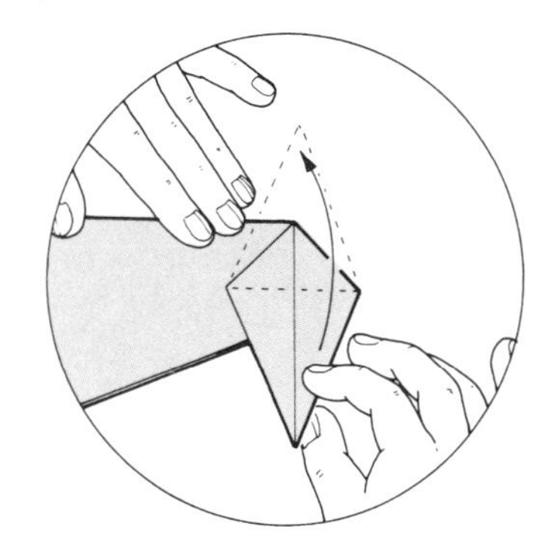

15 To complete the puppet's arms, repeat steps 12 to 14 with the left-hand point.

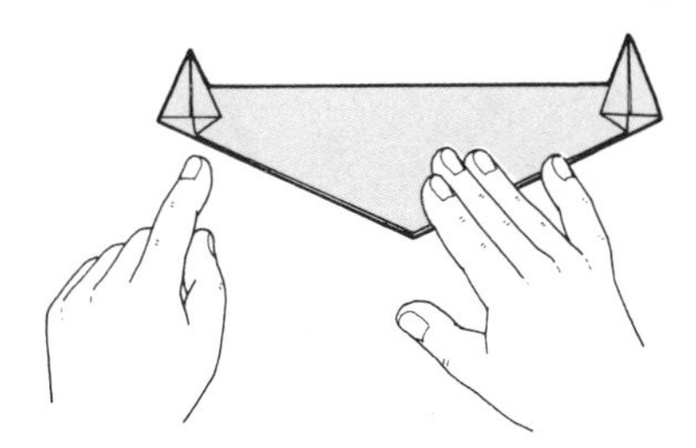

16 *Assembly:* Turn the animal's arms over and glue them on to the body.

17 Turn the animal's body and arms over. Slide the top point of the body inside the animal's face and glue them together.

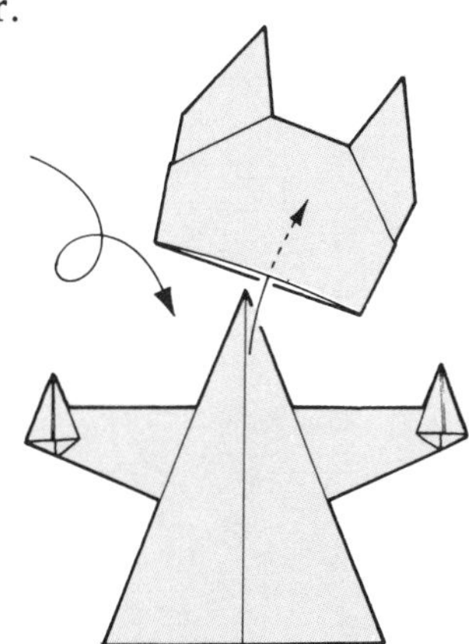

18 To make a puppet, glue the piece of card on to the back of the animal's body.

19 Now make a few more puppets.

Santa Claus

Masao Mizuno

Do try to fold this origami fold accurately. Otherwise your finished Santa Claus will not look neat and tidy.

You will need:
2 squares of paper the same size, red on one side and white on the other
Glue

1 *Body:* Fold one square in half from bottom to top, with the coloured side on top.

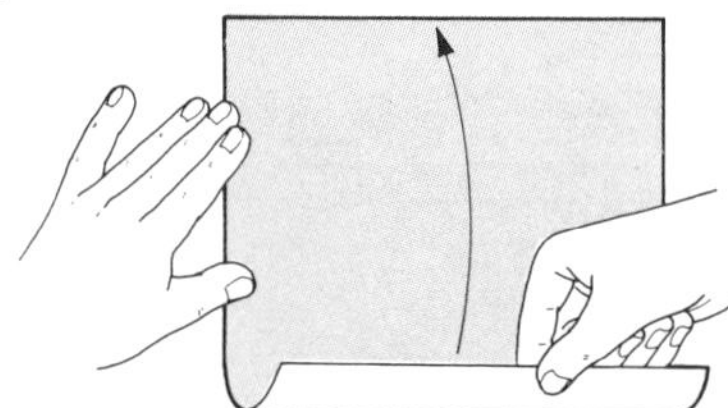

2 Fold it in half from side to side.

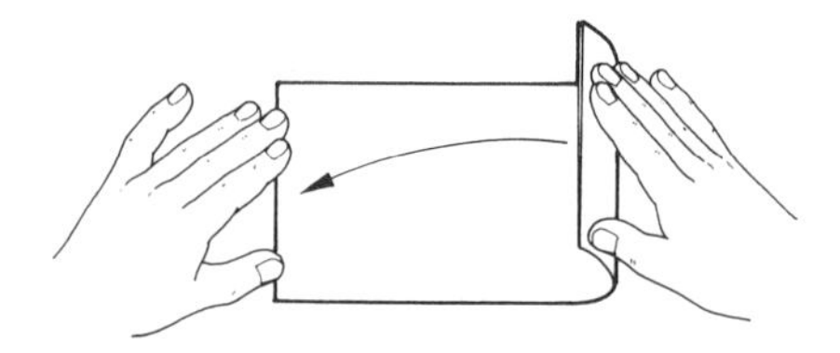

3 Open out the paper completely, back to step 1.

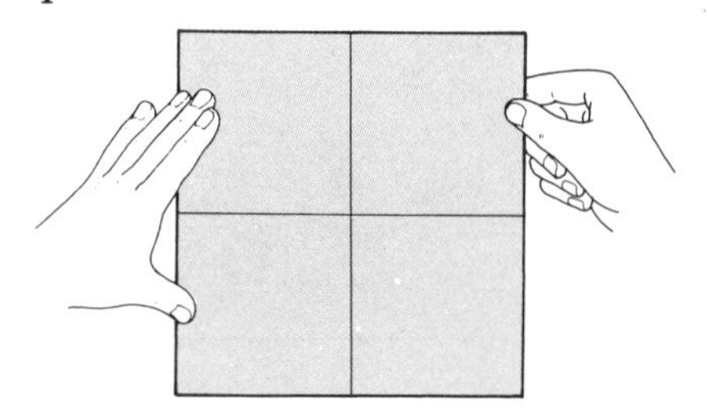

4 Fold in the top and bottom a little.

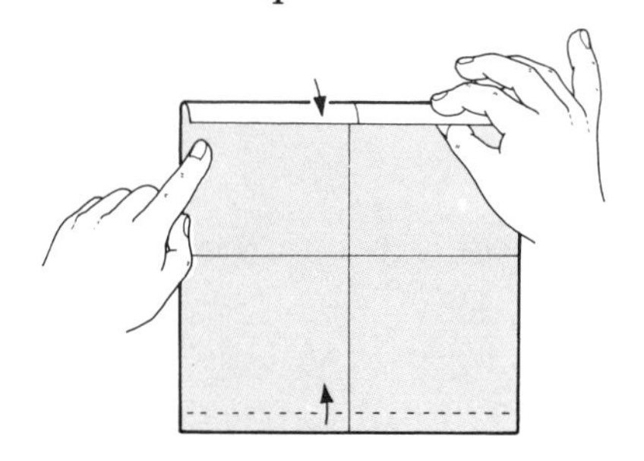

5 Turn the paper over. Fold the sides in to meet the middle fold-line.

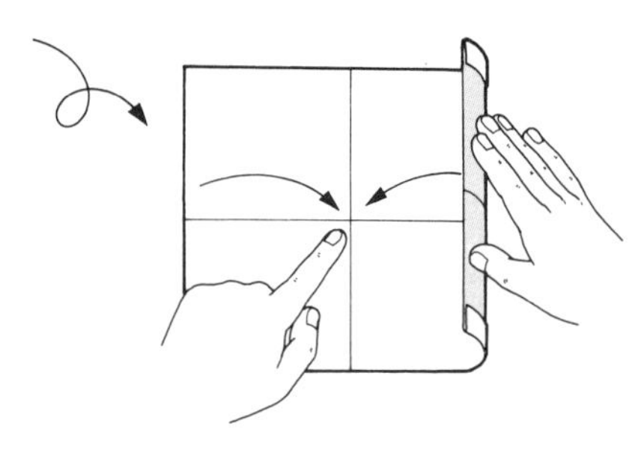

6 This should be your finished result.

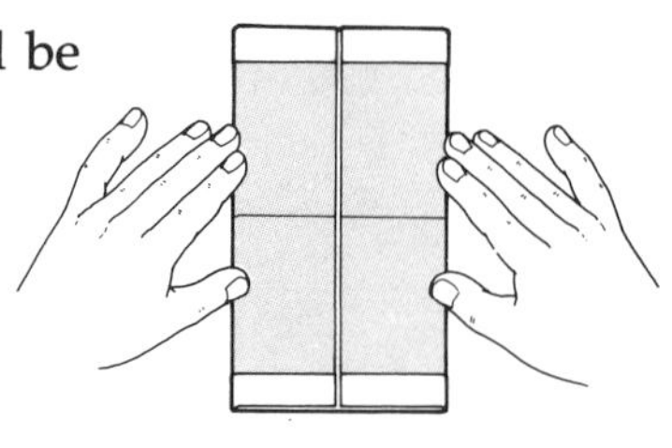

7 Fold the right and left-hand layers of paper over and outwards from the middle, as shown by the dotted lines.

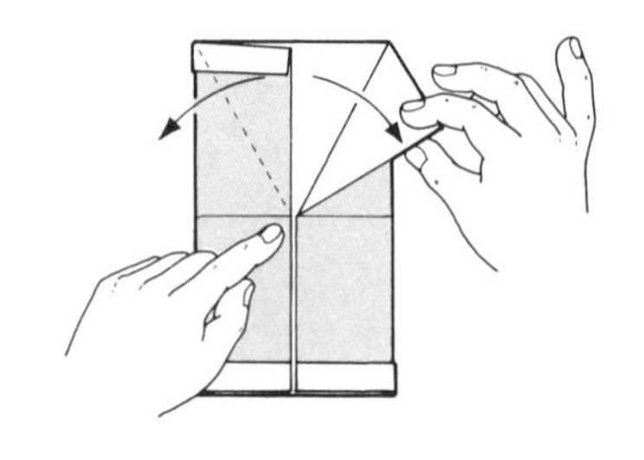

8 Fold the top down as far as shown.

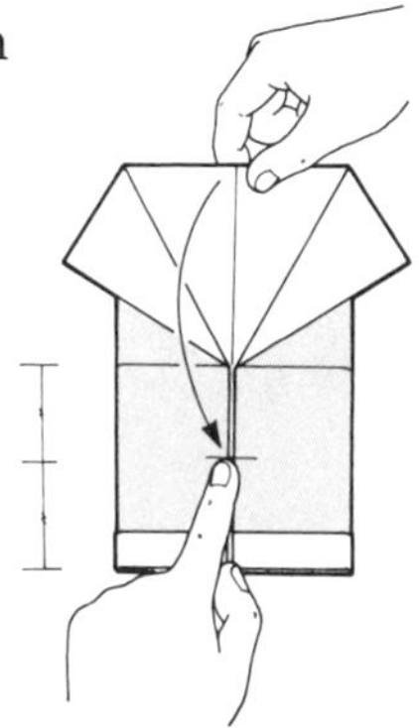

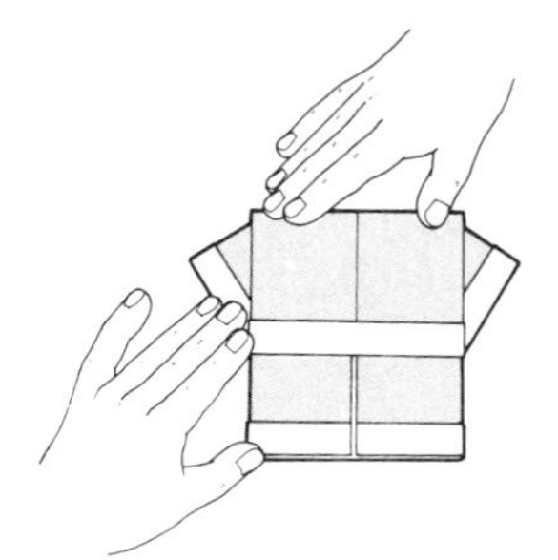

9 Here is the completed body.

10 *Face and hat:* Turn the remaining square around to look like a diamond, with the coloured side on top. From the bottom point, fold the sloping sides in a little as shown.

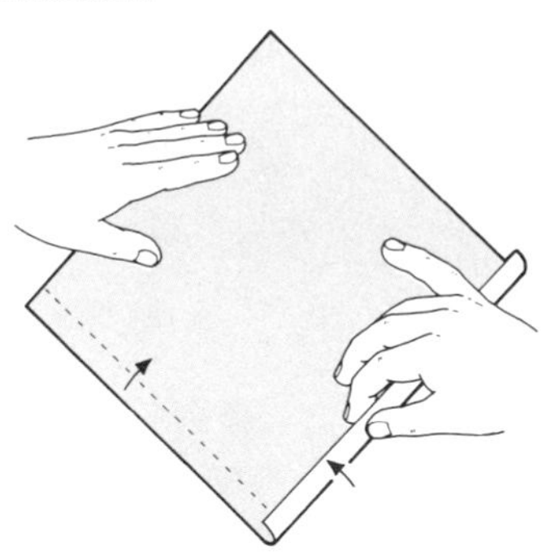

11 Fold the top point over and over a little.

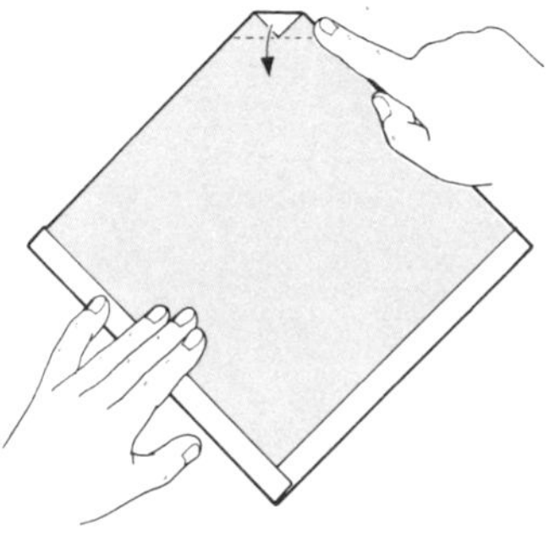

12 Turn the paper over. From the top, fold the left-hand sloping side over one-third of the way.

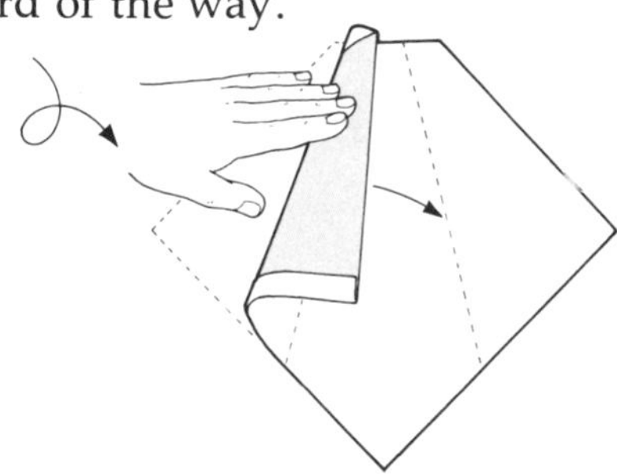

13 Repeat step 12 with the right-hand sloping side.

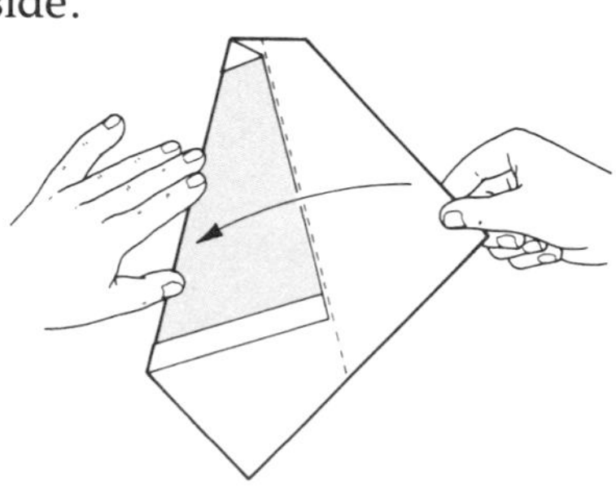

14 Fold the top over and outwards at an angle as shown.

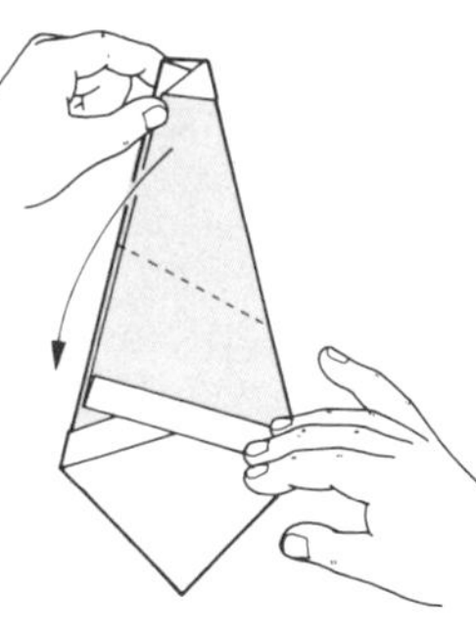

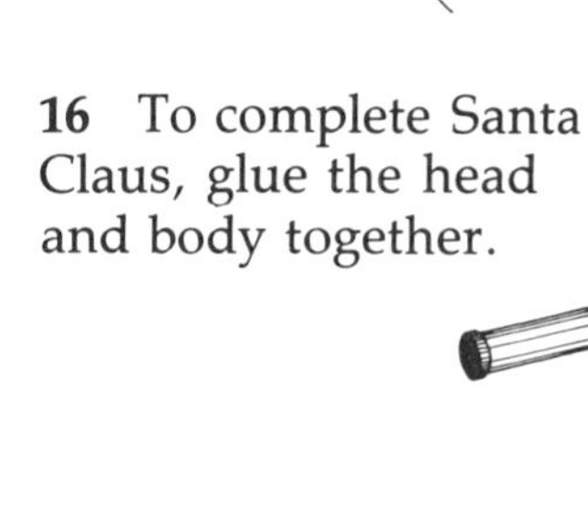

15 Fold behind a little of the bottom point, so suggesting Santa's chin.

16 To complete Santa Claus, glue the head and body together.

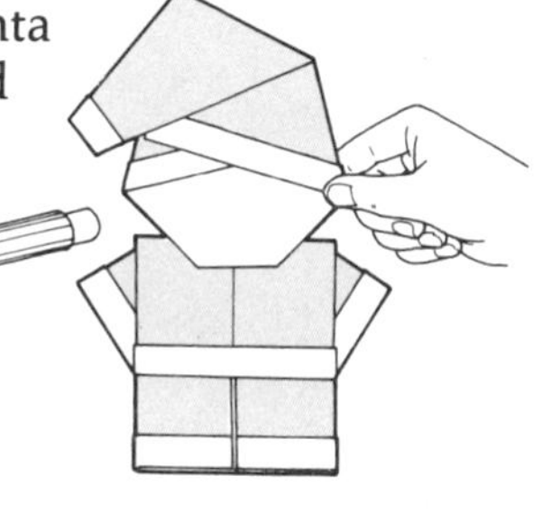

Christmas wreath

Minako Ishibashi

This beautiful origami fold is made by folding eight simple units which are then fitted together. This style of folding is called modular origami.

You will need:
8 squares of paper all the same size, green on one side and white on the other
Glue
Few coloured sticky-backed circles

1 Turn one square around to look like a diamond, with the coloured side on top. Fold and unfold it in half from side to side.

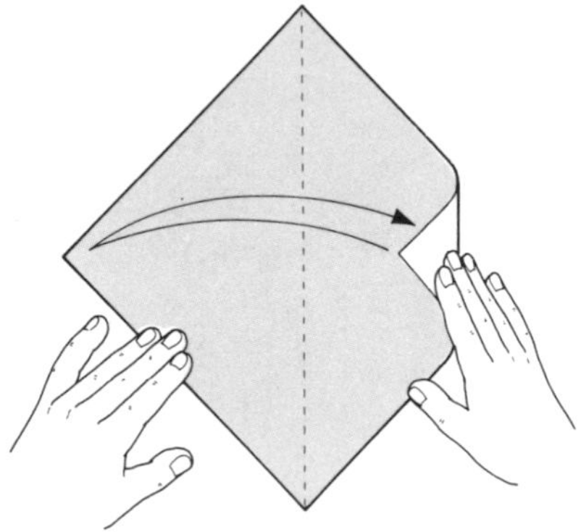

2 Fold it in half from top to bottom.

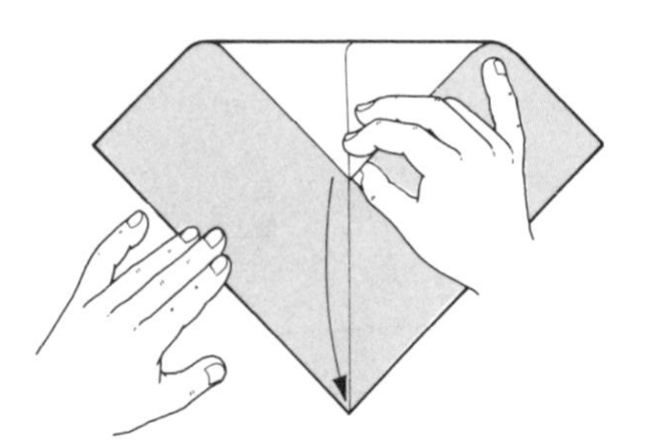

3 Fold the side points in to meet the middle of the top.

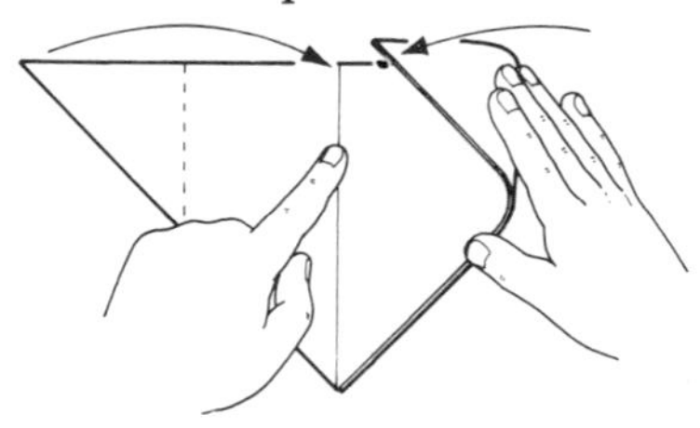

4 Lift up the right-hand point. Start to open out the point and with your free hand . . .

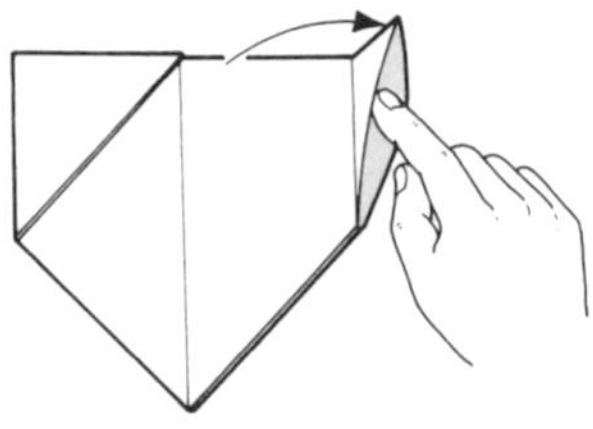

5 press it down neatly into a diamond.

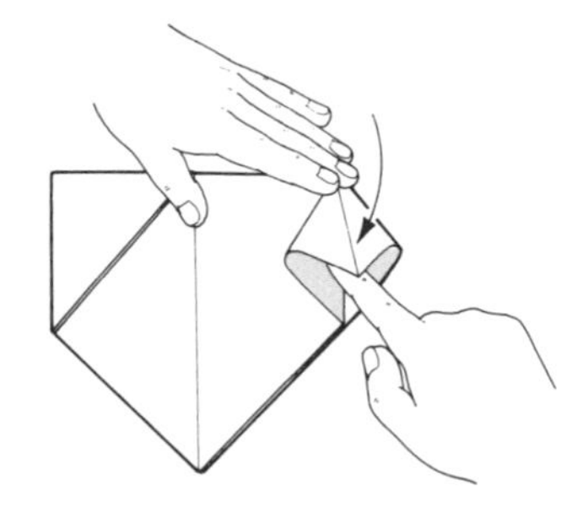

6 Repeat steps 4 and 5 with the left-hand point.

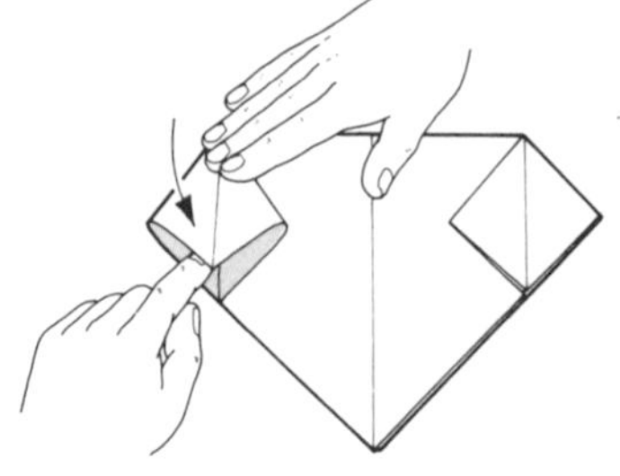

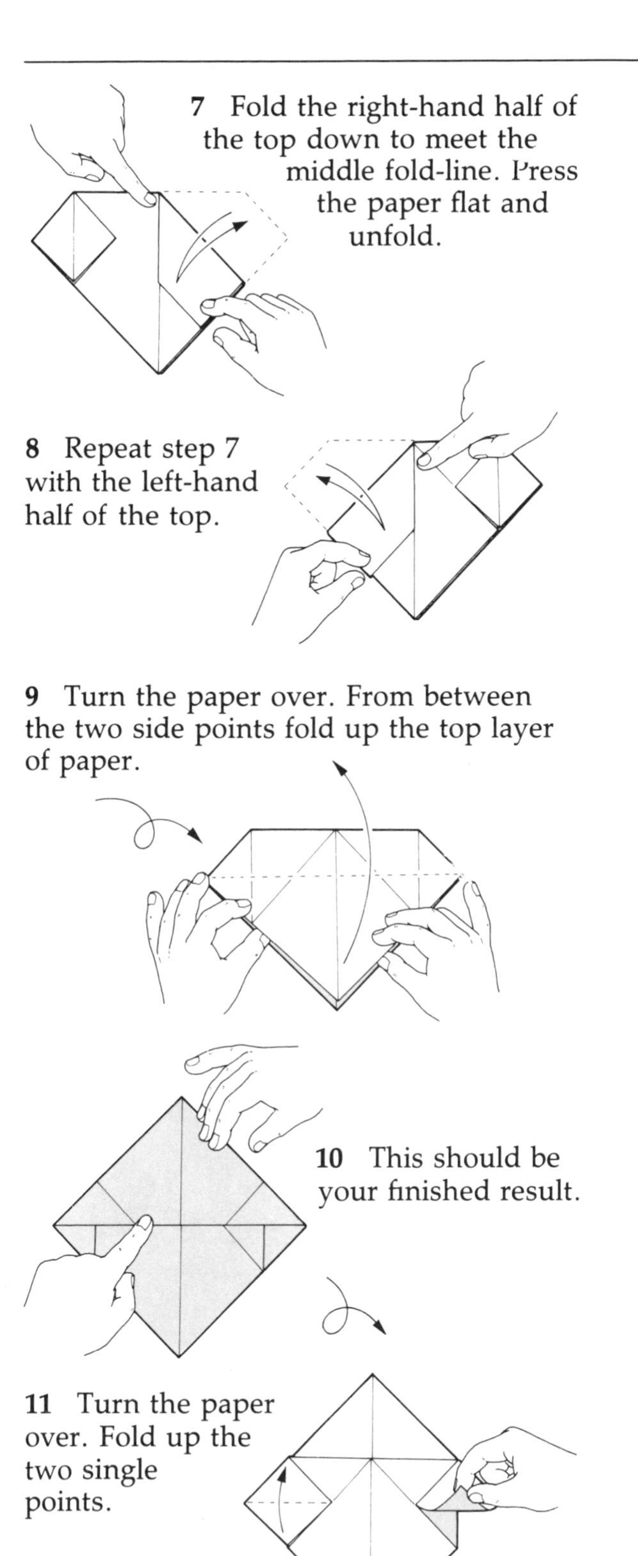

7 Fold the right-hand half of the top down to meet the middle fold-line. Press the paper flat and unfold.

8 Repeat step 7 with the left-hand half of the top.

9 Turn the paper over. From between the two side points fold up the top layer of paper.

10 This should be your finished result.

11 Turn the paper over. Fold up the two single points.

12 Bring the side points together and at same time . . .

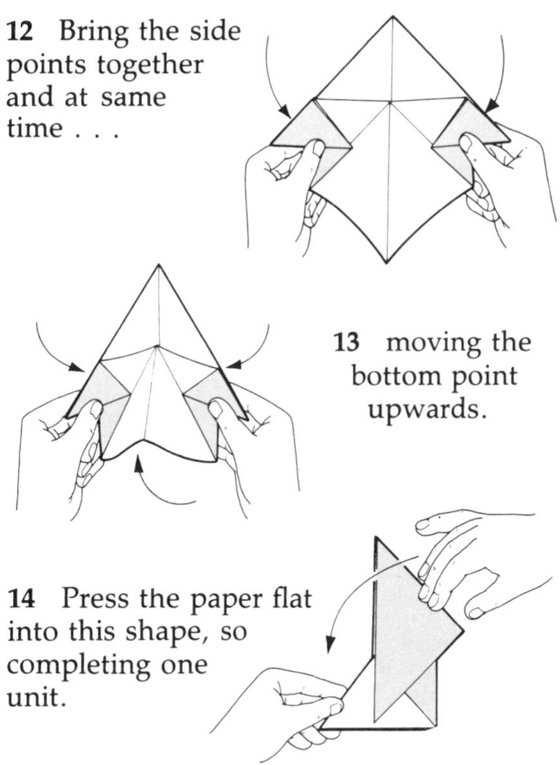

13 moving the bottom point upwards.

14 Press the paper flat into this shape, so completing one unit.

15 *Assembly:* Repeat steps 1 to 14 with the remaining seven squares. Tuck one unit inside another and glue them together.

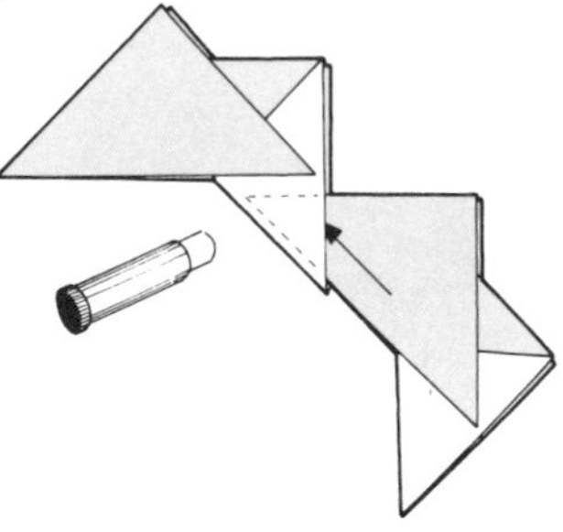

16 Keep on tucking and gluing units together carefully, until you have built up the Christmas wreath. To complete, decorate the wreath with coloured sticky-backed circles.

Balloon decoration

Traditional

Made out of shiny metallic gift paper, this easy origami fold will make an ideal Christmas decoration.

You will need:
Square of paper, coloured on one side and white on the other

1 Fold the square in half from top to bottom, with the white side on top.

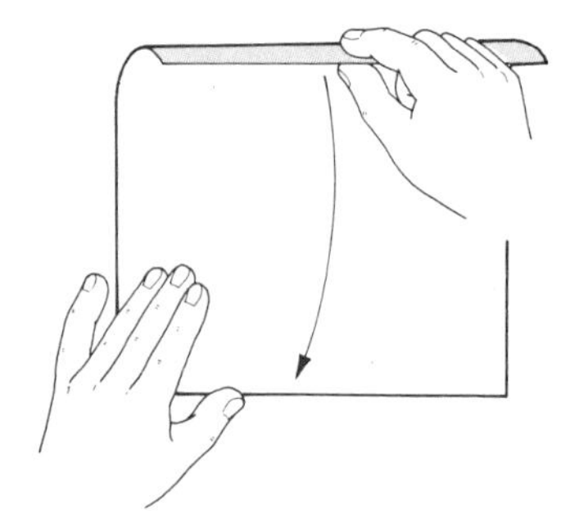

2 Fold it in half from side to side.

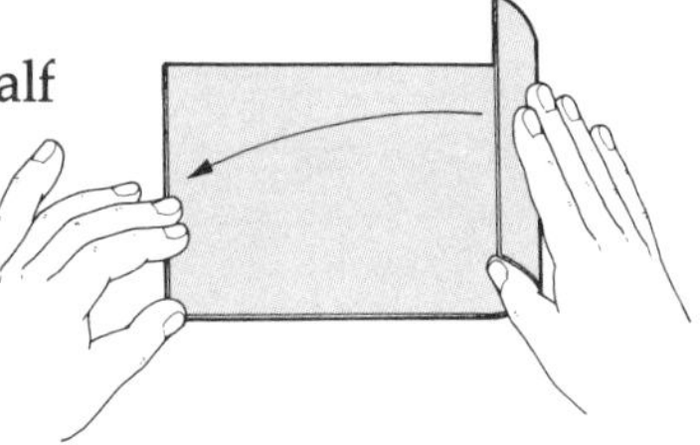

3 Lift the top half up along the middle fold-line. Start to open out the paper and with your free hand . . .

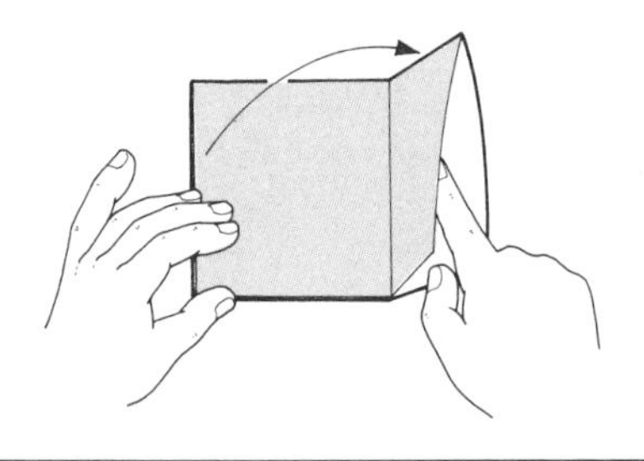

4 press it down neatly into a triangle.

5 Turn the paper over. Repeat step 3.

6 Repeat step 4, so making a shape that in origami is called the waterbomb base.

7 Fold the top bottom points up to meet the top point.

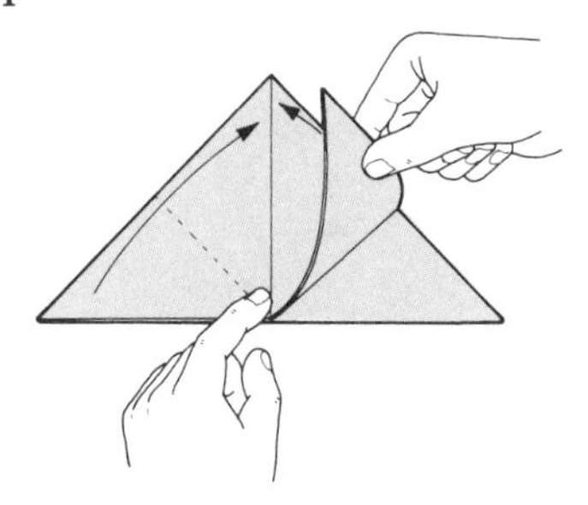

8 Fold the top right and left-hand side points in to meet the middle.

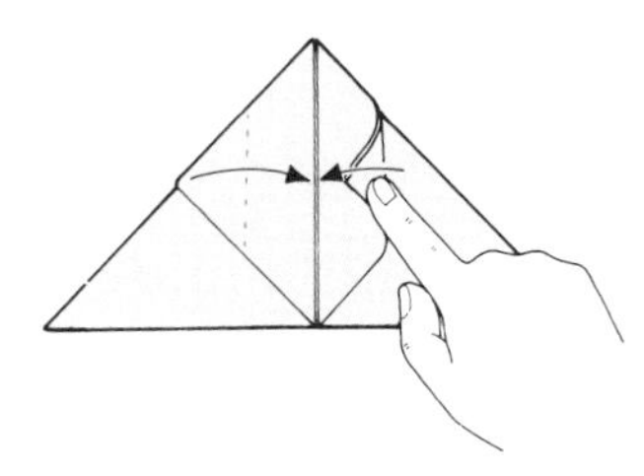

9 Fold the top points down to meet the middle, so making two little triangular flaps.

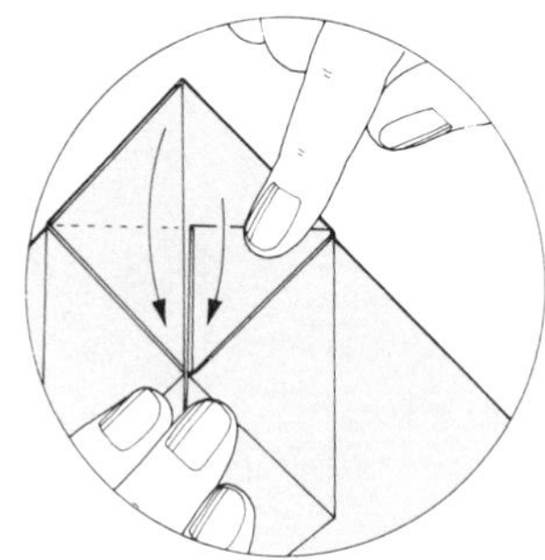

10 Fold the little triangular flaps over and tuck them into the pockets next to them.

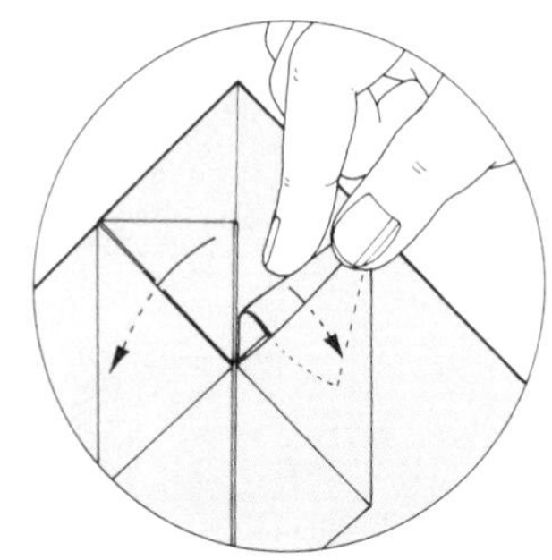

11 This should be your finished result. Turn the paper over. Repeat steps 7 to 10.

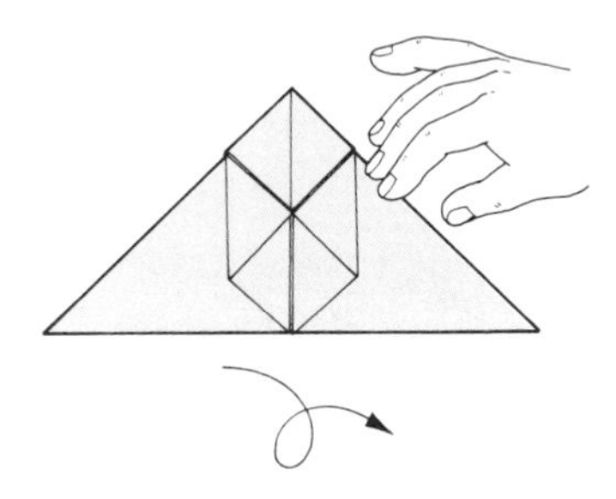

12 Fold the right-hand side over diagonally.

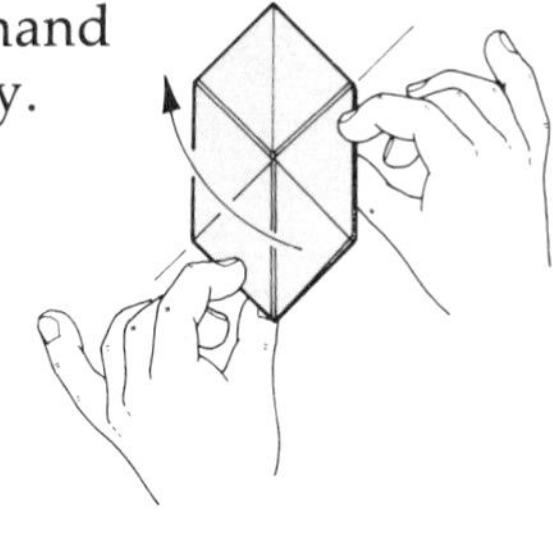

13 Press the paper flat and unfold.

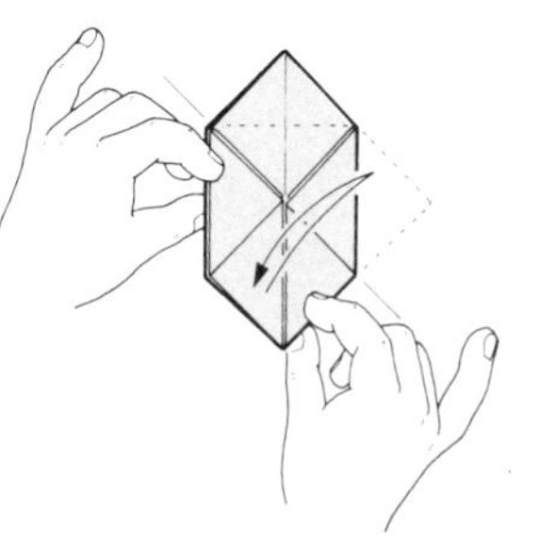

14 Repeat steps 12 and 13 with the left-hand side.

15 Hold the paper very loosely and blow gently into the small hole that you will find at the bottom point. The paper will rise up and form itself into a balloon-like shape.

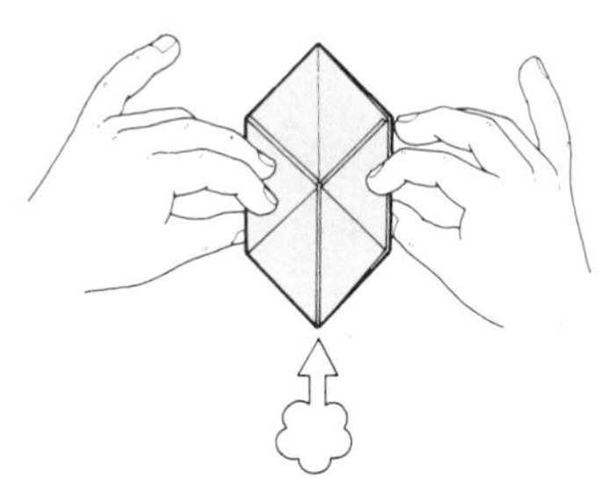

16 To complete the decoration, push in the middle fold-lines of the squares that radiate out from the top and bottom points.

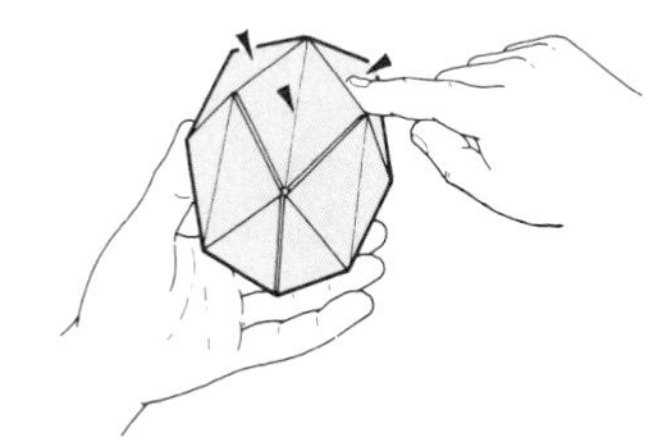

Goldfish

Traditional

This delightful origami fold is thought to have originated in China.

You will need:
Square of paper, coloured on one side and white on the other
Felt-tip pen
Needle and cotton

1 Fold as far as step 6 of the balloon decoration on page 48.

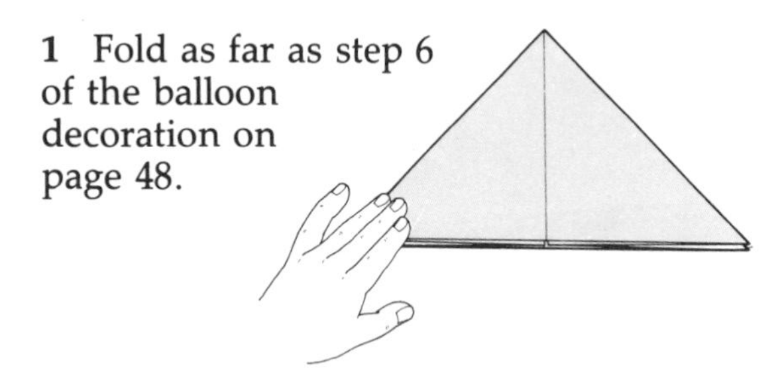

2 With the top bottom points, fold steps 7 to 10 of the balloon decoration on page 48.

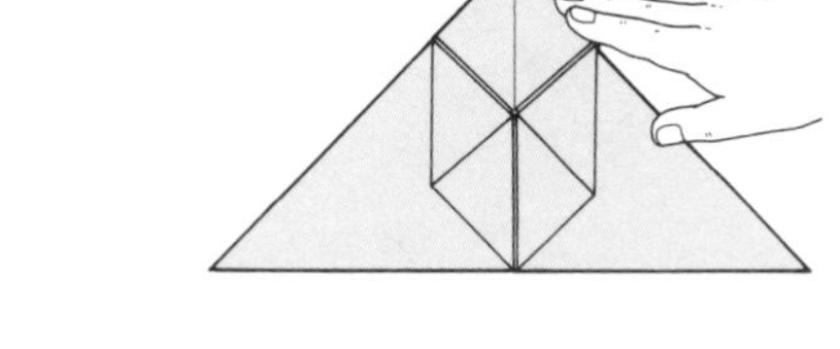

3 Turn the paper over. From the top point, fold the right and left-hand sloping sides over to lie along the middle fold-line.

4 Fold the bottom left-hand point over and outwards into the position as shown by the dotted lines.

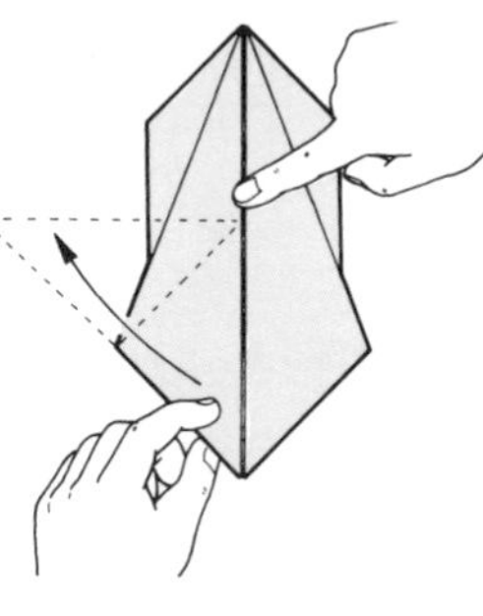

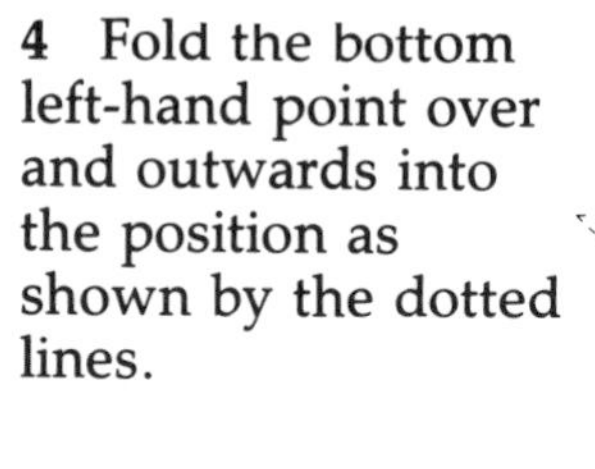

5 Fold the left-hand layer of paper over to the right-hand side, like turning a page of a book.

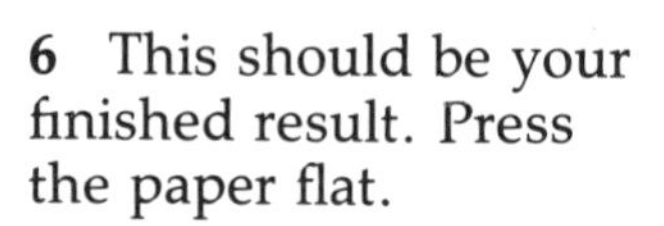

6 This should be your finished result. Press the paper flat.

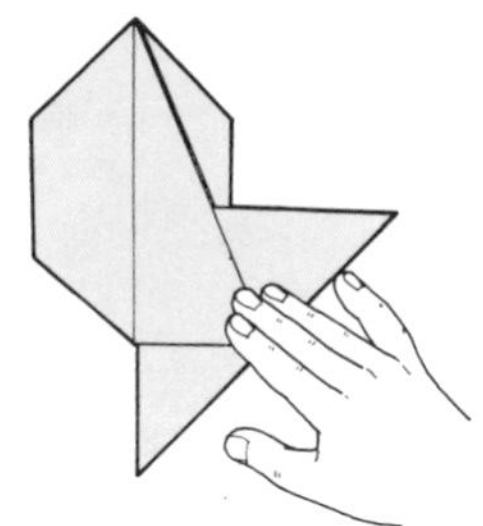

7 Hold the paper very loosely and blow gently into the small hole that you will find at the bottom. The paper will rise up and form itself into the shape of a goldfish.

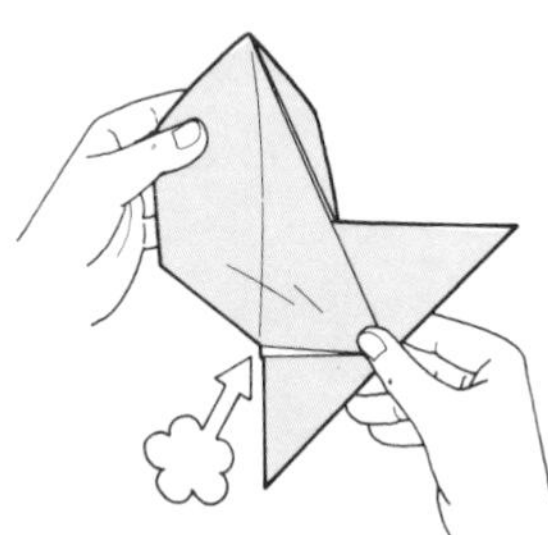

8 Draw on eyes with a felt-tip pen. To complete the goldfish, attach a loop of cotton to the top fin, so that you can turn the goldfish into a mobile.

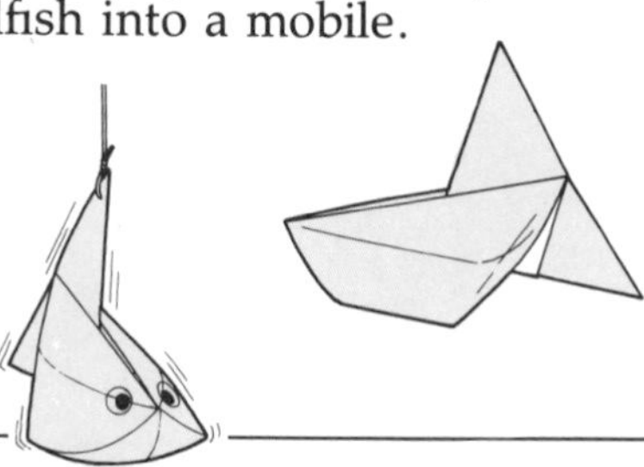

Rabbit

Traditional

Now that you have become an expert, try to take great care in obtaining the right kind of paper to match the origami that you plan to fold. More often than not, this will help to enhance the finished product.

You will need:

Square of paper, pink on one side and white on the other
Felt-tip pen

1 With the pink side on top, fold as far as step 6 of the balloon decoration on page 48.

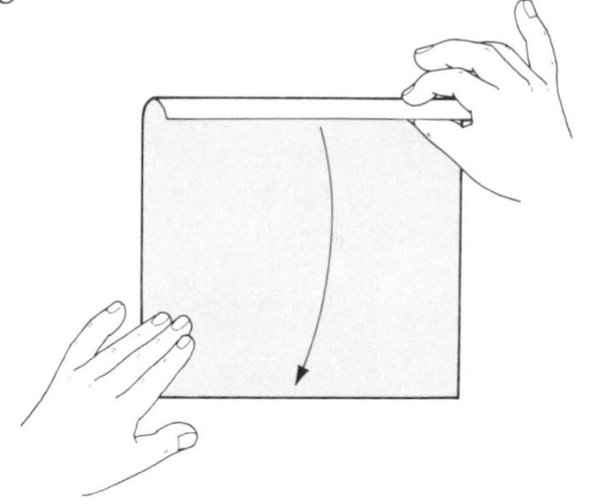

2 With the top bottom points, fold steps 7 to 10 of the balloon decoration on page 48.

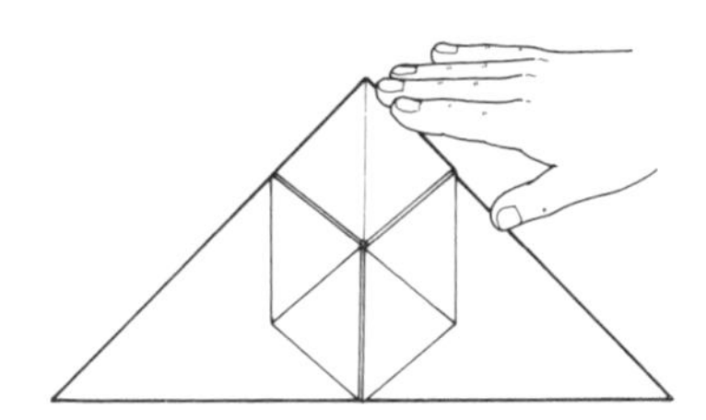

3 Turn the paper over. Fold the bottom points up to meet the top point.

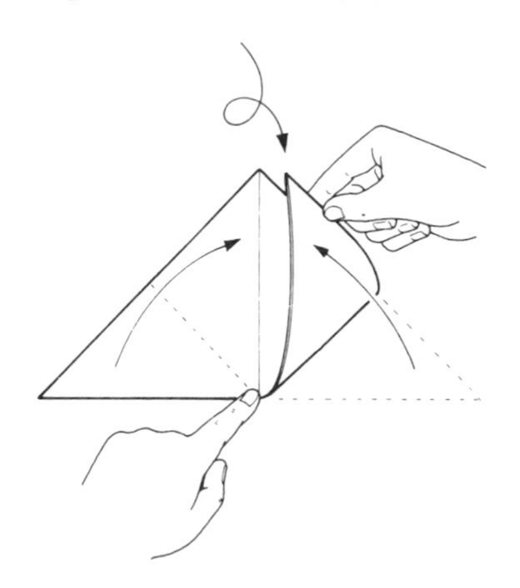

4 Fold the right-hand side over to the left, like turning a page of a book.

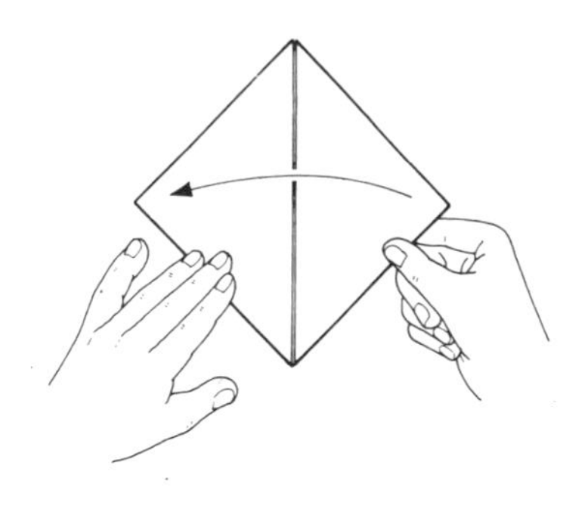

5 Fold the top left-hand point in to meet the middle.

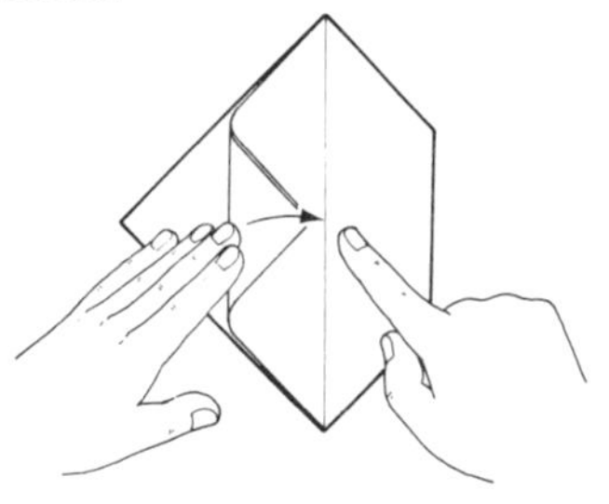

6 Fold the side back over to the right.

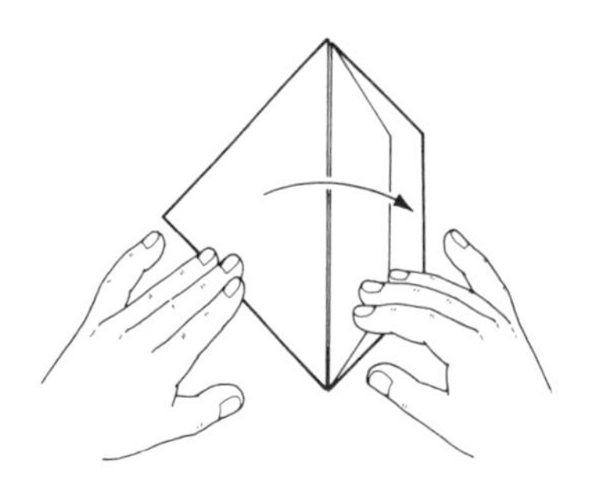

7 Repeat steps 4 to 6 with the left-hand side.

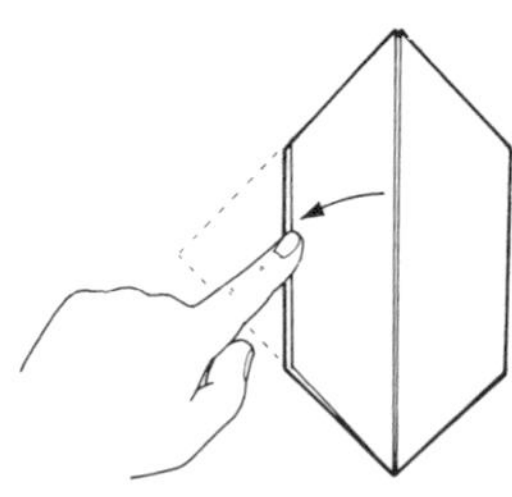

8 Fold the top points over and outwards into the position as shown by the dotted lines.

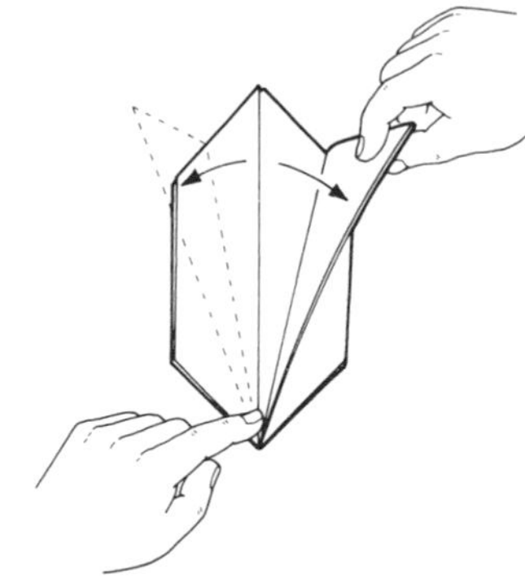

9 Put a finger inside the right-hand point and . . .

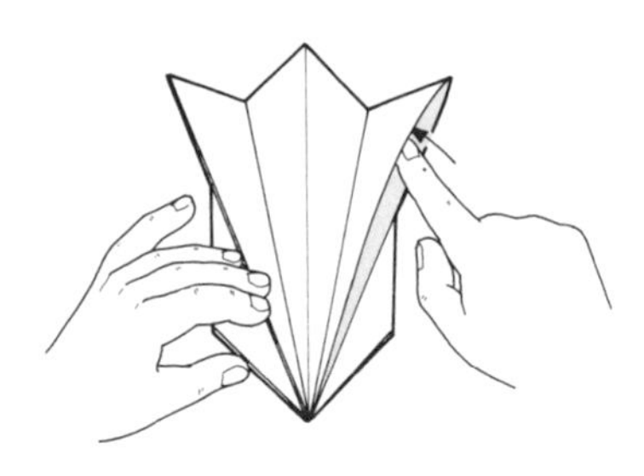

10 open it out into a dish-like shape. Repeat with the left-hand point.

11 Hold the paper very loosely and blow gently into the small hole that you will find at the bottom. the paper will rise up and form itself into the shape of a rabbit.

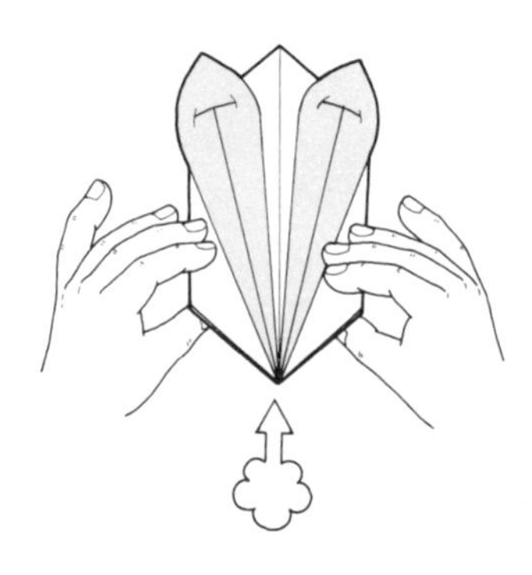

12 To complete the rabbit, draw on its eyes with a felt-tip pen.

Blow top

Traditional

The folding of this particular fold is based around the traditional waterbomb base. Even though it may appear difficult at first, the blow top can be mastered quite easily.

You will need:
6 squares of paper all the same size, coloured on one side and white on the other
Pencil
Needle and cotton

1 Fold each square as far as step 6 of the balloon decoration on page 48. As a help during the assembly, label each waterbomb base from A to F, with the pencil.

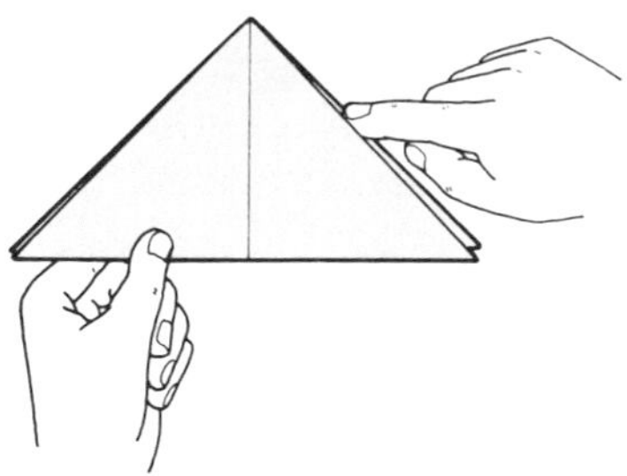

2 Open out each waterbomb base into a star-like shape.

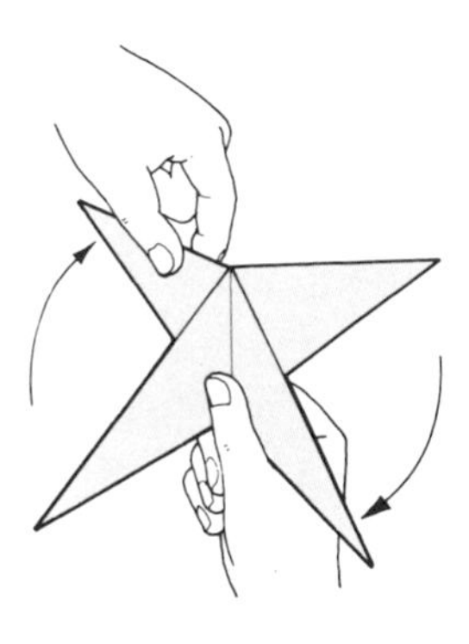

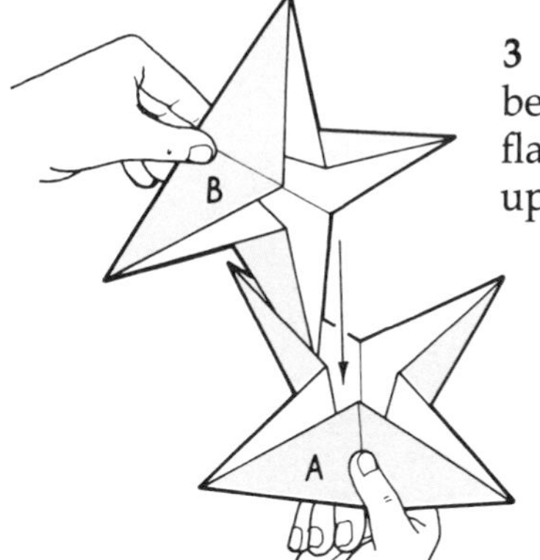

3 Hold piece A between the four flaps, open side up. Tuck piece B into piece A.

4 Tuck piece C into piece B. At the same time tuck piece A into piece C.

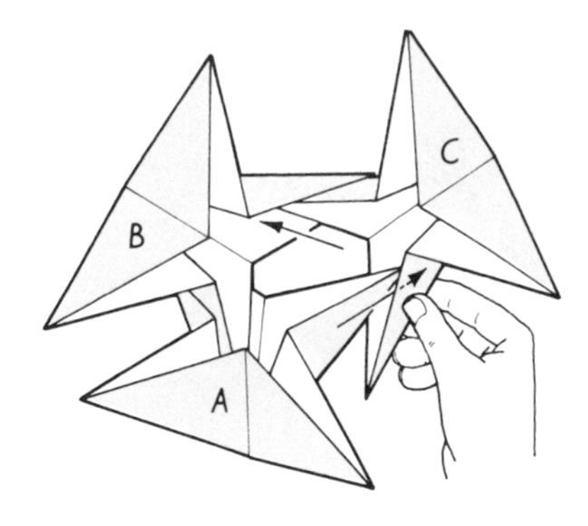

5 Tuck piece A into piece D. Now tuck piece D into piece B.

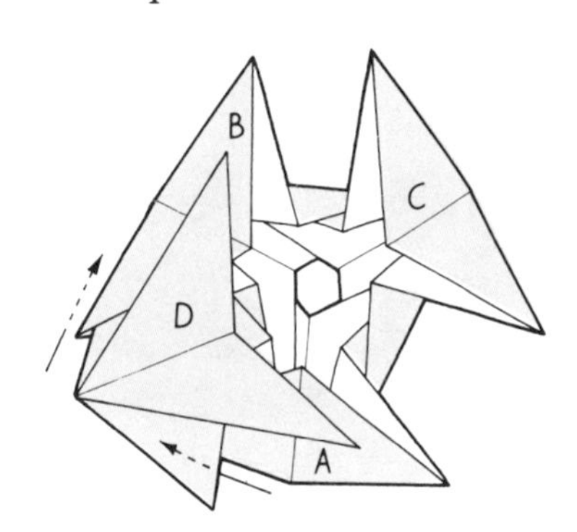

6 Tuck piece E into piece A. Carefully tuck pieces D and C into piece E.

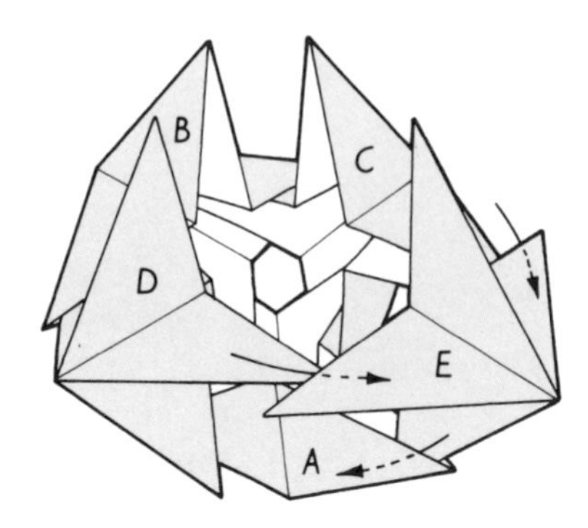

7 Tuck piece F into pieces D and C. Finally tuck pieces B and E into piece F.

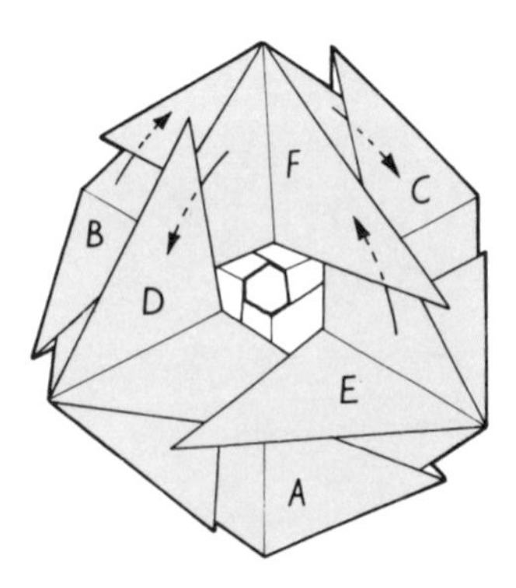

8 Gently push all the waterbomb bases snugly together.

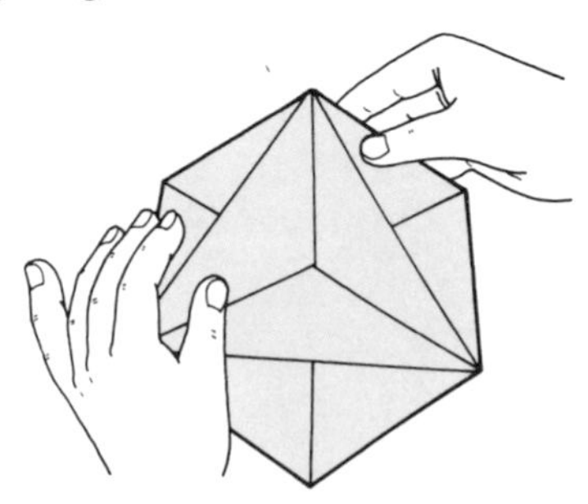

9 To complete the blow top, attach a loop of cotton to the top, so that it can become a hanging ornament.

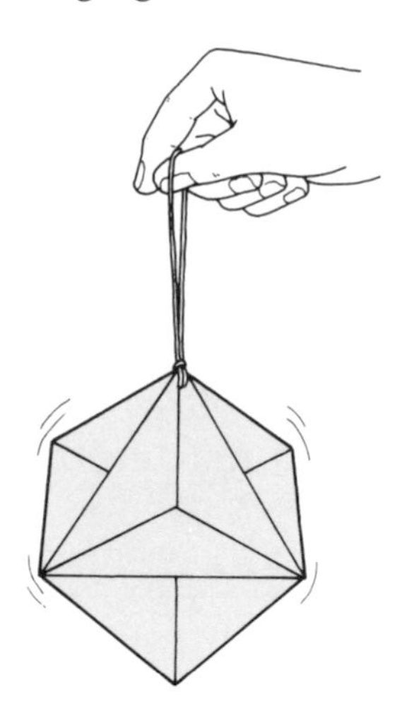

10 Or if you place the blow top between the palms of each hand, and . . .

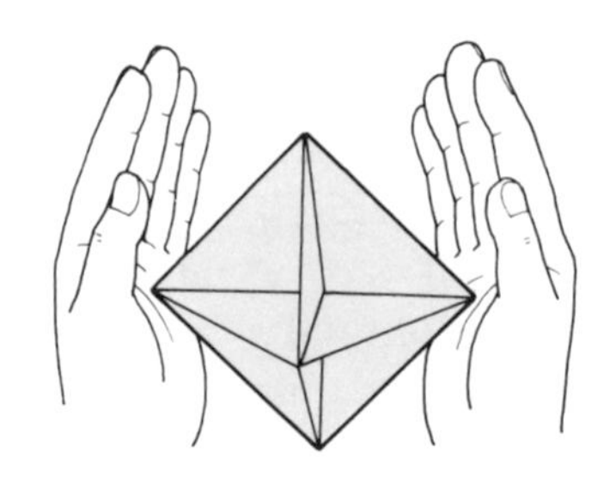

11 softly blow where indicated, the blow top will spin merrily around.

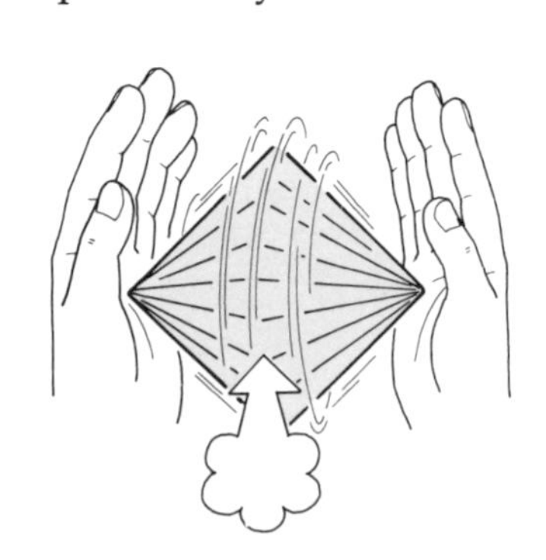

Fruit

Toshie Takahama

By joining together the balloon decoration on page 48 with a stem, it is possible to make many different kinds of fruit.

You will need:
Few squares of paper all the same size, coloured on one side and white on the other (try to fold each fruit in the correct colour of paper – orange, green, brown, red and purple)
Scissors
Glue

1 *Orange:* Fold an orange square, with the white side on top, as far as step 11 of the balloon decoration on page 48. Now repeat step 15 of the same decoration on page 48. To complete, cut out a green centre and glue it over the small hole.

2 *Apple:* Fold a green square, with the white side on top, as above. To complete, cut out a brown stalk and glue it inside the small hole.

3 *Cherries:* Fold two red squares, with the white side on top, as above. (Use paper that is 9cm square for a perfect result.) To complete, cut out a thin strip of brown paper. Fold the strip in half and glue a cherry on to each end.

4 *Grapes:* Fold a few purple squares, with the white side on top, as above. (Use paper that is 9cm square for a perfect result.) Cut out a strip of brown paper and glue it inside the small hole of one grape. To complete, glue the remaining grapes around in a bunch.

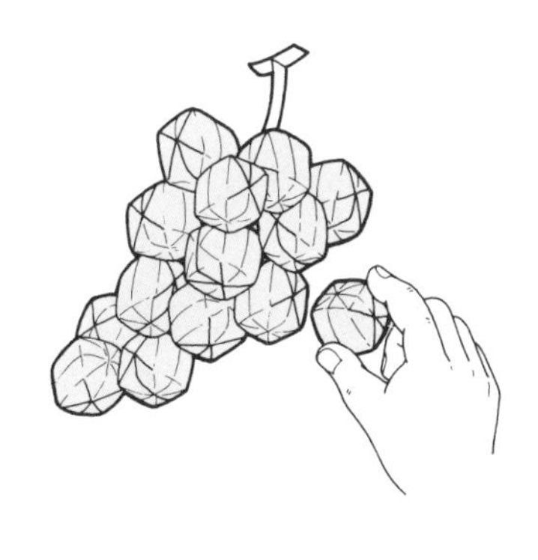

Bananas

Hiroshi Kumasaka

To complete your origami fruit bowl, here's how to make a bunch of bananas.

You will need:
Square of paper, yellow on one side and white on the other

1 Fold in a little of each corner of the square, with the white side on top. Now fold as far as step 6 of the balloon decoration on page 48.

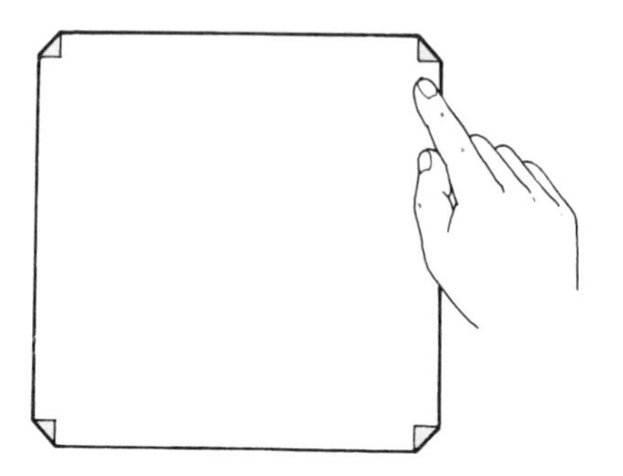

2 Fold the waterbomb base in half from side to side.

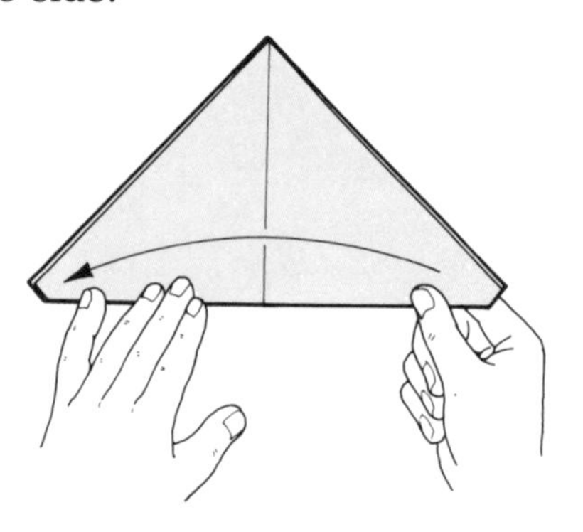

3 Fold the bottom right-hand point up into the position as shown by the dotted lines.

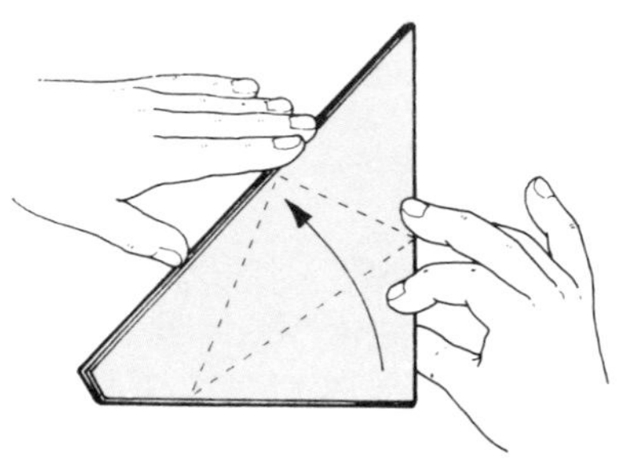

4 From the bottom left-hand point pull the topmost layer of paper upwards. Press it flat into the position as shown, by rearranging the layers of paper.

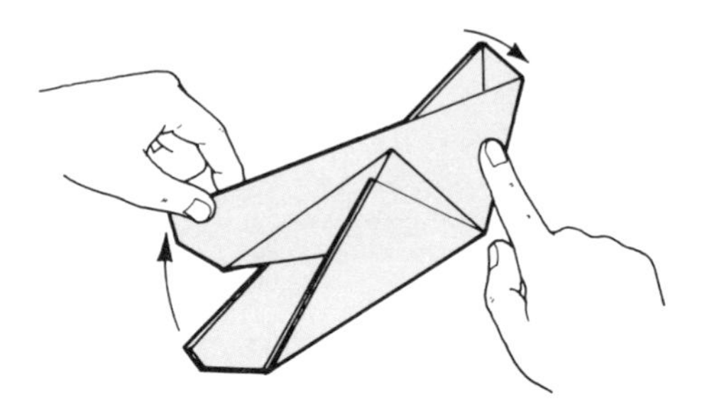

5 Repeat step 4 with the next layer of paper.

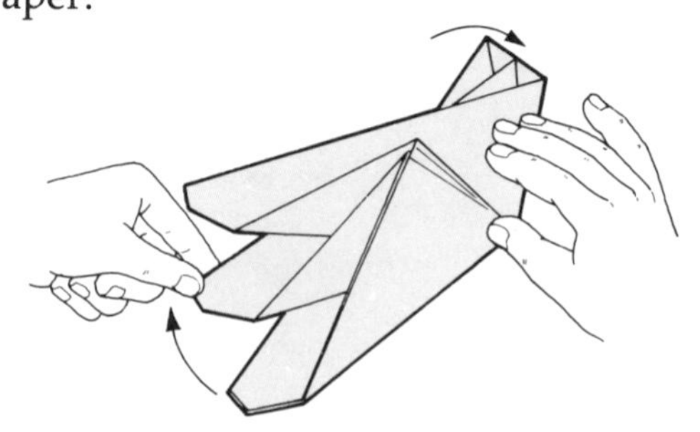

6 Finally repeat step 4 with the remaining layer of paper, so making four bananas.

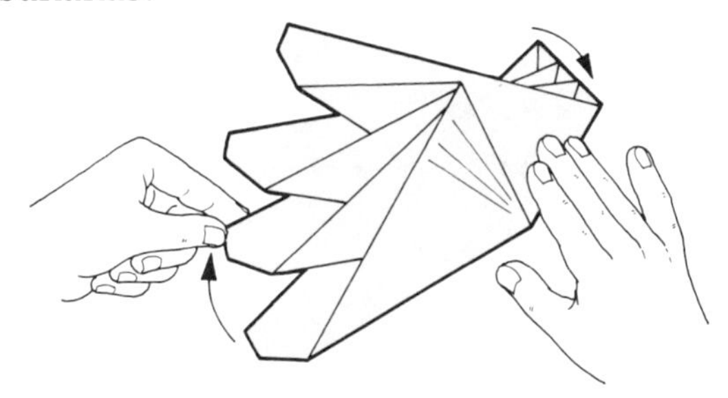

7 Fold the top right-hand point down.

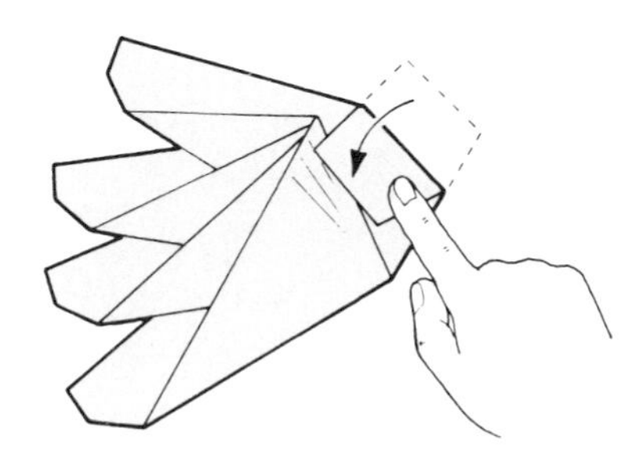

8 Fold the top right-hand point back up, so making a small pleat.

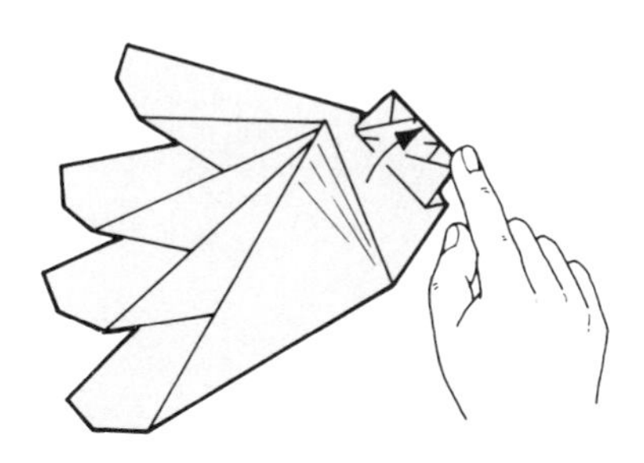

9 Fold the right-hand side point over.

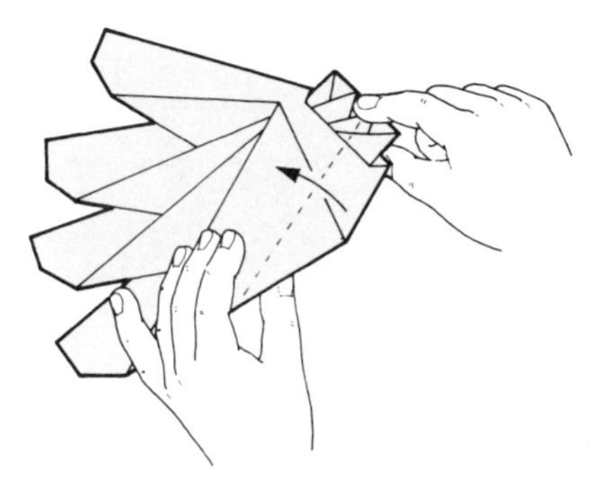

10 This should be your finished result. Press the paper flat.

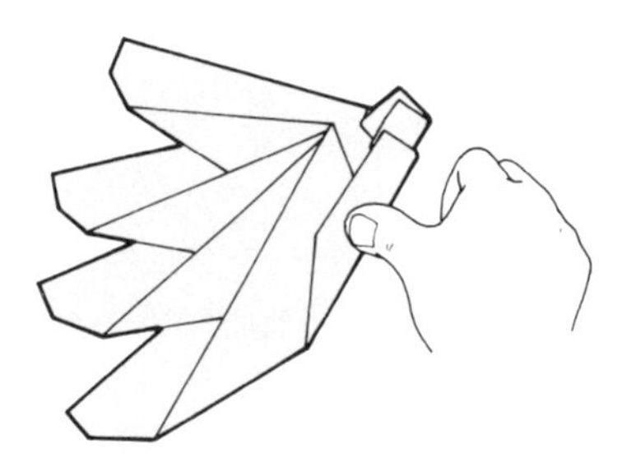

11 Turn the paper over from side to side. Press each banana into shape.

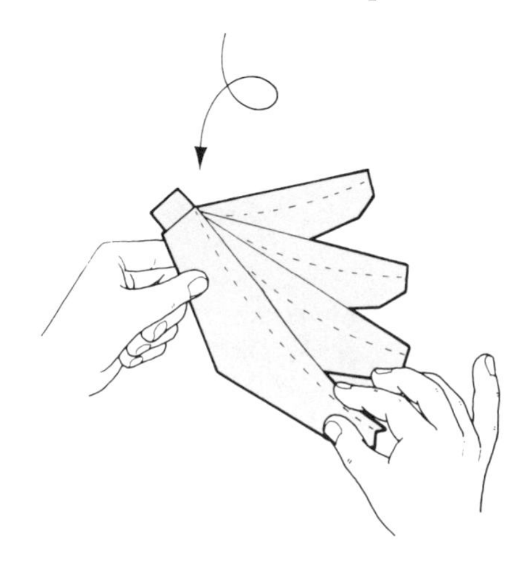

12 Here are the completed bananas.

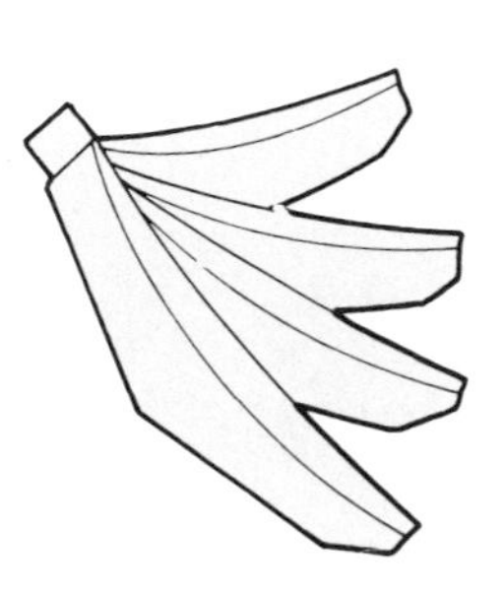

Shirt

Toshie Takahama

This charming fold makes an ideal package for containing all sorts of small items, such as postage stamps and coins.

You will need:
Square of paper, coloured on one side and white on the other Scissors

1 Fold and unfold the square in half from bottom to top, with the coloured side on top. Cut along the middle fold-line, so making two rectangles.

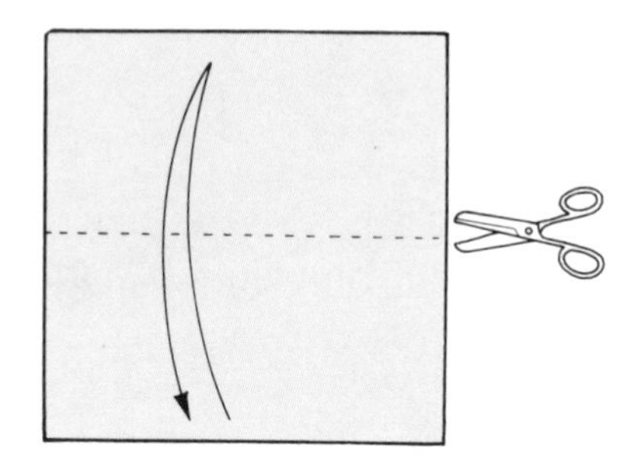

2 Place one rectangle sideways on, with the coloured side on top. Fold in the left-hand side a little.

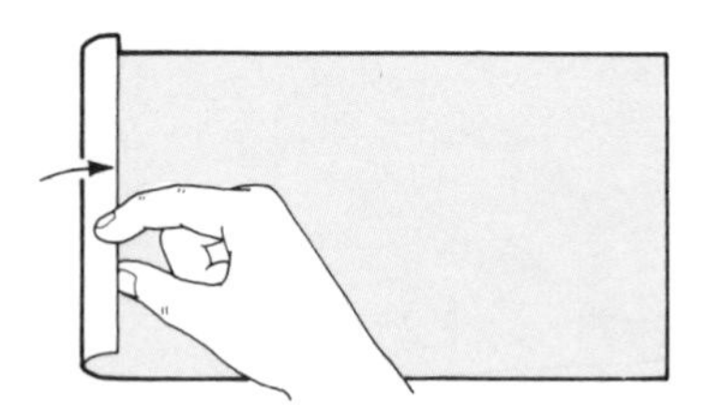

3 Turn the paper over. Fold and unfold it in half from bottom to top.

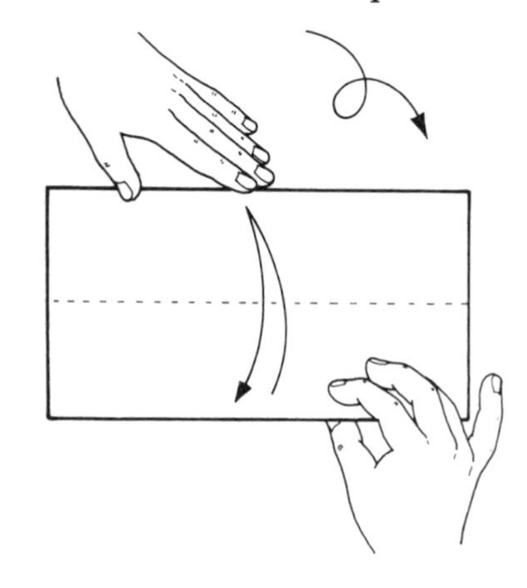

4 Fold the top and bottom in to meet the middle fold-line.

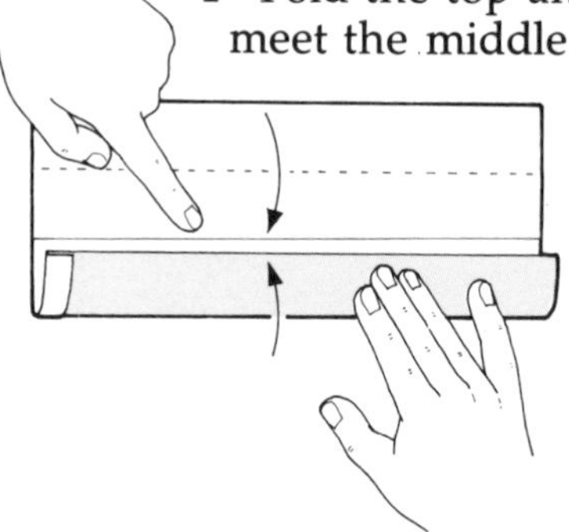

5 Fold a little of the right-hand centre layers outwards on a slant.

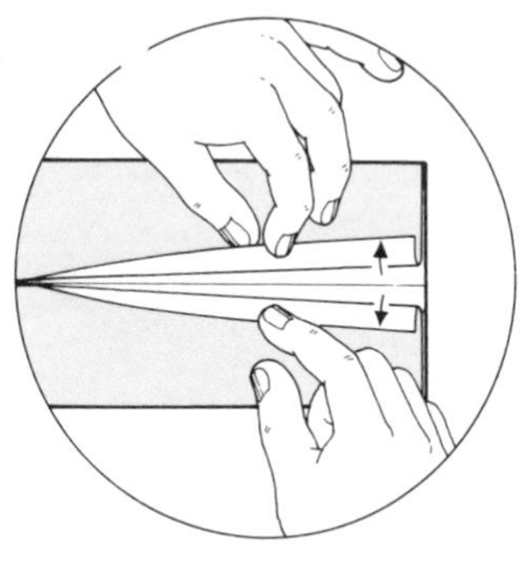

6 Open out the paper back to step 3. But do *not* unfold step 5.

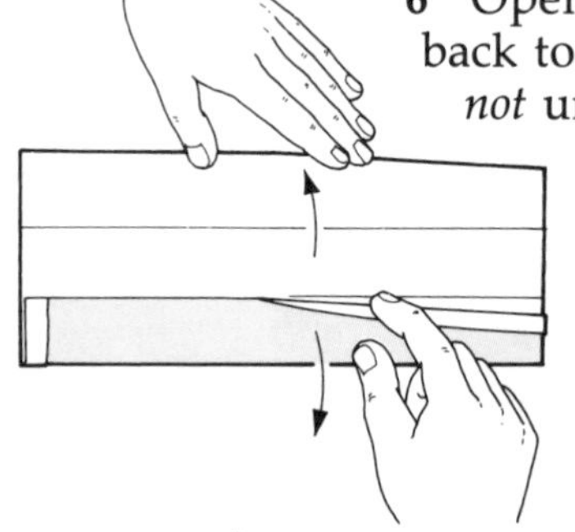

7 Fold and unfold the paper in half from side to side, being careful to press the paper only a little in the middle.

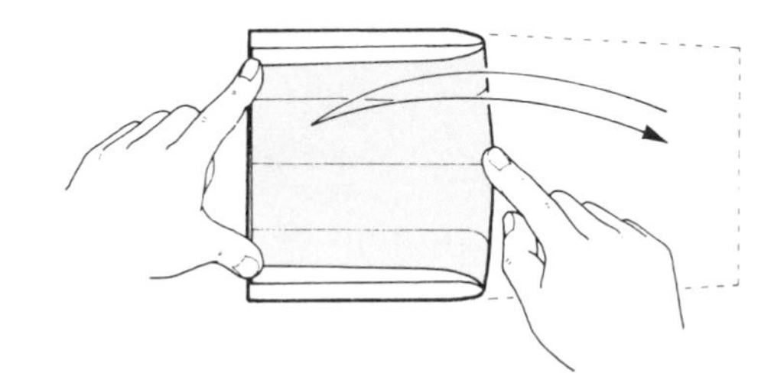

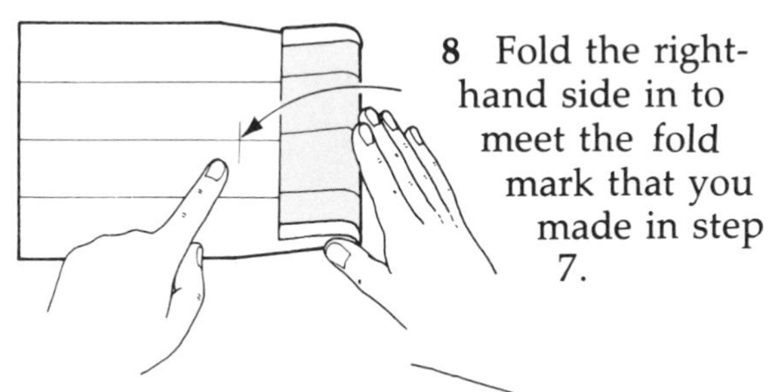

8 Fold the right-hand side in to meet the fold mark that you made in step 7.

9 Fold the top and bottom in to meet the middle fold-line.

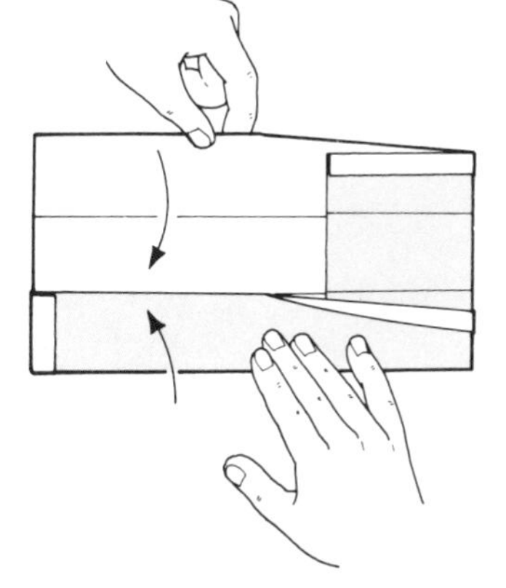

10 Fold the right-hand top layers of paper outwards into the position as shown by the dotted lines.

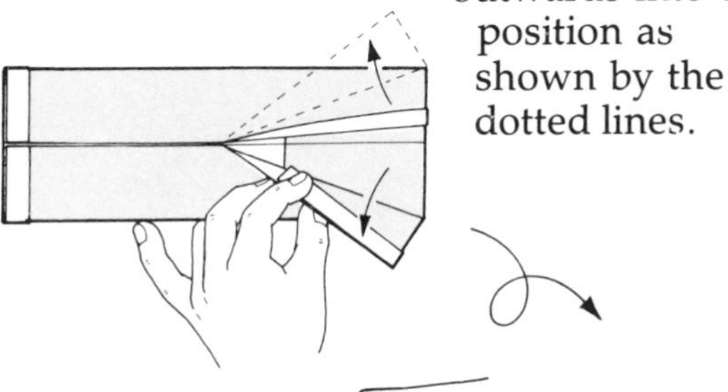

11 Turn the paper over. Fold the band of white paper over on itself.

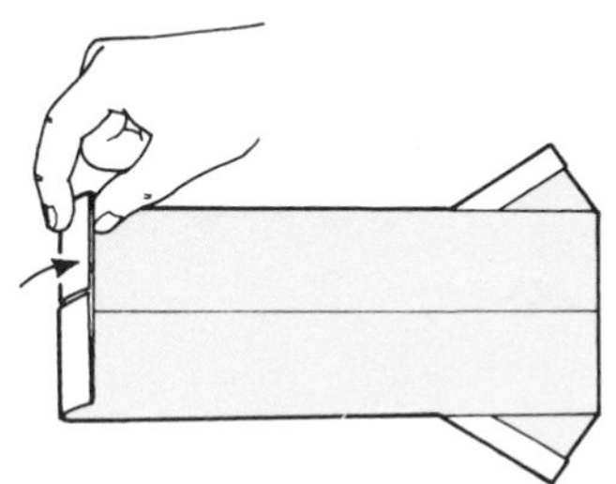

12 Turn the paper over. Fold the top and bottom left-hand points in on a slant to meet the middle fold-line, so making the shirt's collar.

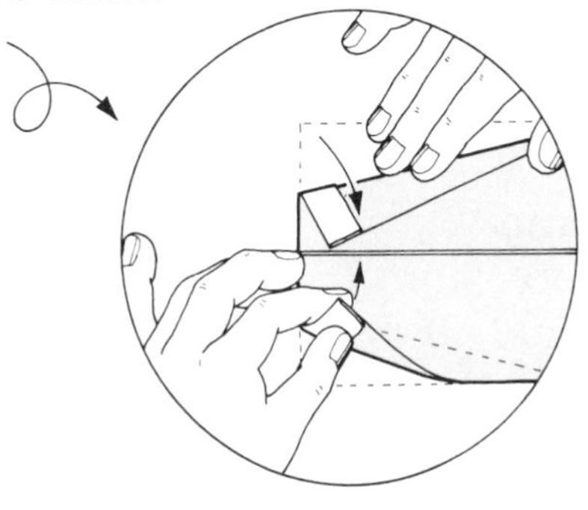

13 Tuck the right-hand side underneath the collar. At this stage in the folding you can place any small items inside.

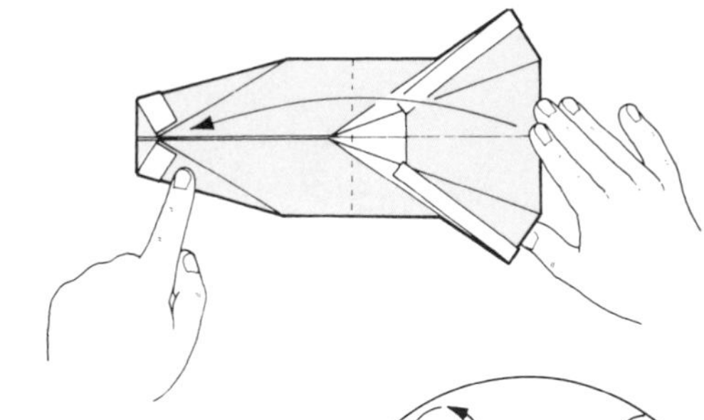

14 To make the tucking easier, turn the shirt around.

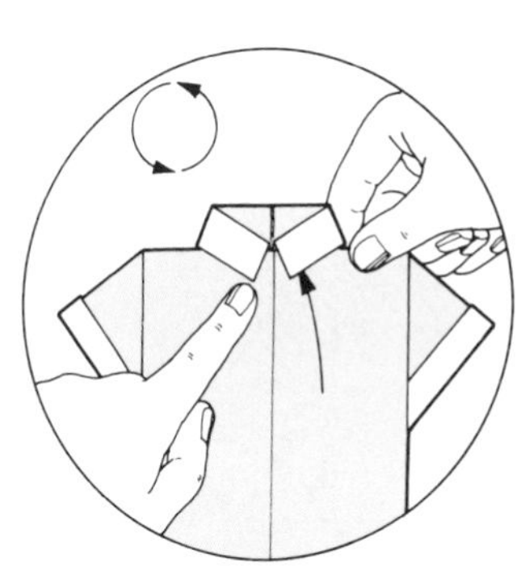

15 Here is the completed shirt. Try folding another shirt, so that the coloured side of the paper is on the inside.

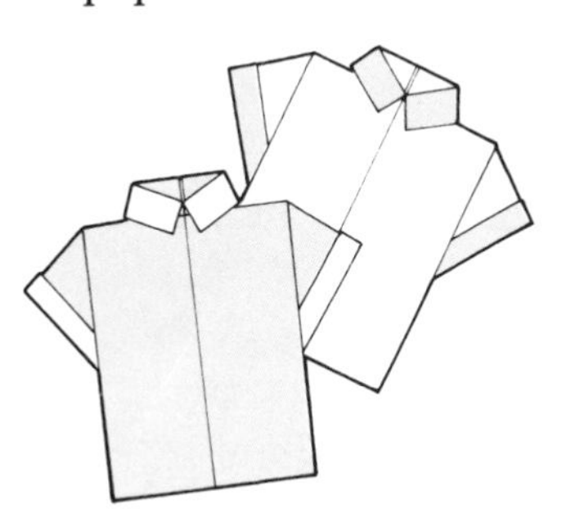

Napkin boot

Traditional

To decorate your table for a very special occasion, try this simple napkin fold. If you use a cloth napkin, make sure that it is well starched, so that it can hold the folds.

You will need:
Paper or cloth napkin

1 As a napkin is usually folded into quarters, open it out completely. Fold it in half from bottom to top.

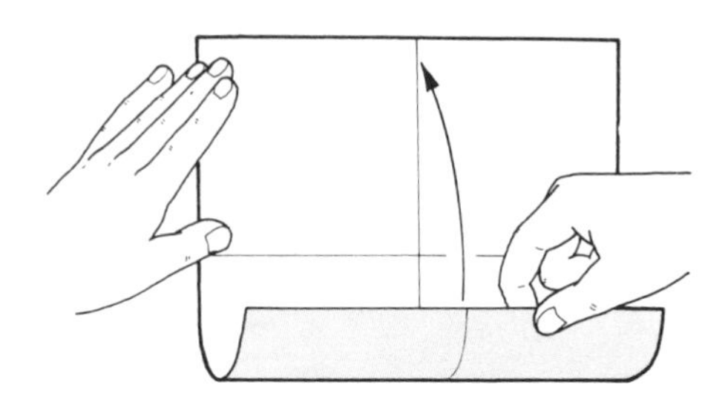

2 Once again, fold the napkin in half from bottom to top.

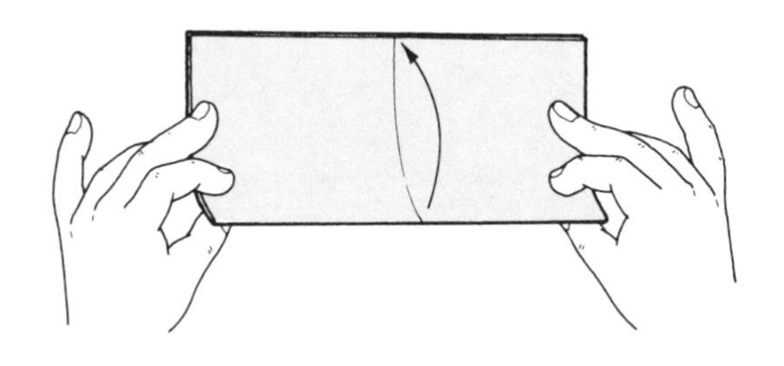

3 Fold the right-hand half of the top down to meet the middle fold-line.

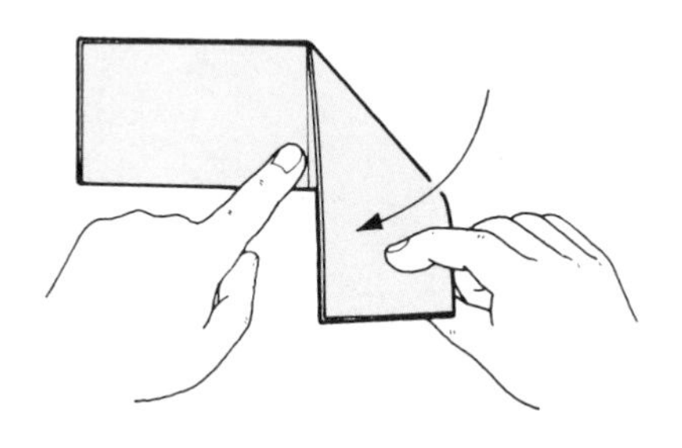

4 Repeat step 3 with the left-hand half.

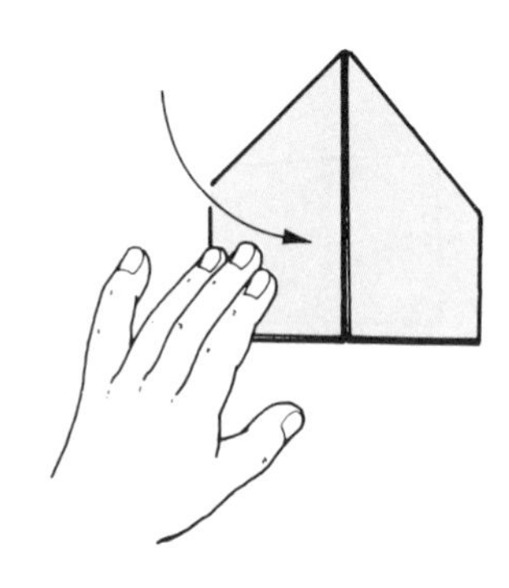

5 From the top point, fold the right and left-hand sloping sides in to meet the middle fold-line.

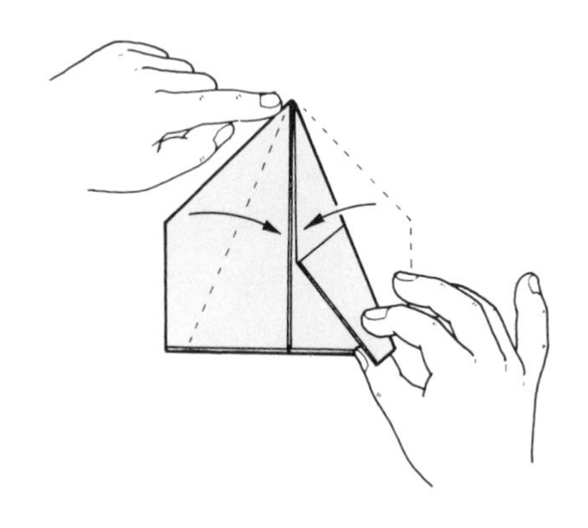

6 Fold the napkin in half from side to side.

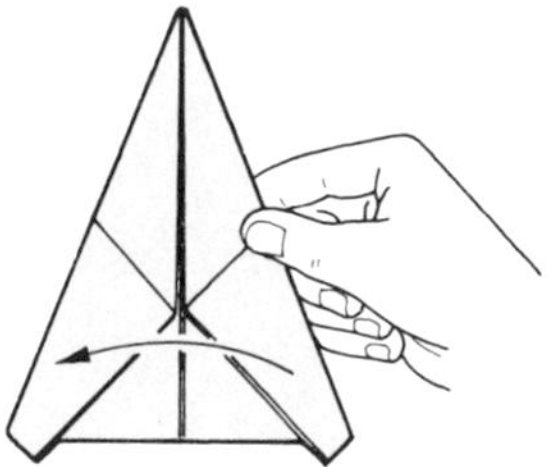

7 Turn the fold around so that it points towards the left.

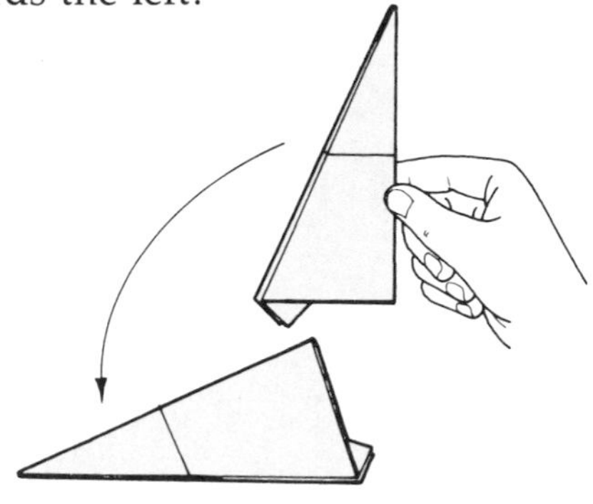

8 Fold the top right-hand flap of paper over into the position as shown by the dotted lines.

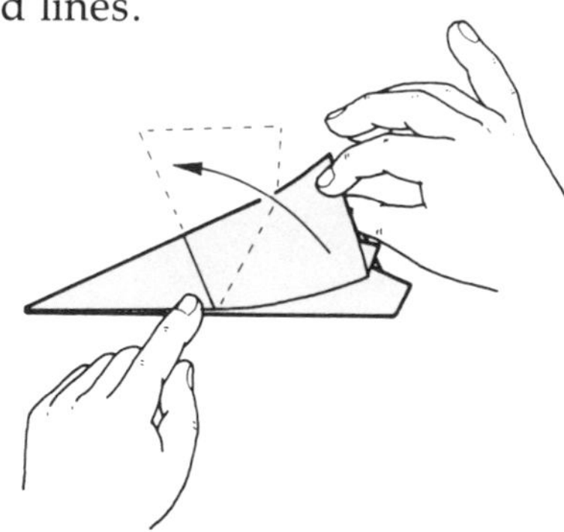

9 Fold the back right-hand flap of paper down, so narrowing it.

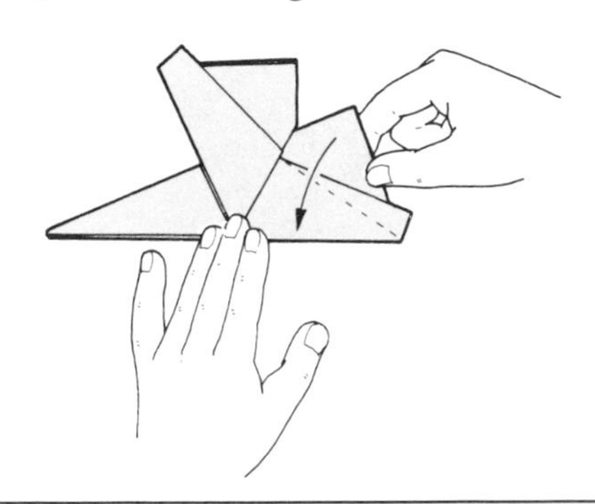

10 Fold the back flap around the heel of the boot and tuck it deep inside the toe pocket.

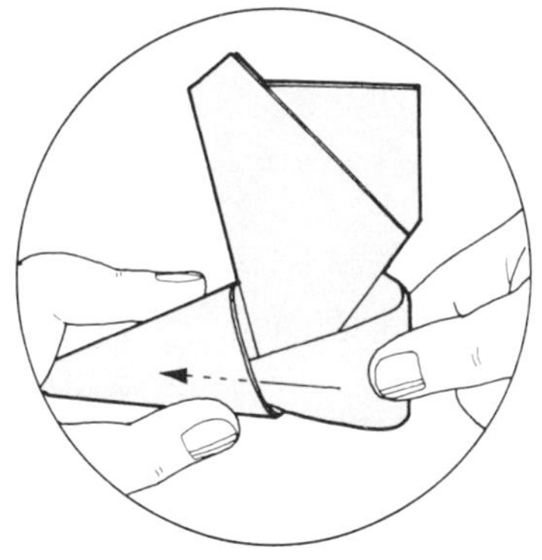

11 This should be your finished result.

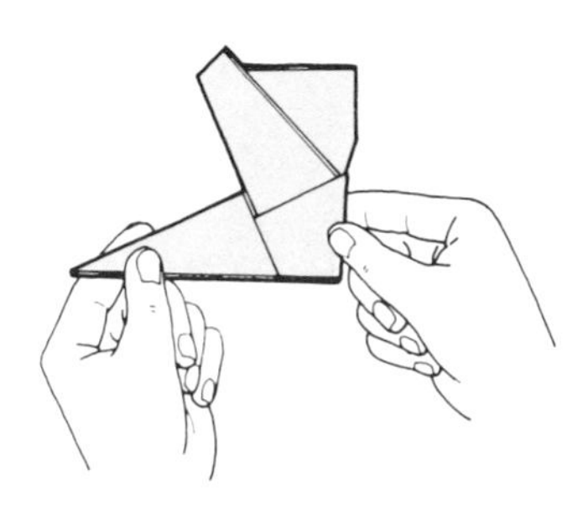

12 To complete, open the boot out so that it will stand up. Now have a go at making a pair of boots.

Napkin bunny

Steve Biddle

This second napkin fold will make an ideal table decoration for Easter.

You will need:
Paper or cloth napkin

1 Fold the napkin as far as step 4 of the napkin boot on page 60.

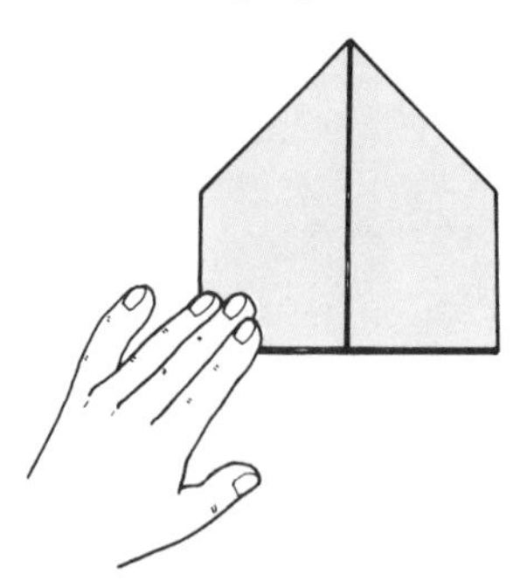

2 Turn the fold around. Fold the top corners down to meet the middle fold-line.

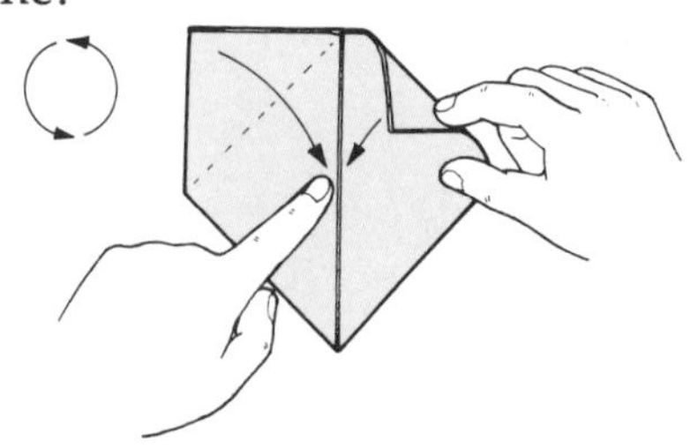

3 From the top points, fold the right and left-hand sloping sides in to meet the middle fold line.

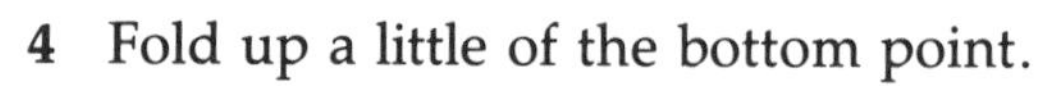

4 Fold up a little of the bottom point.

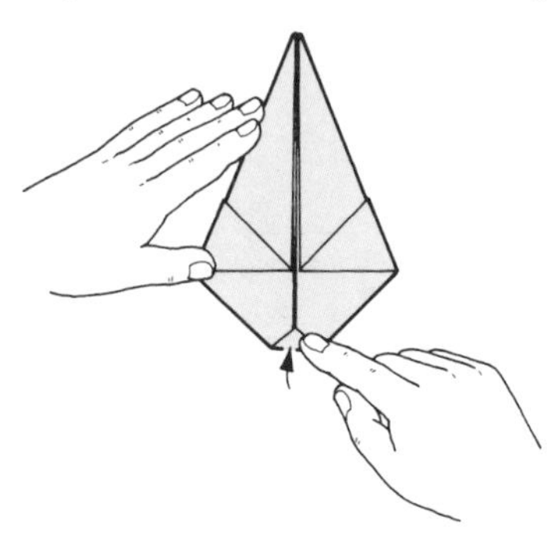

5 Turn the napkin over. Fold the top points outwards.

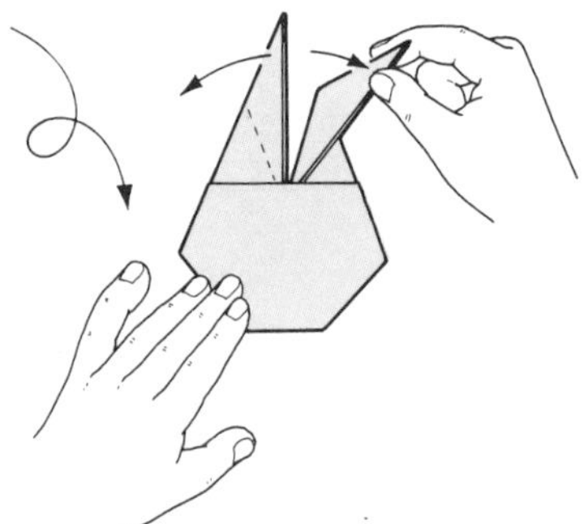

6 Open out each point into a dish-like shape.

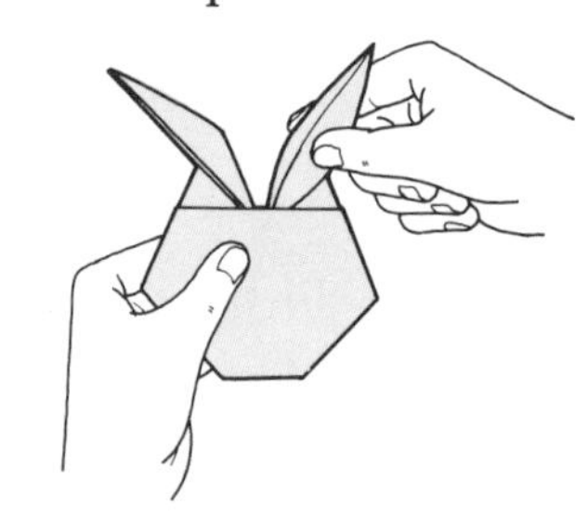

7 Here is the completed napkin bunny.

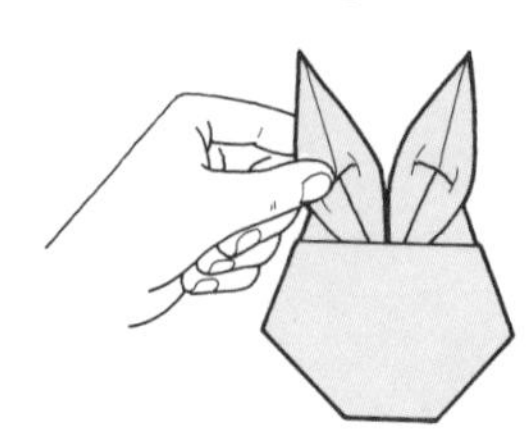

Sweet dish

Traditional

You may already know this fold. In America it is called the 'cootie catcher', but you may know it as the 'salt cellar' or 'fortune teller'.

You will need:
Square of paper, coloured on one side and white on the other

1 Fold and unfold the square in half from side to side, with the white side on top.

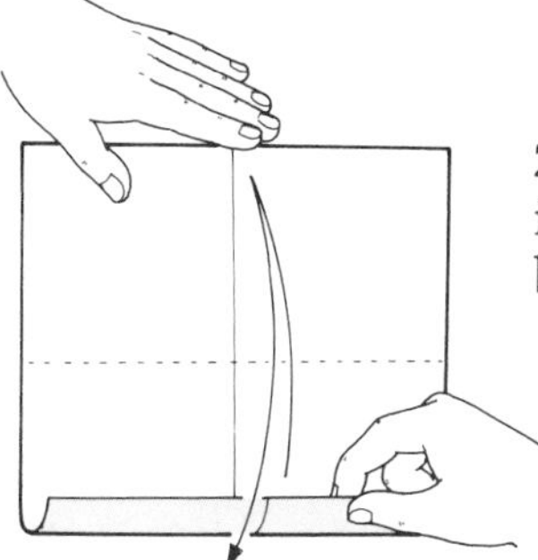

2 Fold and unfold it in half from bottom to top.

3 Fold the corners in to meet the middle, so making the blintz base.

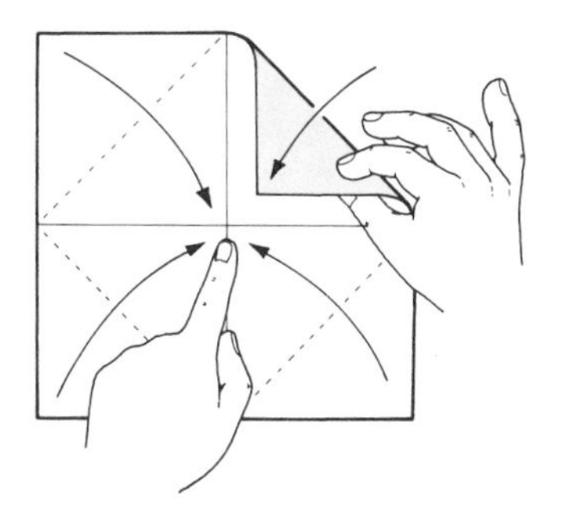

4 Turn the paper over. Once again, fold the corners in to meet the middle.

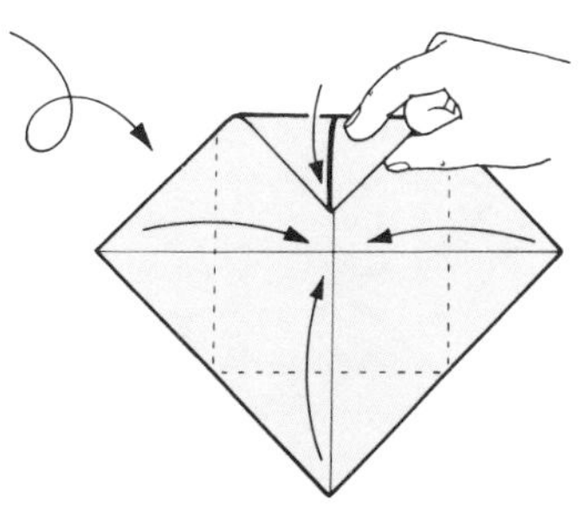

5 Turn the paper around so that it looks like a diamond. Fold it in half from top to bottom, so making a triangle.

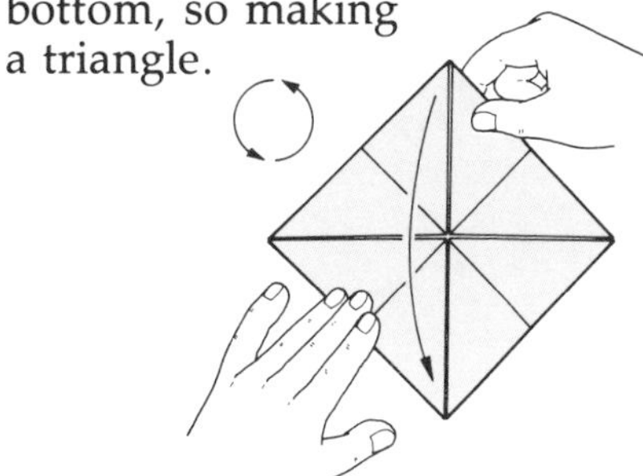

6 Fold the triangle in half from side to side.

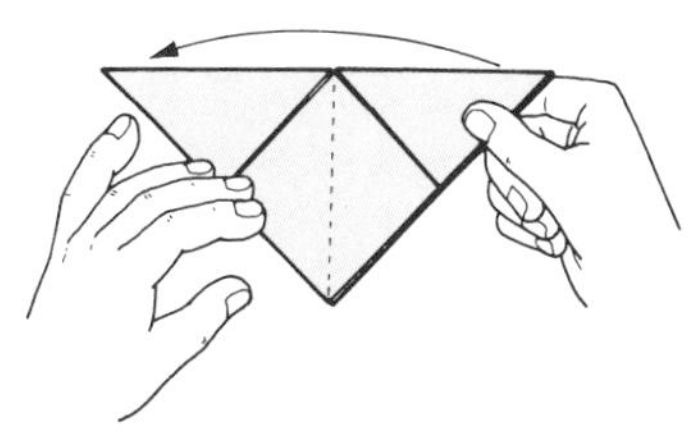

7 Lift the top half up along the middle fold line. Start to open the paper out and with your free hand . . .

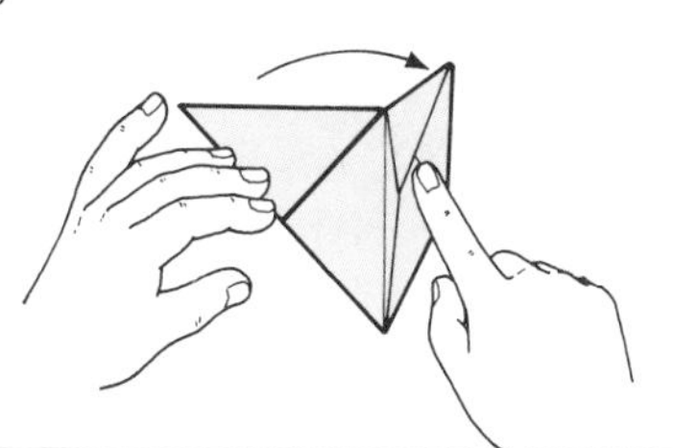

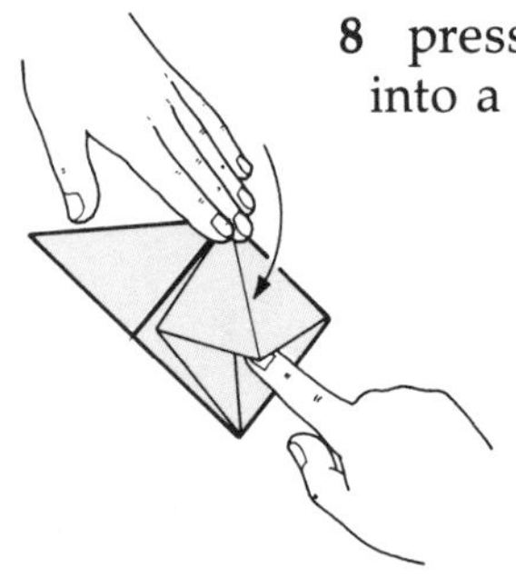

8 press it down neatly into a diamond.

9 Turn the paper over. Repeat step 7.

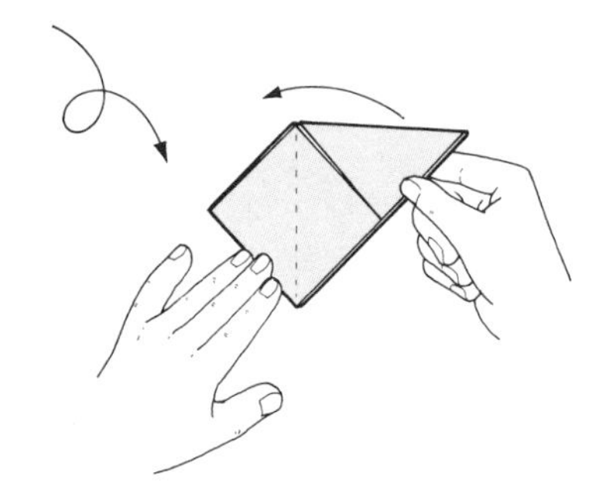

10 Carry on repeating step 7.

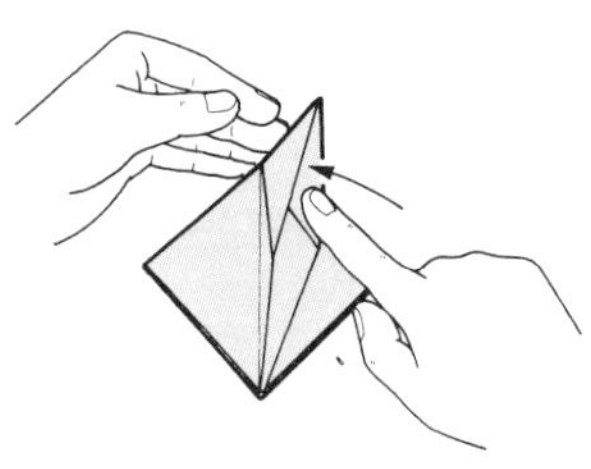

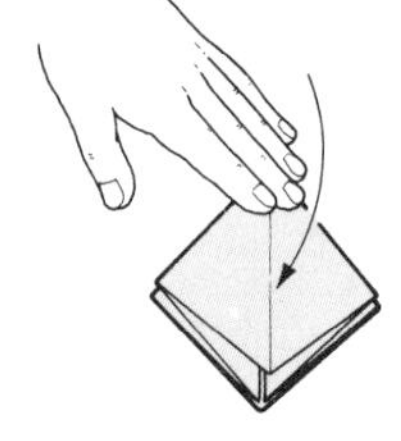

11 Repeat step 8.

12 Pull out the four flaps and push them into place to form . . .

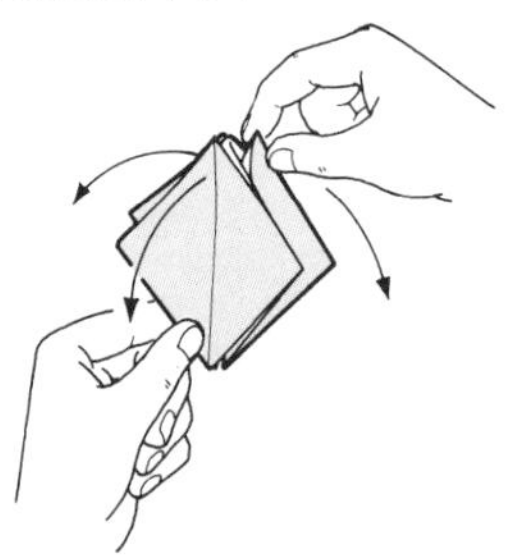

13 the sweet dish or the salt cellar.

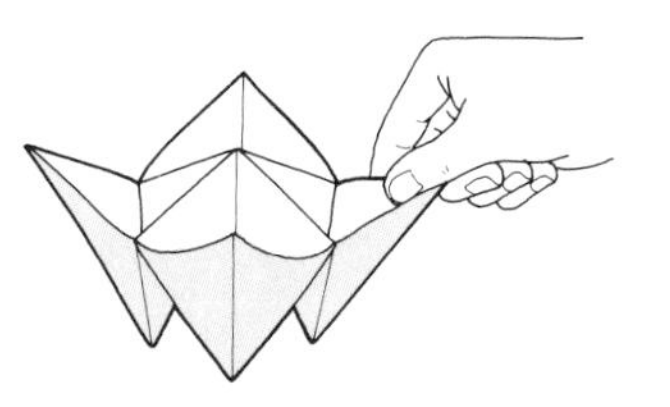

14 Turn it over to make the fortune teller.

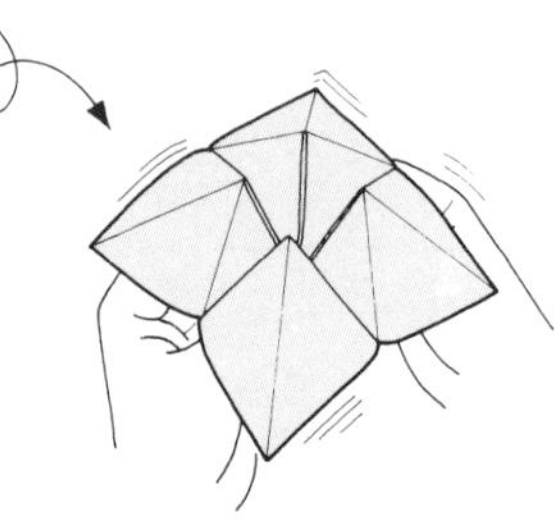

15 *Christmas bauble:* With the coloured side on top in step 1, fold six fortune tellers. Glue four fortune tellers together into a ring, with all the flaps on the outside. To complete, glue one into the top and bottom of the ring and attach a loop of cotton to the top point.

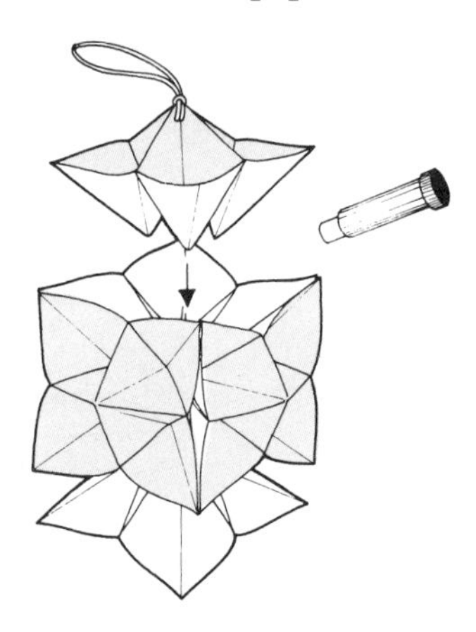

16 If made from a large square of colourful paper, the sweet dish becomes an ideal party food container.

Yakko san/crown

Traditional

Many Japanese children are able to fold this simple origami figure. Yakko san is thought to be one of the oldest folds known in origami.

You will need:
Few squares of paper all the same size, coloured on one side and white on the other
Glue

1 Fold one square as far as step 4 of the sweet dish on page 63.

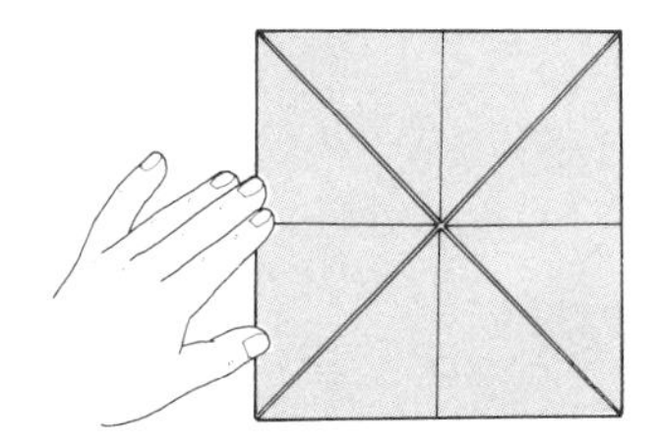

2 Turn the paper over. Once again, fold the corners in to meet the middle.

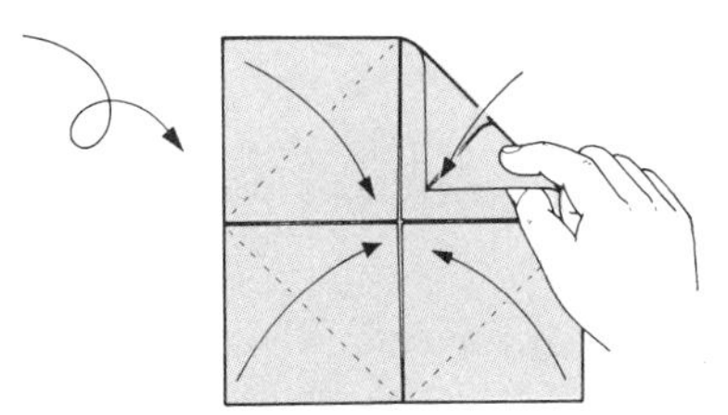

3 Turn the paper over. Open out the right-hand little corner square and . . .

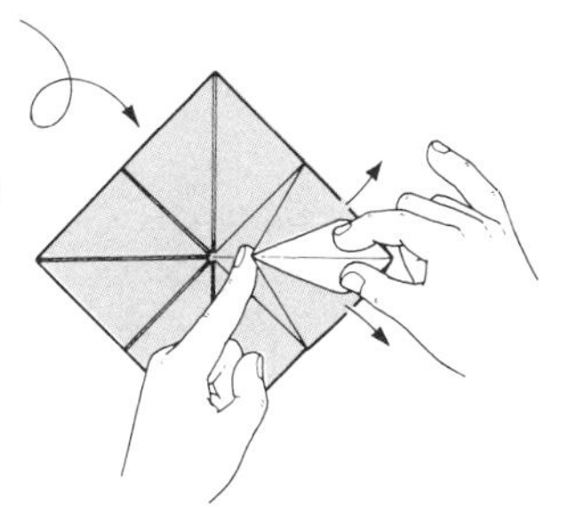

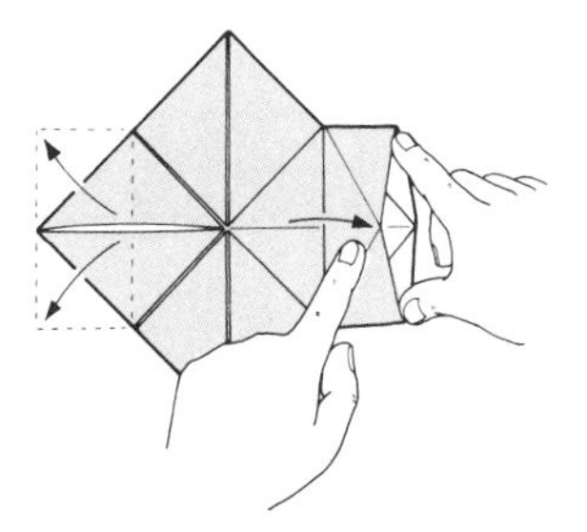

4 press it down neatly into a rectangle. Repeat with the left-hand little corner square.

5 To complete Yakko san, repeat steps 3 and 4 with the bottom little corner square. Can you see his coat, sleeves, and diamond-shaped face?

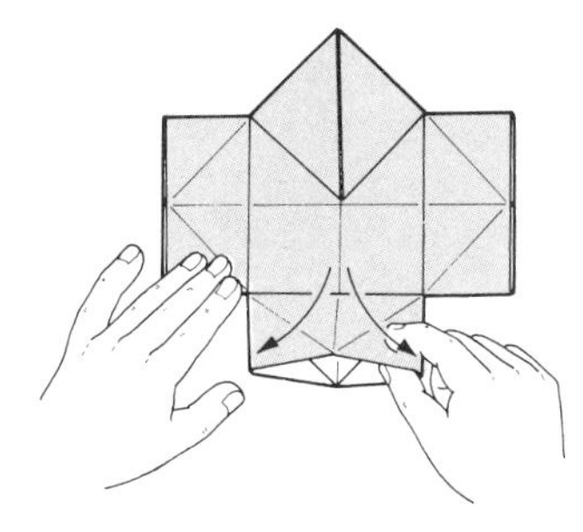

6 *Crown:* Repeat steps 1 through to 5 with the remaining squares. Tuck one Yakko san inside another and glue them together.

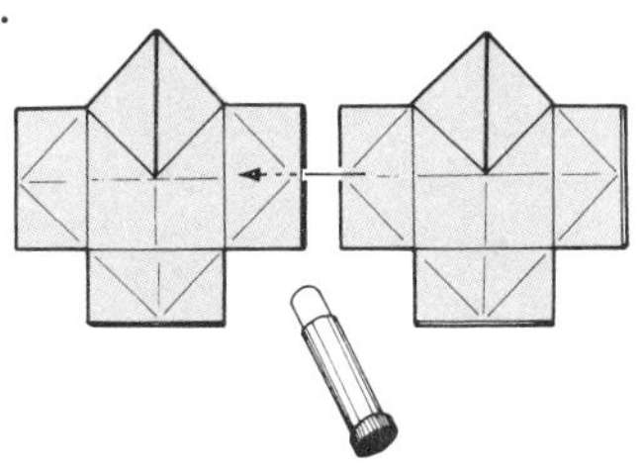

7 Keep on tucking and gluing Yakko sans together until you have built up a crown that fits on your head.

Jumping frog

Traditional

The secret to this delightful fold is in the paper. Try to find a piece that is light and springy, so that the frog will jump up into the air.

You will need:
Square of paper, coloured on one side and white on the other

1 Fold the square in half from side to side, with the white side on top.

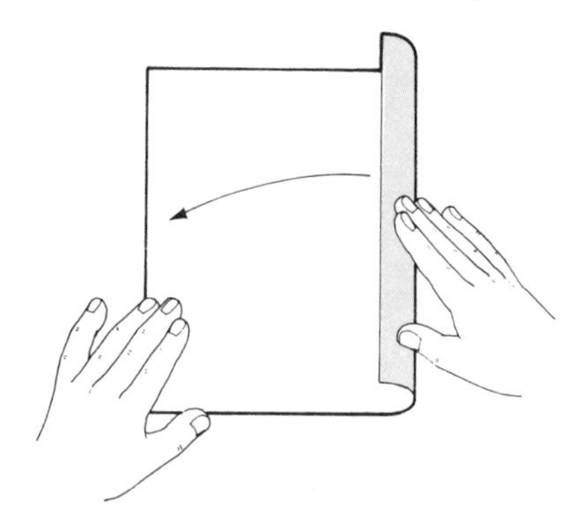

2 Fold the top over to lie along the left-hand side. Press the paper flat and unfold.

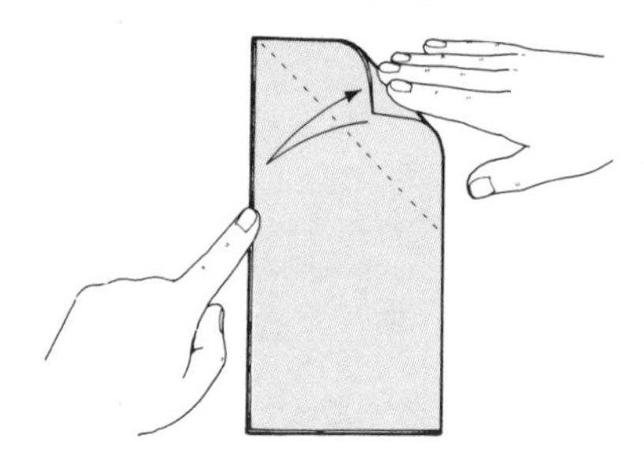

3 Fold the top over to lie along the right-hand side. Press the paper flat and unfold.

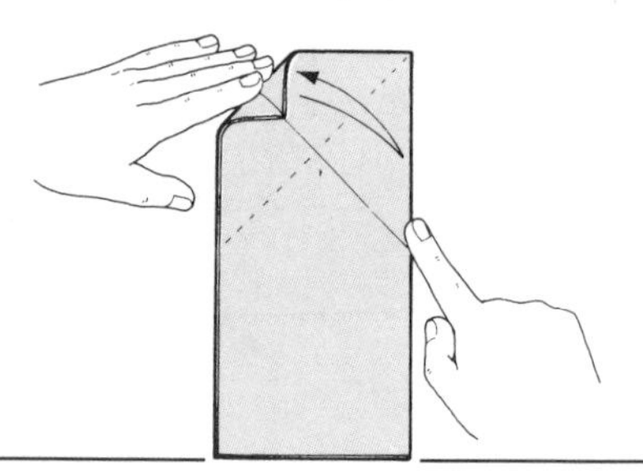

4 Turn the paper over. Fold the top down to meet the middle.

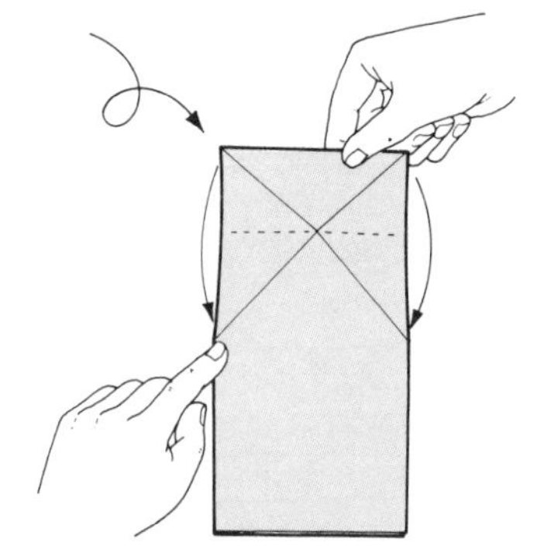

5 Press the paper flat and unfold.

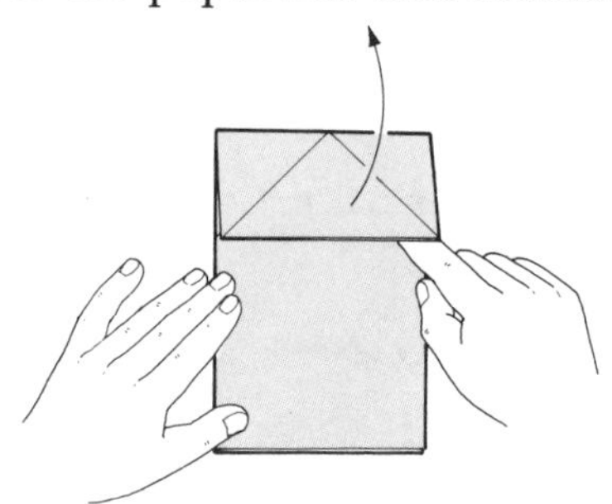

6 Turn the paper over. Put a finger into the middle of the fold-lines. Push down until the sides pop up.

7 Place a finger against both sides.

8 Using the fold-lines as a guide, bring the sides together and down towards you.

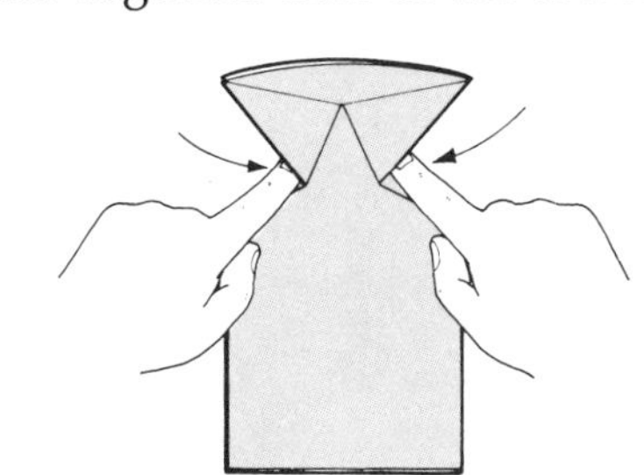

9 Press the top down neatly into a triangle.

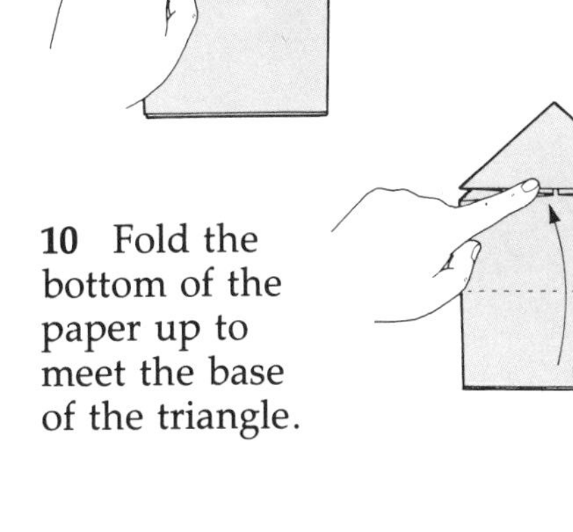

10 Fold the bottom of the paper up to meet the base of the triangle.

11 Fold the sides in to meet the middle.

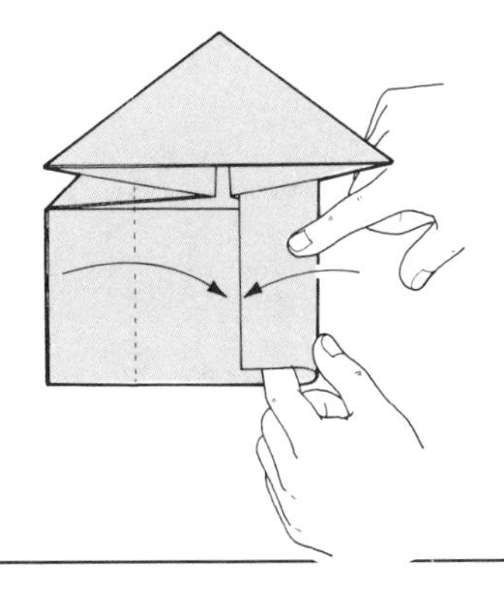

12 Once again, fold the bottom up to meet the base of the triangle.

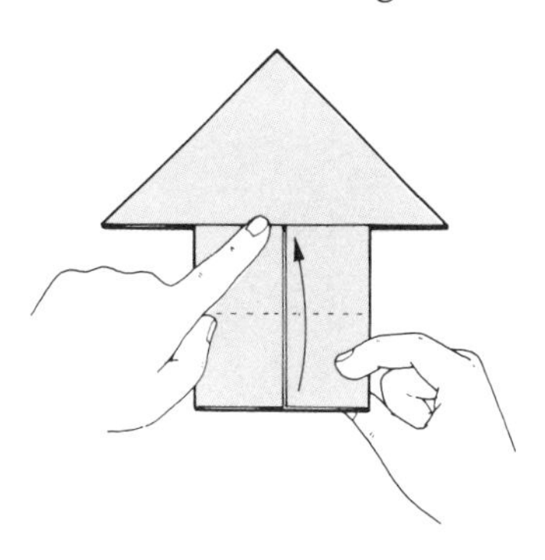

13 Fold the two top side points of the front flap down to meet the bottom.

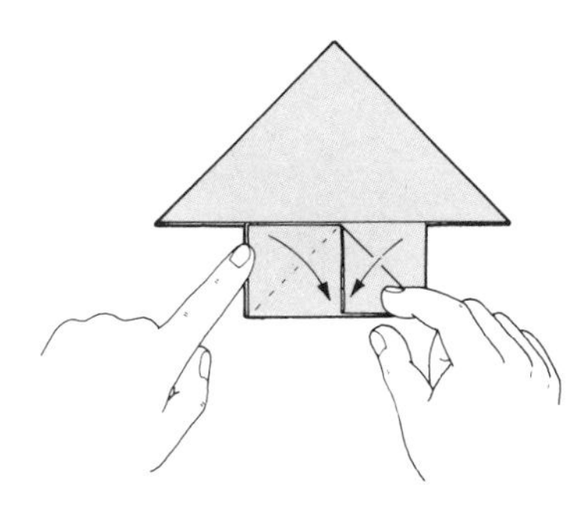

14 Pinch the two middle points and pull the outer layers apart . . .

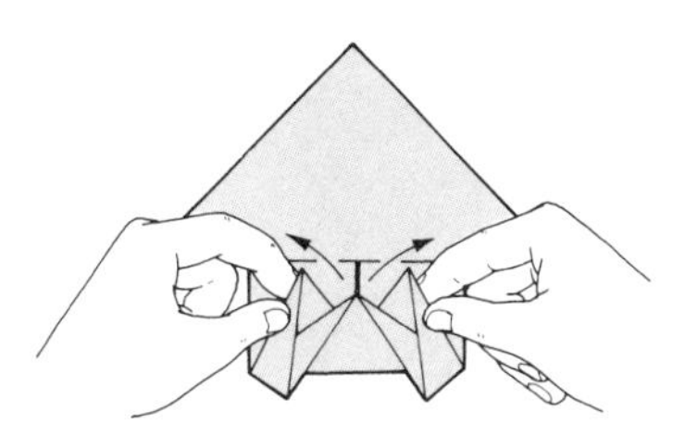

15 into this position. Press the paper flat.

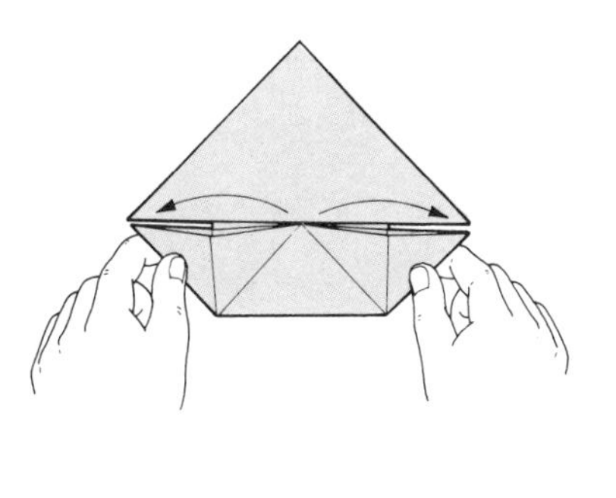

16 Fold the middle points down.

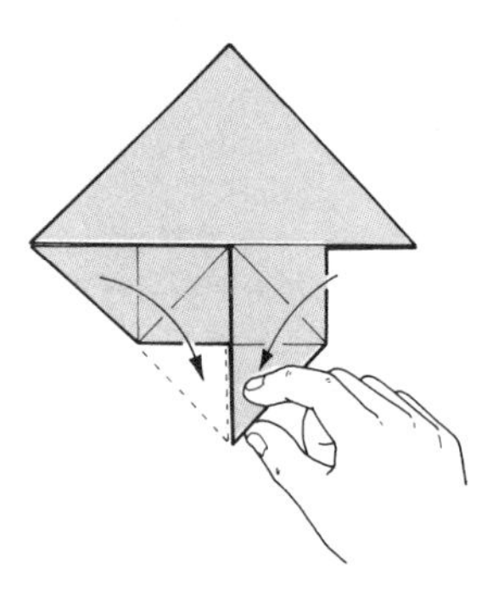

17 Fold the middle points over into the position as shown by the dotted lines.

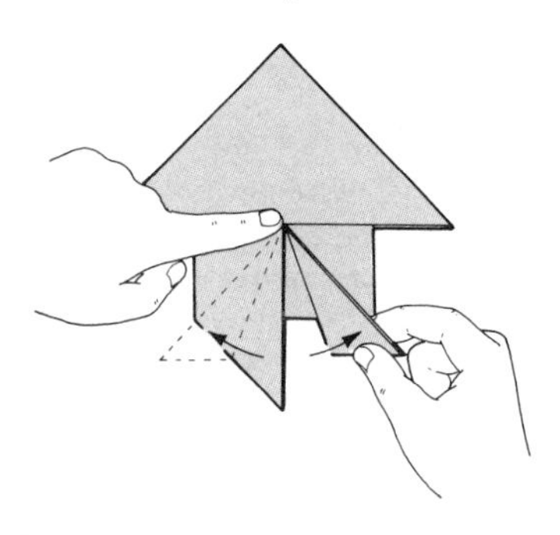

18 Fold the triangle's bottom points up into the position as shown by the dotted lines.

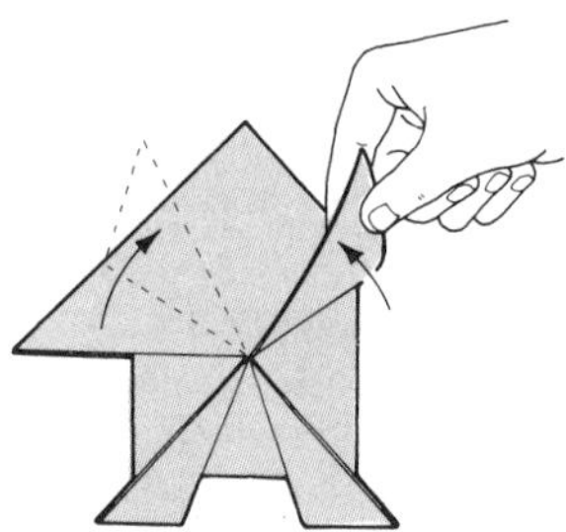

19 Fold the bottom section up along the middle.

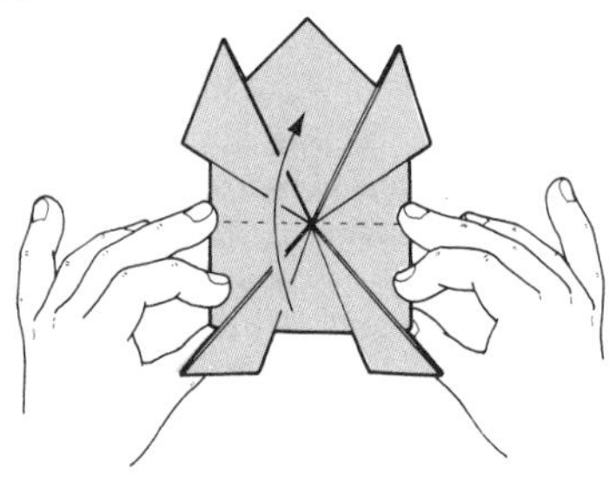

20 Fold the bottom section down, so making a small pleat. Be careful not to press the pleat down very hard.

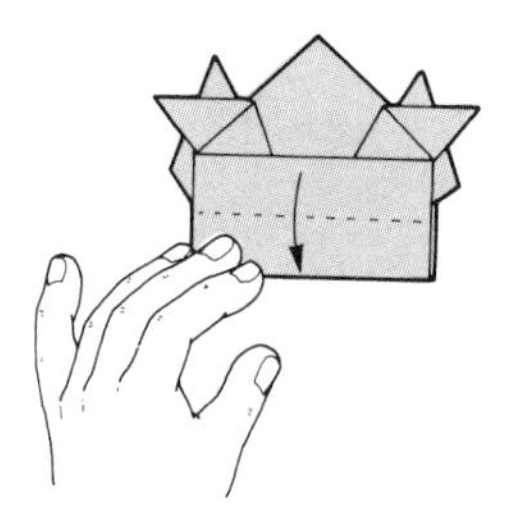

21 This should be your finished result.

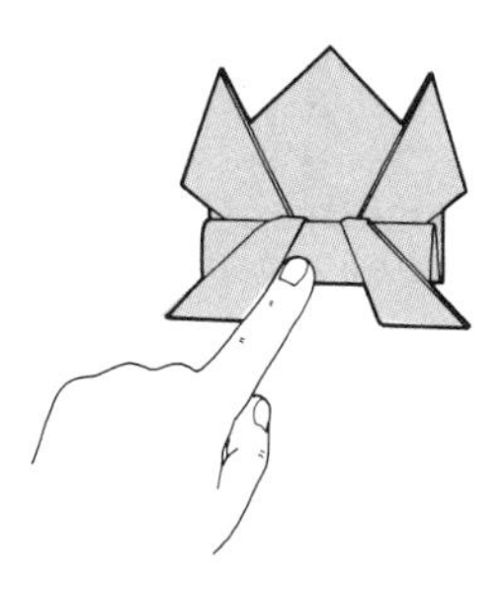

22 To complete the jumping frog, turn the paper over.

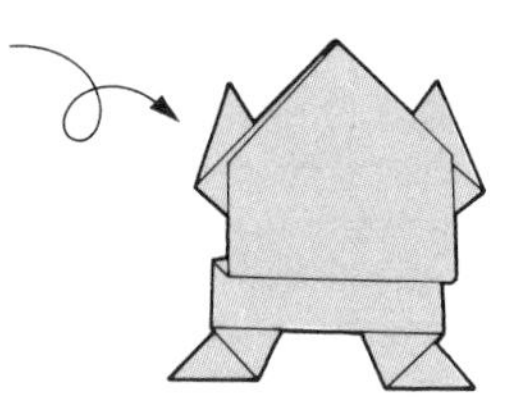

23 If you place the frog on a flat surface and run a finger down its back, pressing firmly, he will jump up into the air and may even turn a complete somersault.

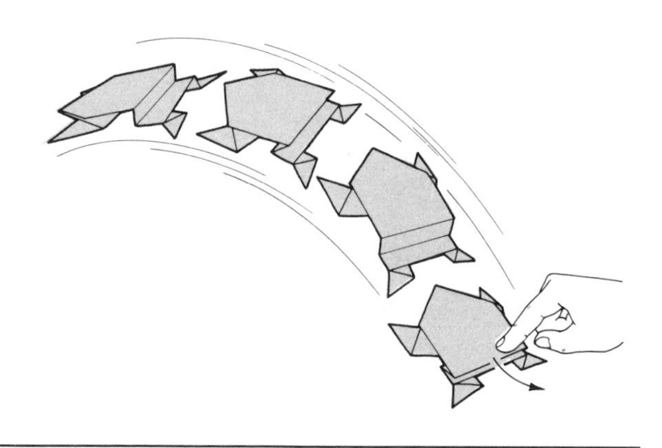

Water lily

Traditional

Be very careful not to tear the paper when folding this pretty flower.

You will need:

Square of thin but strong paper, coloured on one side and white on the other (airmail paper is ideal)

1 Fold as far as step 3 of the sweet dish on page 63.

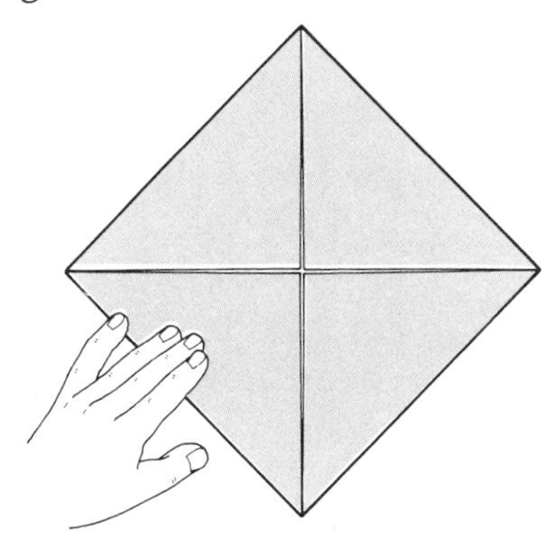

2 Again, fold the corners in to meet the middle.

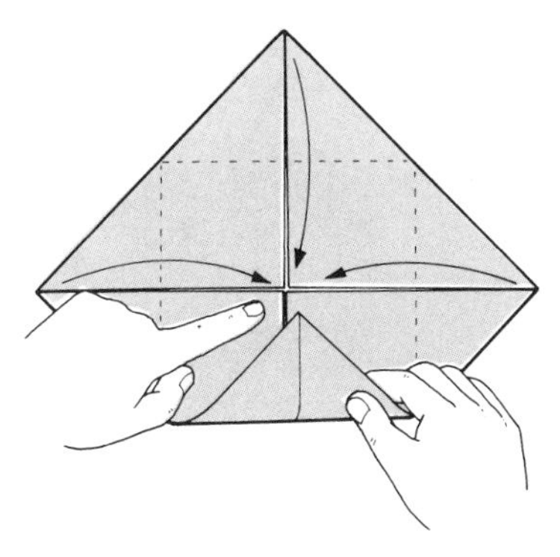

3 Fold the corners in to meet the middle once again.

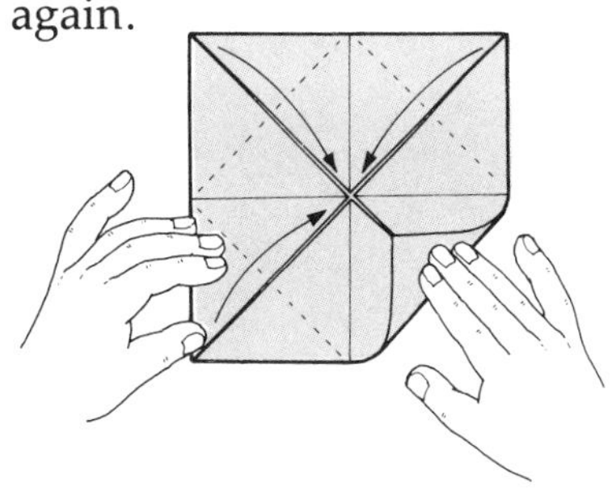

4 This should be your finished result – three layers of paper containing twelve corners (which will become the petals later on).

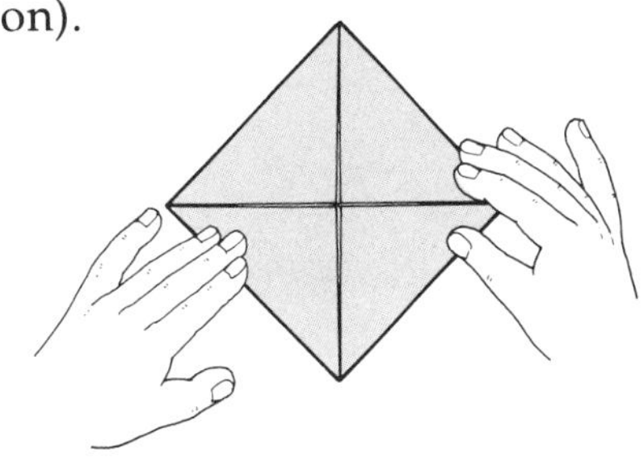

5 Turn the paper over. Fold each of the corners in to meet the middle for the final time.

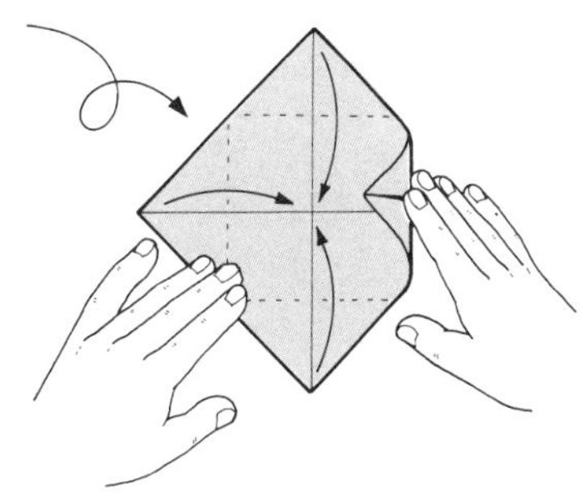

6 Fold over a little of one corner.

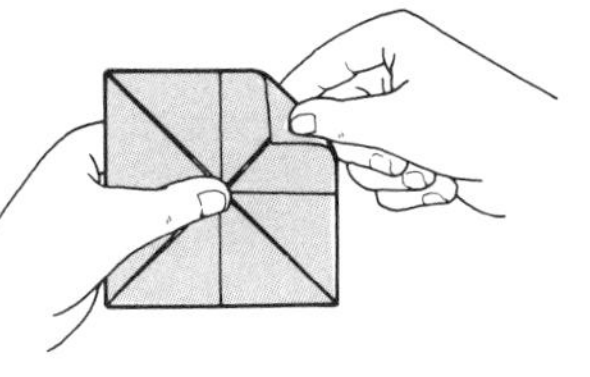

7 Hold the paper as shown. From the top layer of paper, pull over a corner from 'behind'.

8 Stand the corner upright and shape it to look like a petal.

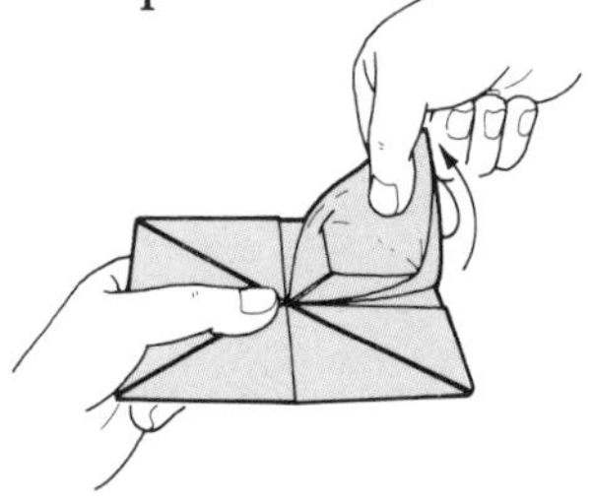

9 Repeat step 6 with the next corner.

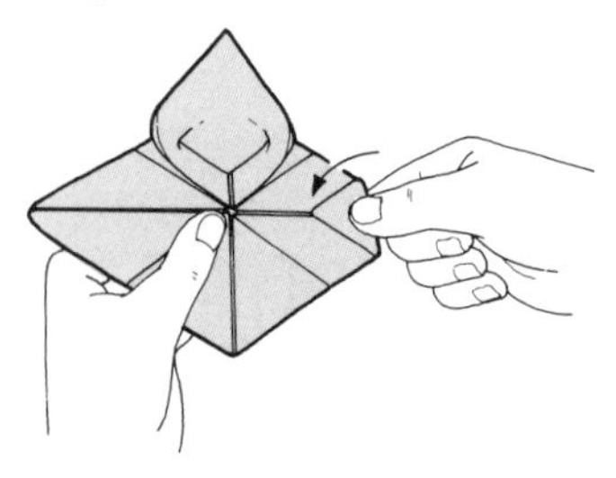

10 Repeat steps 7 and 8.

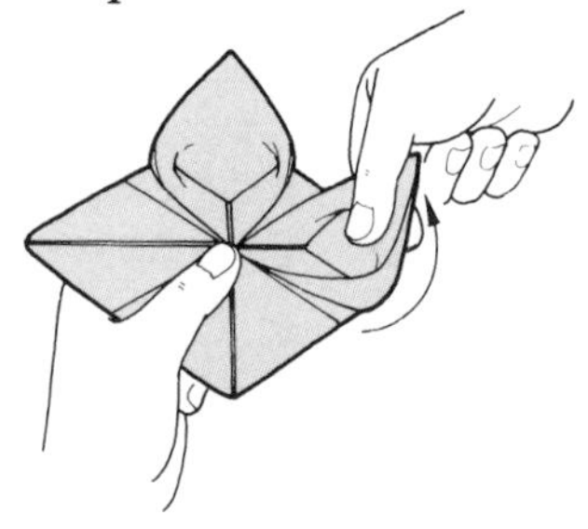

11 Repeat steps 6 to 8 with the remaining corners, so making the first layer of petals.

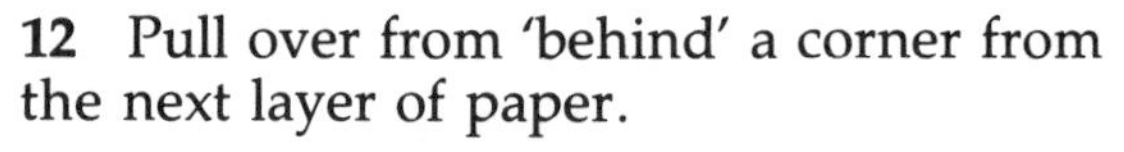

12 Pull over from 'behind' a corner from the next layer of paper.

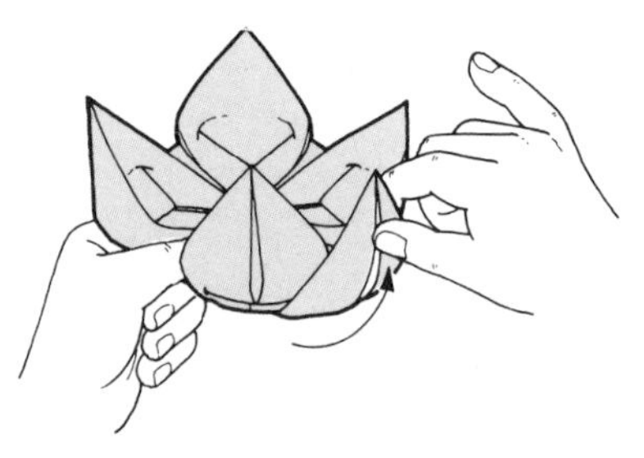

13 Repeat step 12 three more times, so making the second layer of petals.

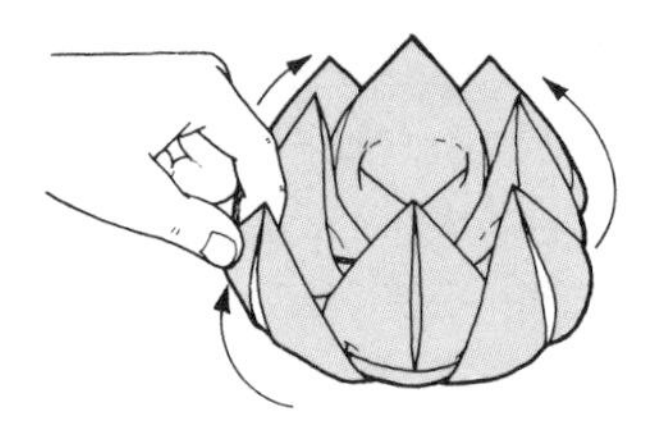

14 Pull over from 'behind' a corner from the final layer of paper.

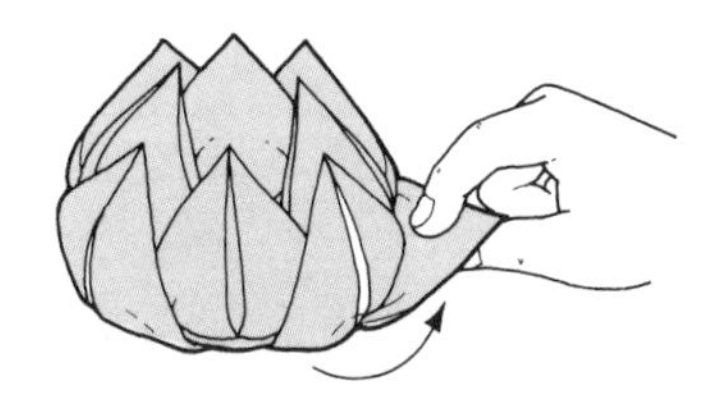

15 Repeat step 14 two more times.

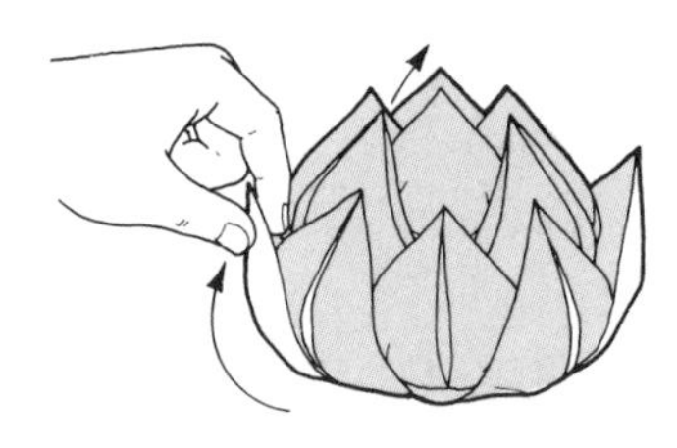

16 To complete the water lily, pull over the remaining corner, so making the third layer of petals. If you make your water lily out of a starched cloth napkin, it will make a perfect table decoration.

Water lily leaf

Megumi Biddle

This very simple fold is based on a Japanese paper-cutting technique called kirigami.

You will need:
Square of paper, green on one side and white on the other
Scissors

1 Fold the square in half from side to side, with the green side on top.

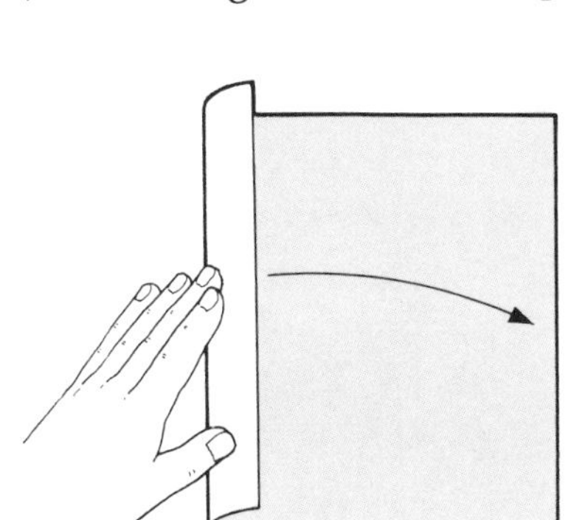

2 From the open side, cut away the shaded parts.

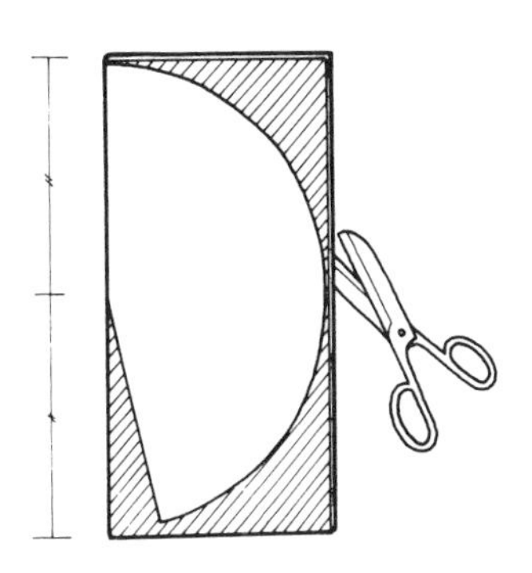

3 To complete the water lily leaf, unfold the paper. The leaf looks perfect when it is displayed alongside the water lily and jumping frog.

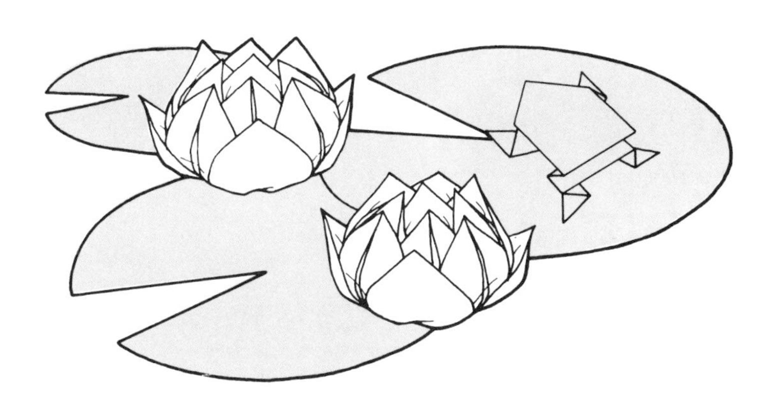

Talking crow

Makoto Yamaguchi

We were shown how to fold this delightful piece of action origami by its creator, when we were in Japan a while ago.

You will need:
Square of paper, coloured on one side and white on the other
Felt-tip pen

1 Turn the square around to look like a diamond, with the white side on top. Fold and unfold it in half from side to side.

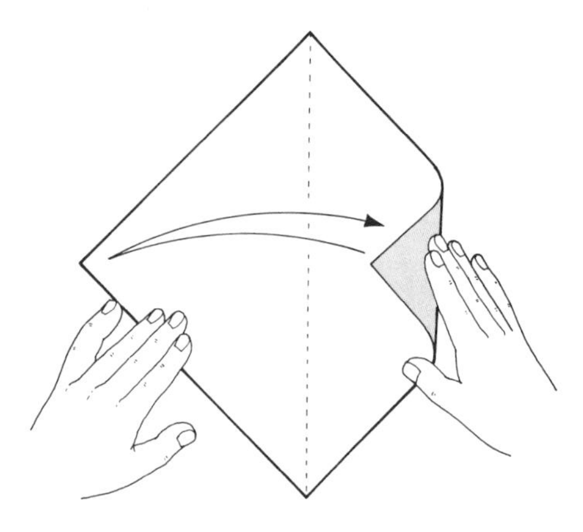

2 Fold it in halt from bottom to top.

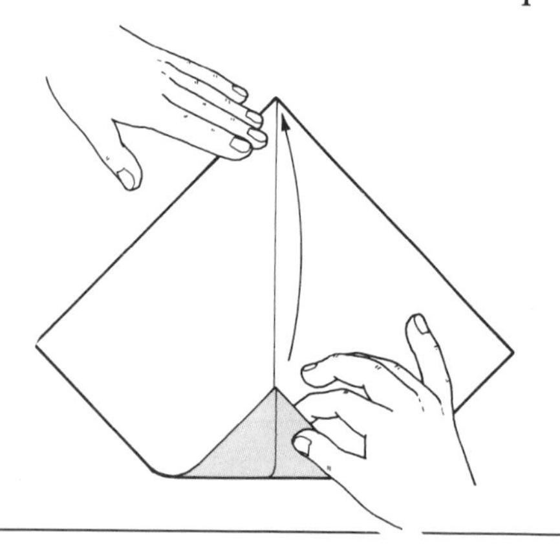

3 From the top point, fold the sloping sides in to meet the middle fold-line.

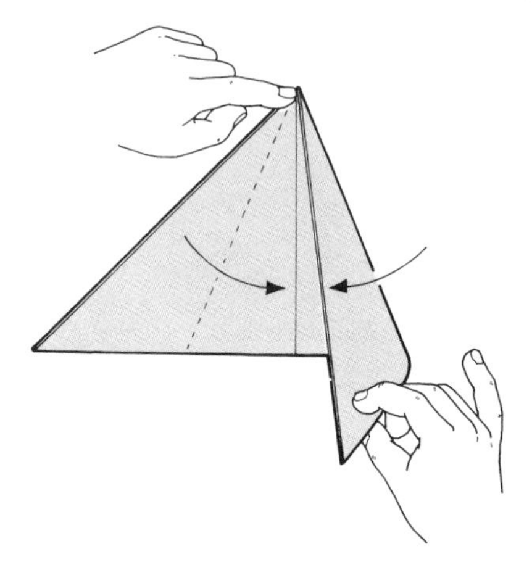

4 Fold the bottom points up into the position as shown by the dotted lines.

5 This should be your finished result.

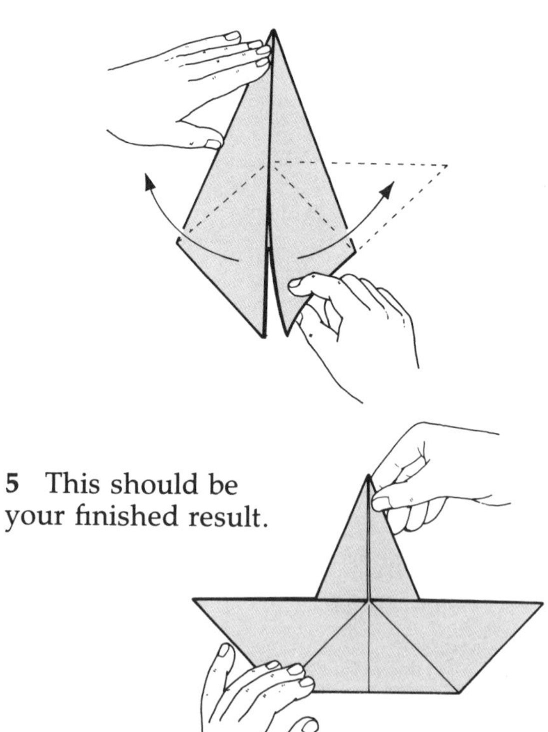

6 From the top point, pull the inside layer out.

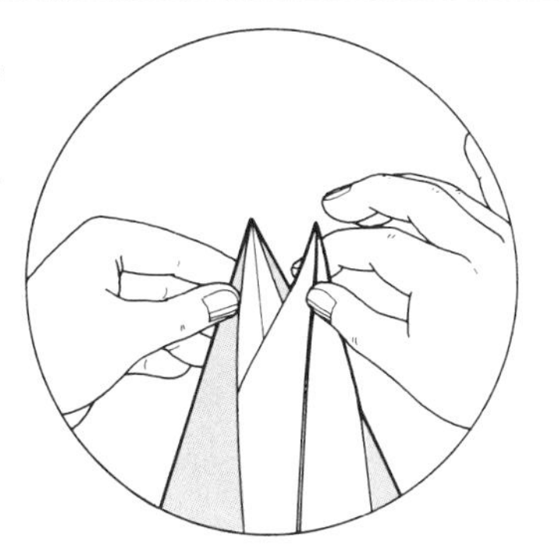

7 Keep on pulling, until you can . . .

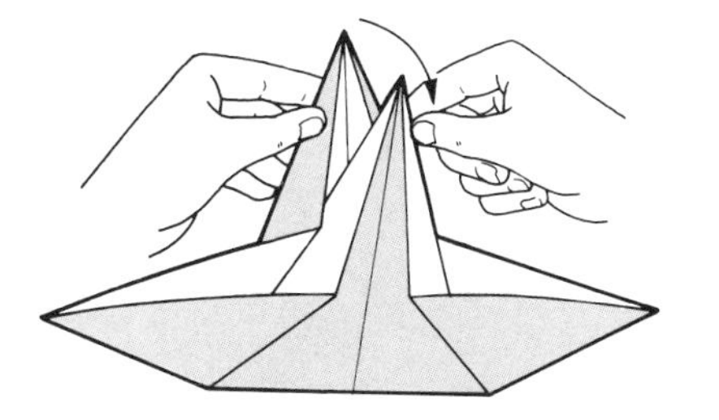

8 arrange the layers into this position.

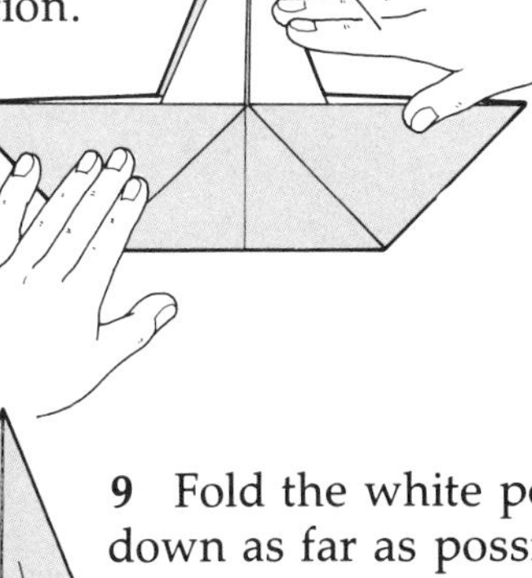

9 Fold the white point down as far as possible.

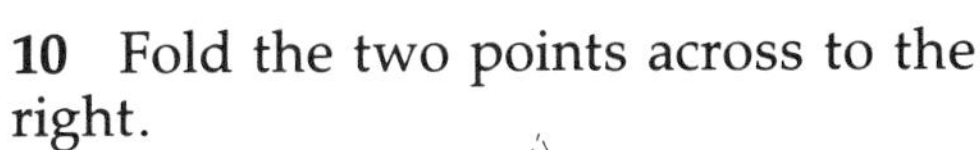

10 Fold the two points across to the right.

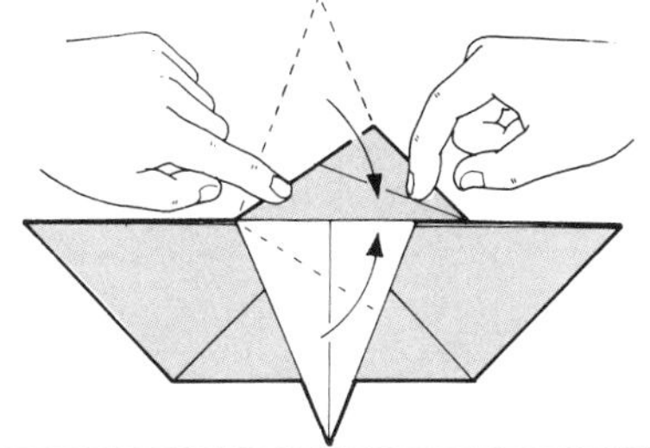

11 Turn the paper over. Fold it in half from side to side.

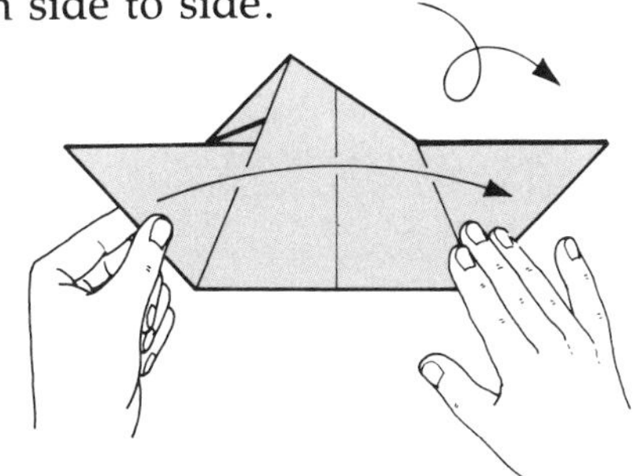

12 Pull the points across to the left and . . .

13 press them down neatly, so making the crow's beak.

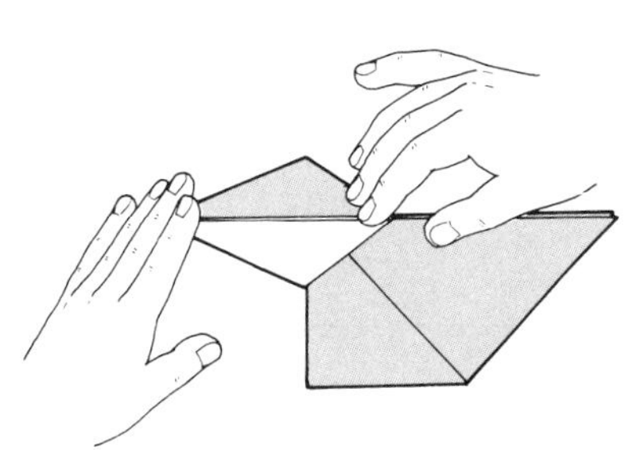

14 To complete the crow, draw on eyes with a felt-tip pen.

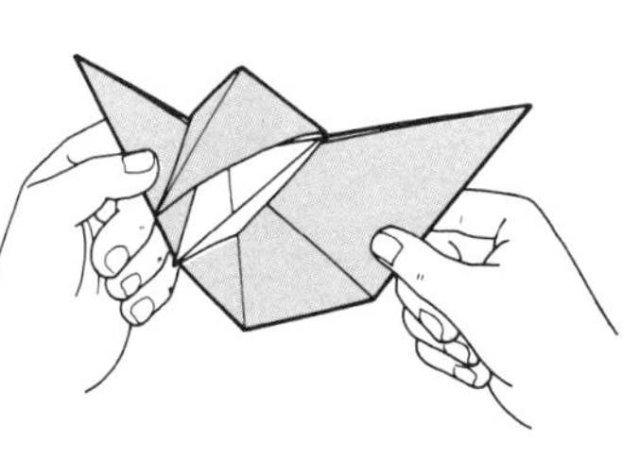

15 Open and close the crow's wings to make him talk. It is even possible to pick up small lightweight objects in the crow's beak.

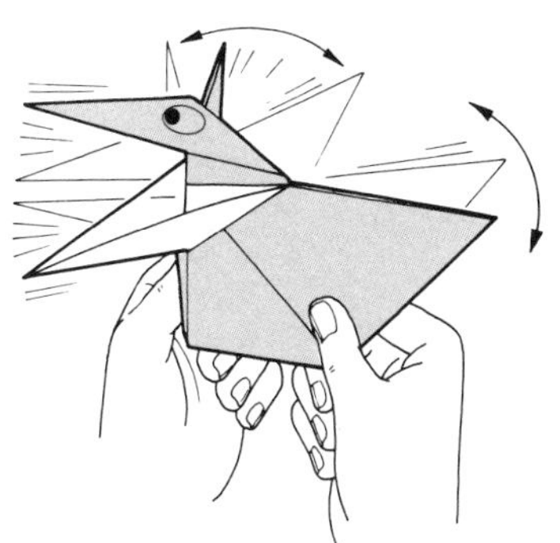

Koron-koron

Isamu Asahi

As koron-koron is made up of similar units, be very careful not to get the folding steps mixed up.

> **You will need:**
> 6 squares of paper all the same size, coloured on one side and white on the other
> Glue

1 *Unit A:* Fold one square in half from top to bottom, with the coloured side on top.

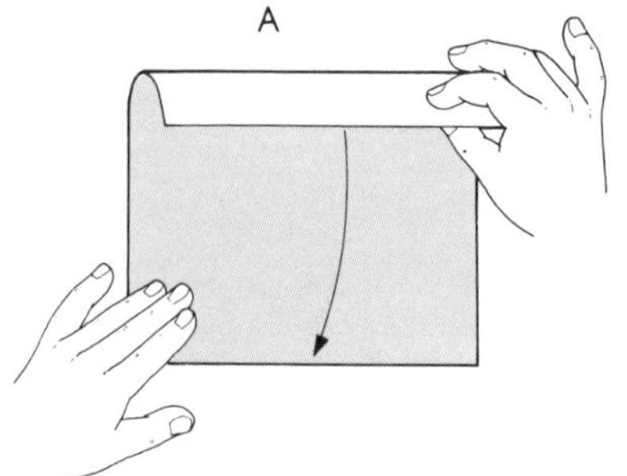

2 Fold the top layer of paper up to meet the top. Press it flat and unfold.

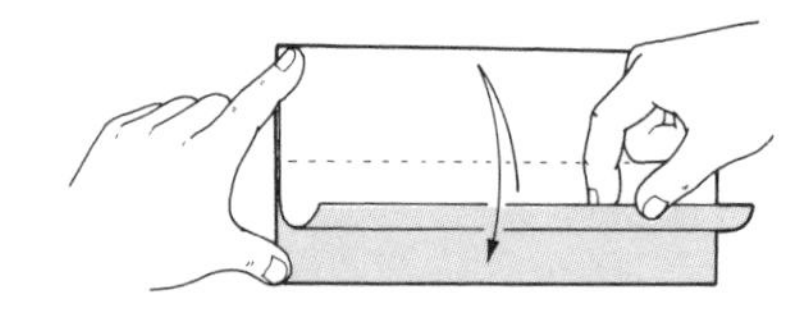

3 Fold the bottom left-hand corner of the top layer of paper up to meet the middle fold-line.

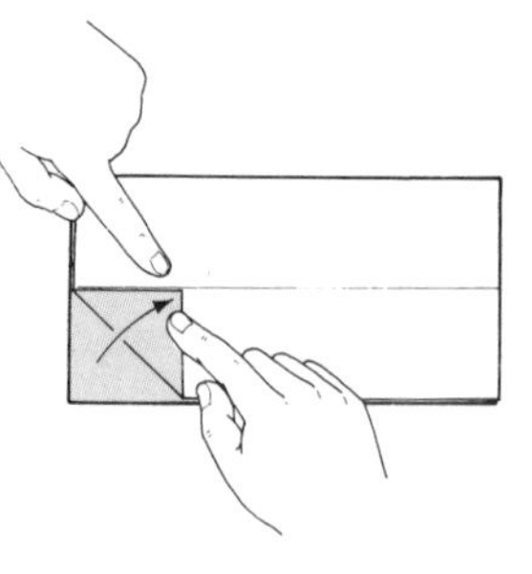

4 Repeat step 2 but do *not* unfold.

5 Turn the paper over. Repeat step 2.

6 Fold the topmost corners of the top layer of paper down to meet the middle fold-line. Press them flat and unfold.

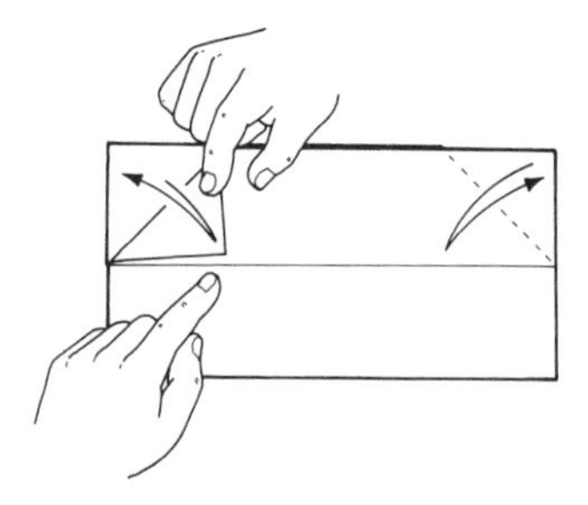

7 Repeat step 2 but do *not* unfold.

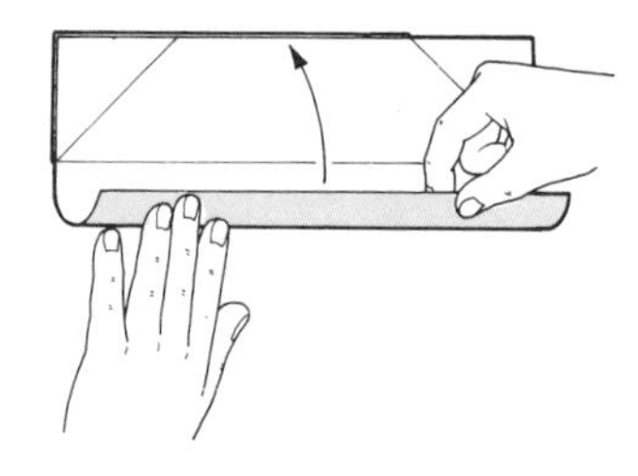

8 Fold the sides in to meet the middle.

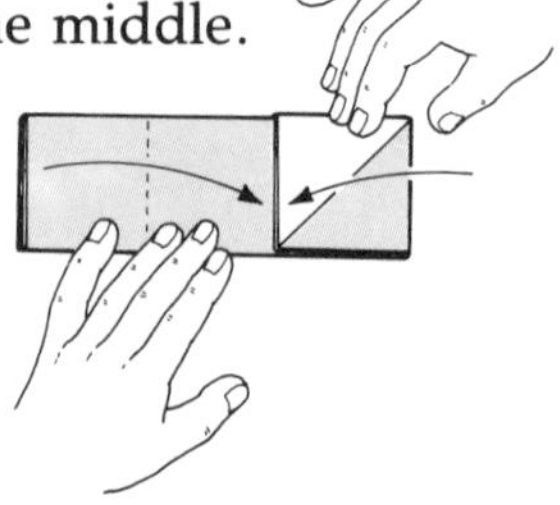

9 Stand the right-hand side upright. Put a finger in between the layers of paper.

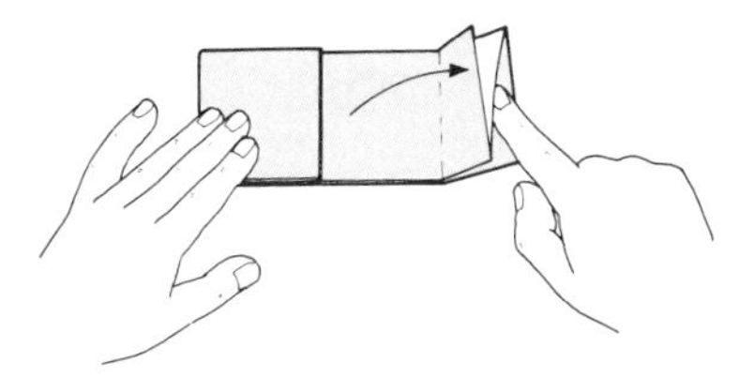

10 Open out the layers and press them down neatly into a triangle and flap.

11 Repeat steps 9 and 10 with the left-hand side.

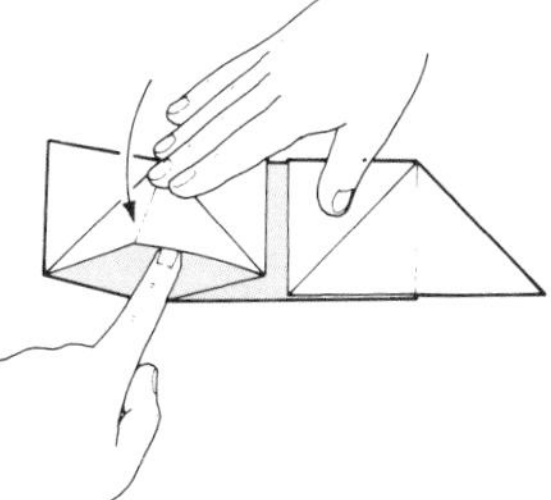

12 Fold the flaps out to either side.

13 Give the middle section a gentle curve.

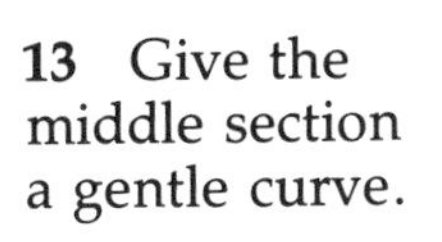

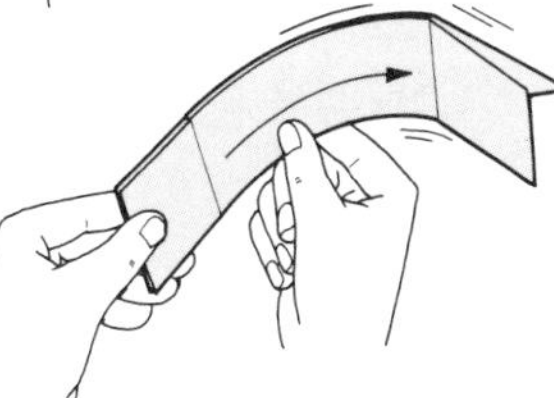

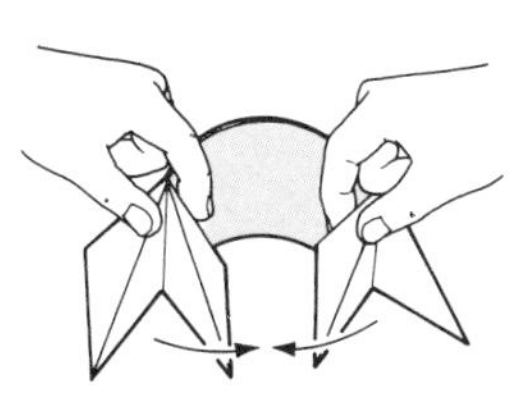

14 Fold the flaps back in.

15 Tuck the right-hand flap inside the left-hand flap and glue them together, so completing unit A.

16 *Unit B:* Repeat steps 1 and 2 of unit A with another square.

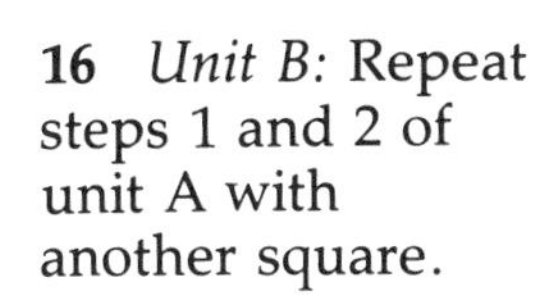

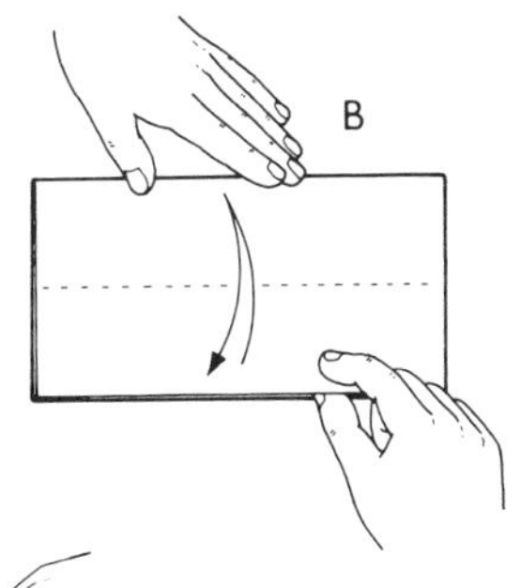

17 Fold the bottom right-hand corner of the top layer of paper up to meet the middle fold-line.

18 Repeat steps 4 to 15 of unit A.

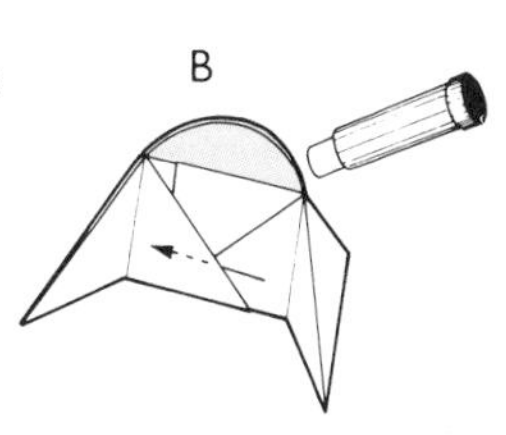

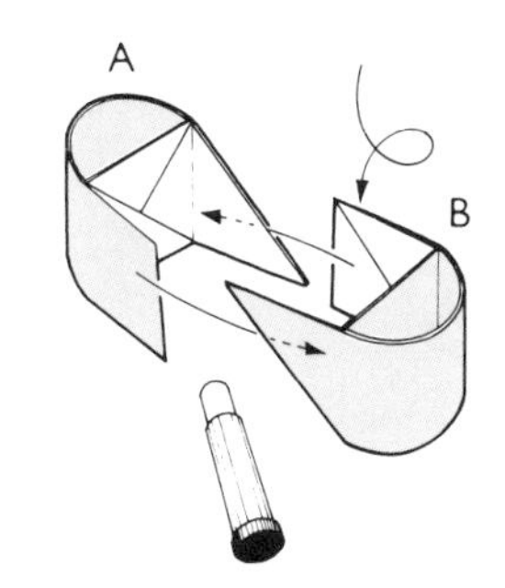

19 Turn unit B upside-down. Tuck and glue units A and B together, so making . . .

20 one oval-shaped unit. Repeat steps 1 to 19 with another two squares, so making one more oval-shaped unit.

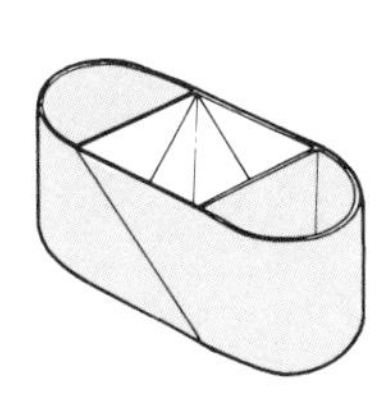

21 *Pieces A and B:* You should now have two squares left.

22 Fold and unfold one square in half from side to side, with the white side on top.

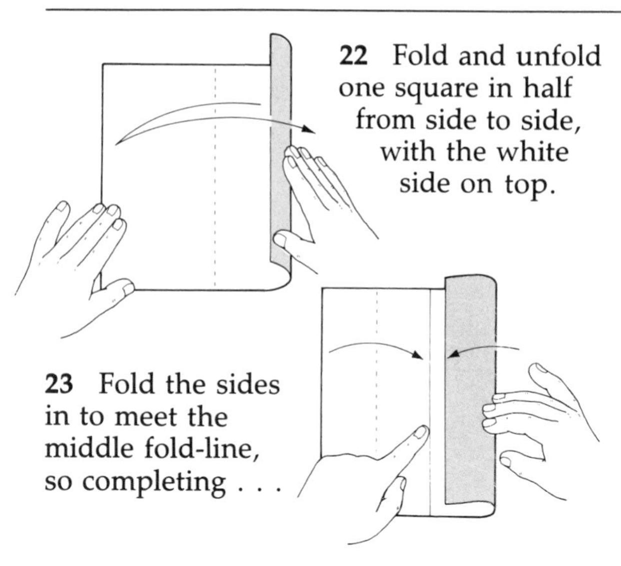

23 Fold the sides in to meet the middle fold-line, so completing . . .

24 piece A. With the remaining square repeat steps 22 and 23, so making piece B.

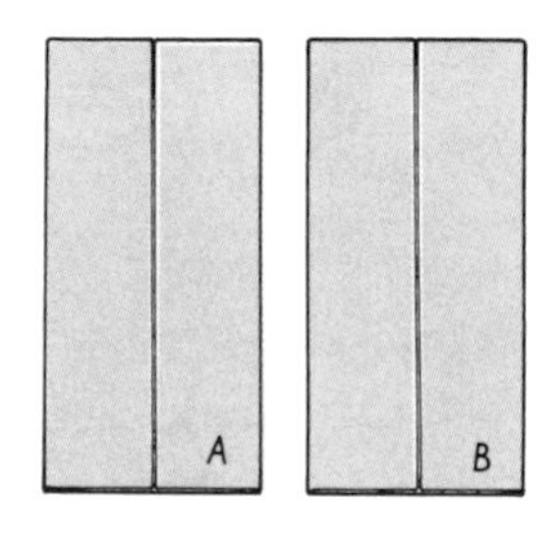

25 Unfold piece A.

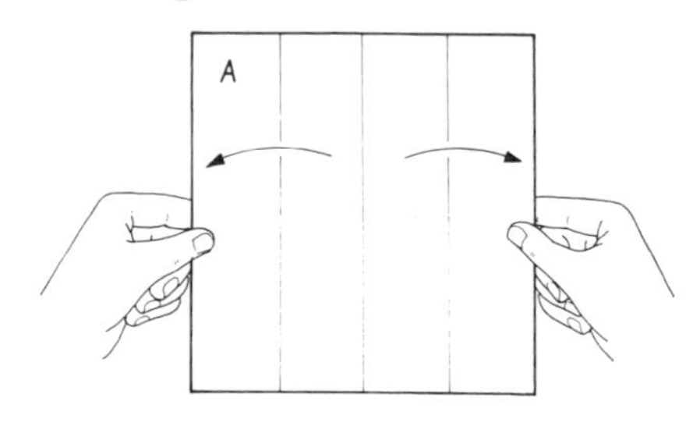

26 Turn piece B over. Place it centrally on top of piece A. Fold the sides of piece A over piece B and glue them down.

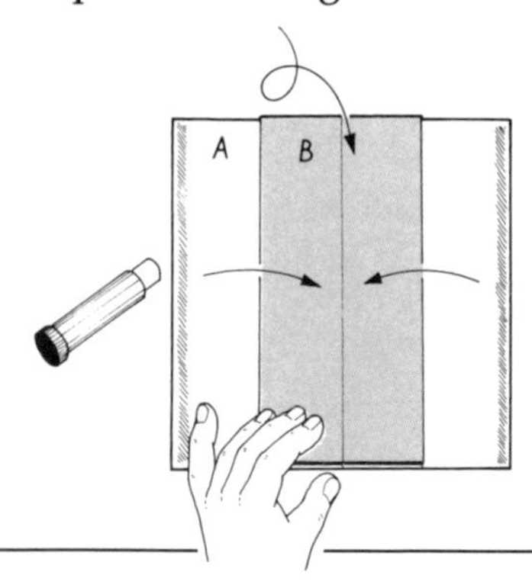

27 Carefully open out pieces A and B into a tube.

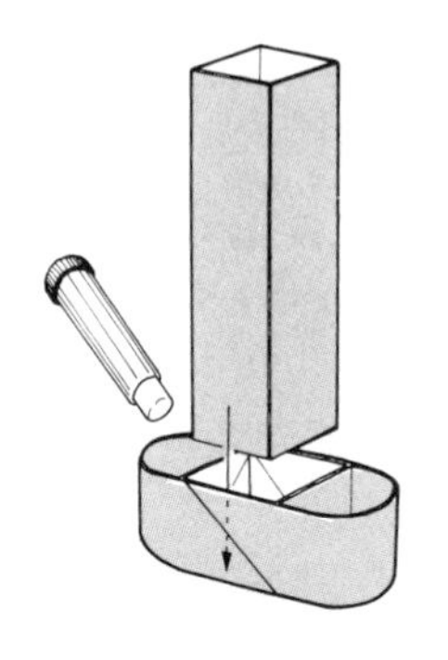

28 *Assembly:* Slide the tube into an oval unit. Glue them together.

29 Slide the opposite end of the tube into the remaining oval unit at 90° to the other oval unit. Glue them together.

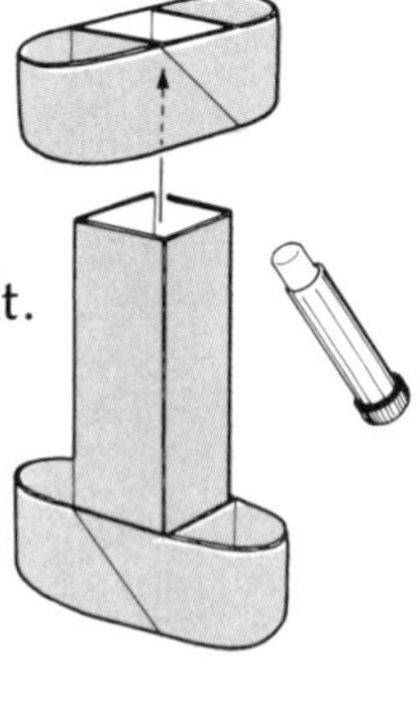

30 Here is the completed koron-koron.

31 When placed upon a sloping surface, this puzzling piece of origami will roll forwards, turning somersaults with a 'koron-koron' sound.

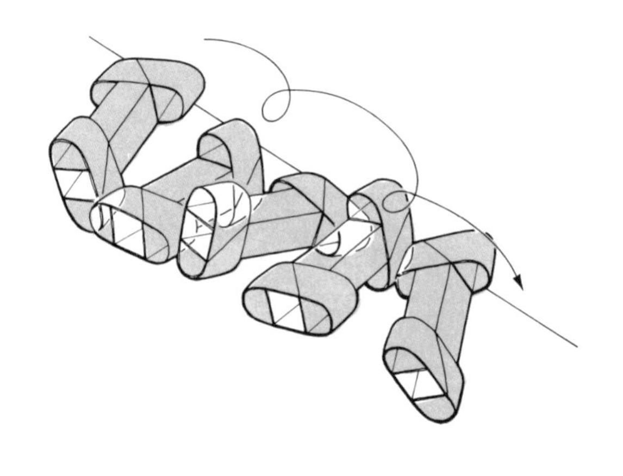

Rolling ball

Isamu Asahi

Even though this fold may at first appear daunting, it is very easy. Remember, as with any fold, do look carefully at each illustration to see what you should do.

You will need:
6 squares of paper all the same size, coloured on one side and white on the other
Glue

1 Fold and unfold one square in half from side to side, with the white side on top.

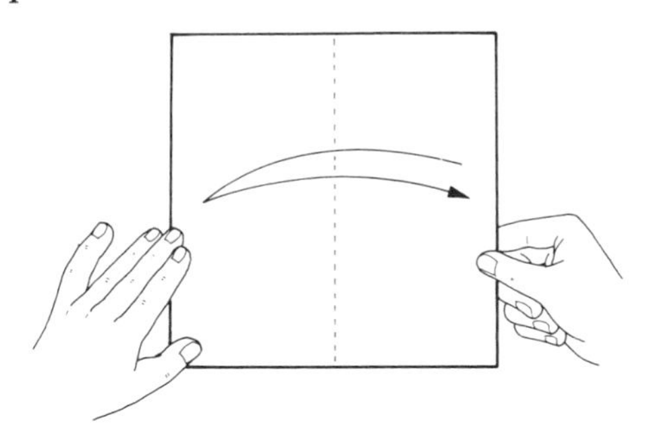

2 Fold the sides in to meet the middle fold-line.

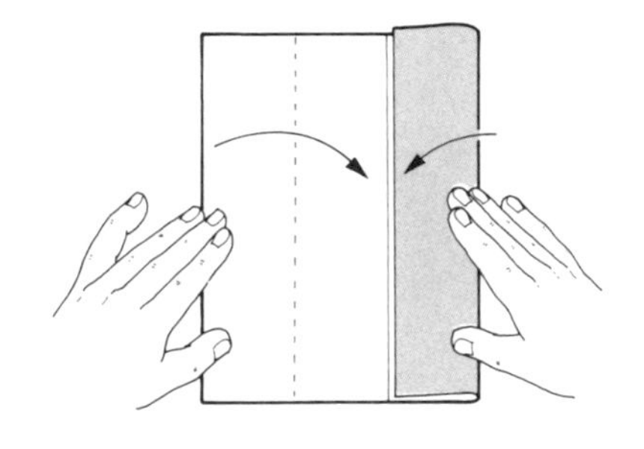

3 Turn the paper over. Pleat the paper by folding the sides in to meet the middle fold-line, while at the same time . . .

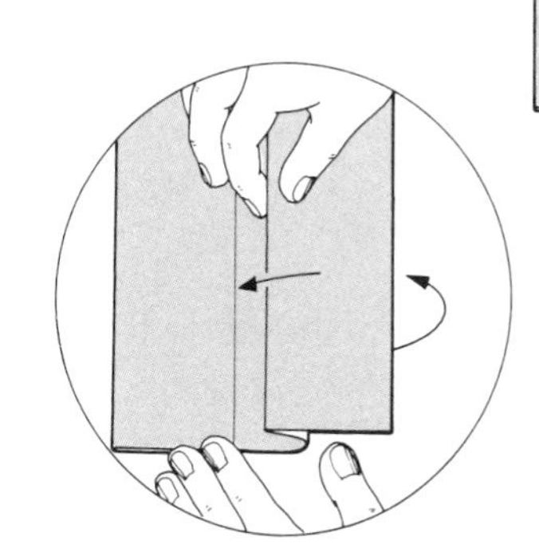

4 letting the paper from underneath flick up.

5 Fold the paper in half from top to bottom.

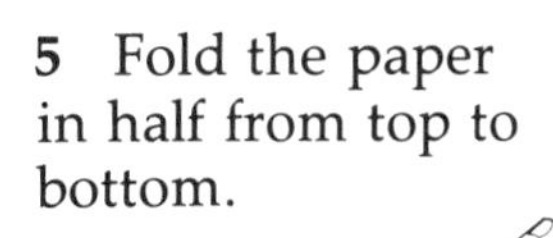

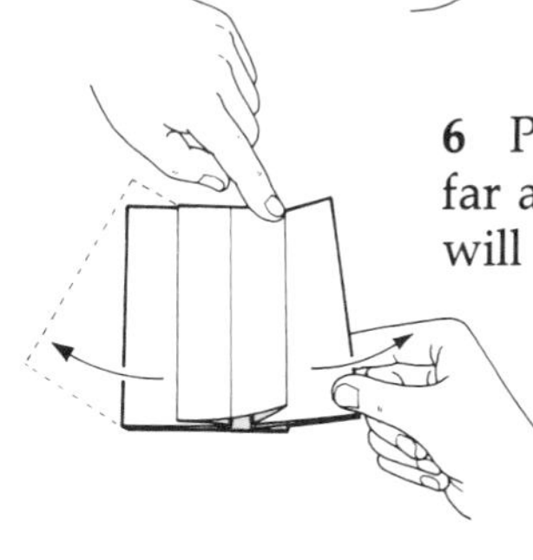

6 Pull the sides up as far as the hidden pleat will allow you.

7 This should be your finished result. Repeat steps 1 to 7 with the remaining five squares.

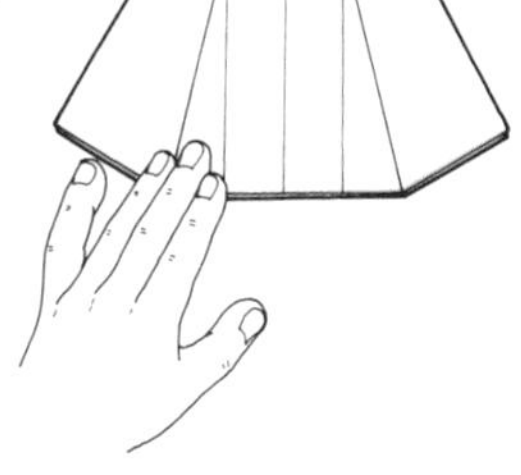

8 Working on a flat surface, tuck one piece inside another and glue them together.

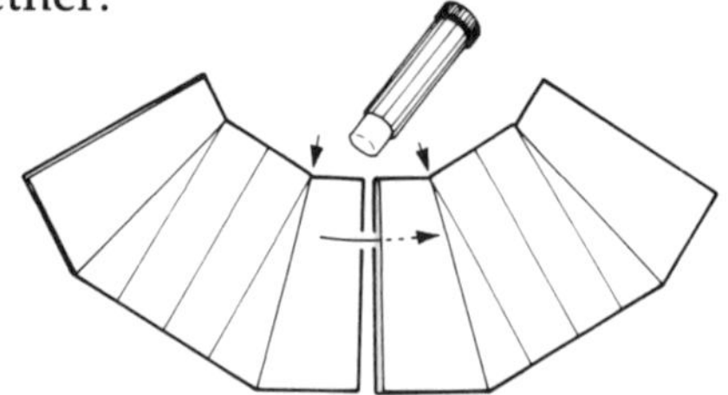

9 Keep on tucking and gluing the six pieces together until you have built up a doughnut-like shape.

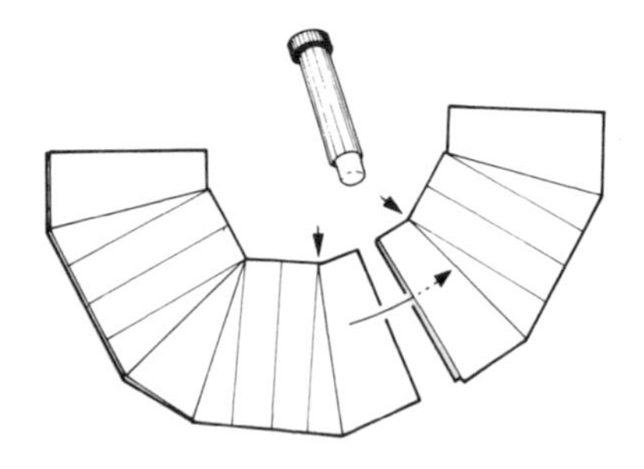

10 Working around the 'doughnut', fold the topmost layer of paper up to meet the centre hole.

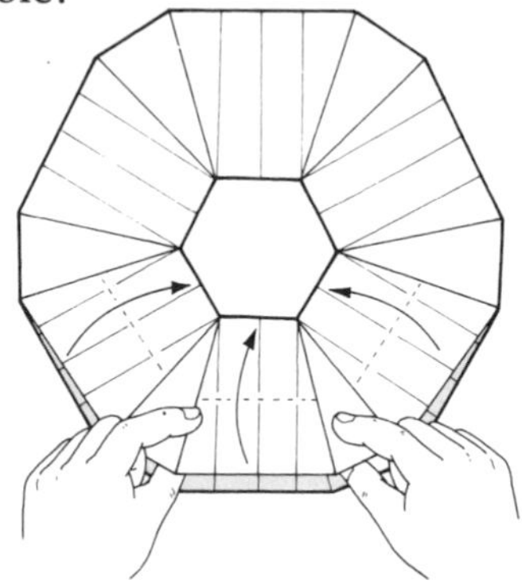

11 This shows you step 10 in more detail. See how the joined sections of the 'doughnut' form themselves into little squares.

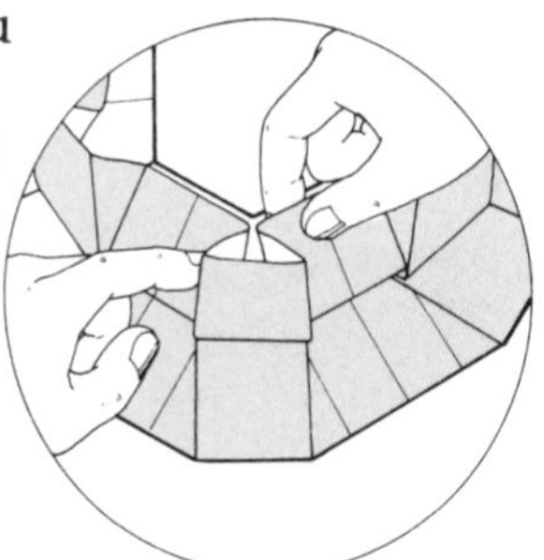

12 This should be your finished result.

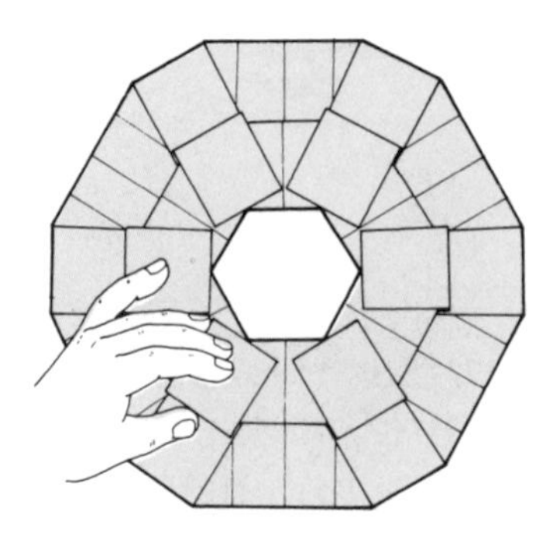

13 Turn the 'doughnut' over. Repeat steps 10 and 11. Press the paper flat.

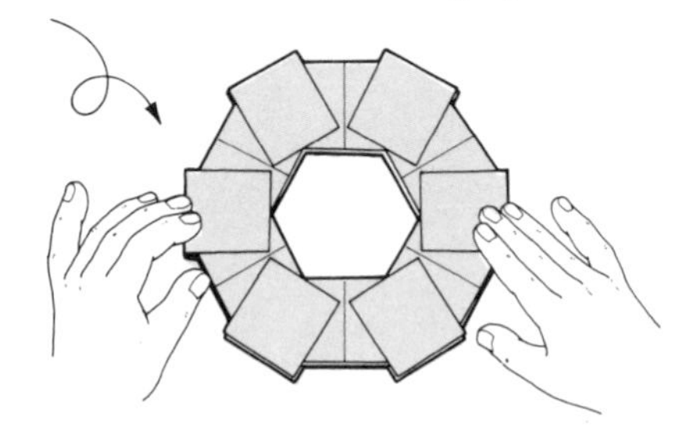

14 Fold back the top corners of each little square on both sides of the 'doughnut'.

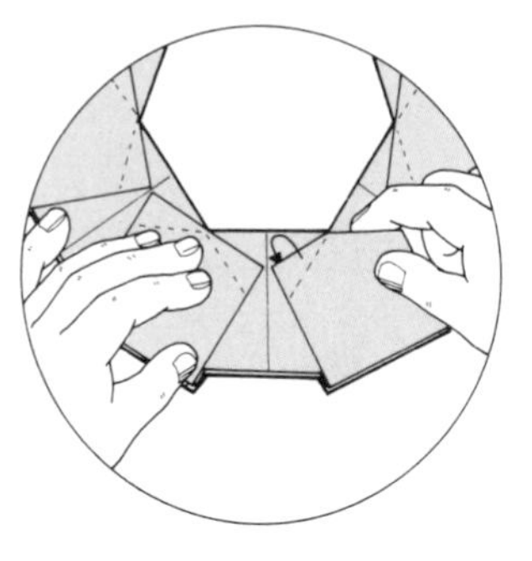

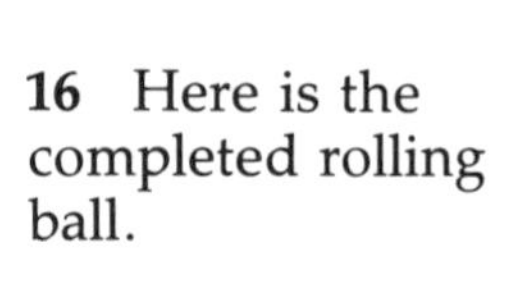

15 Carefully open out the 'doughnut', so making it take on a three-dimensional form.

16 Here is the completed rolling ball.

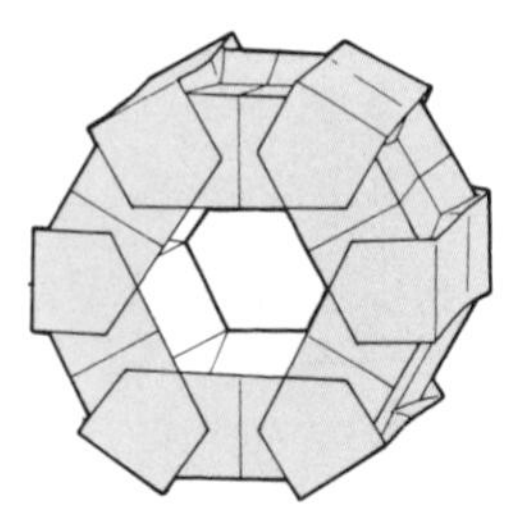

Skittles

Isamu Asahi

You can have a lot of fun and enjoyment with this origami game.

You will need:
10 squares of paper all the same size, coloured on one side and white on the other
10 small animal faces
Glue

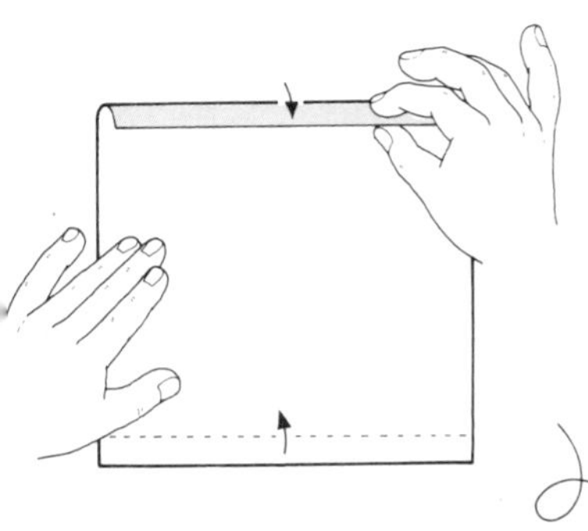

1 Fold in the top and bottom of one square a little way, with the white side on top.

2 Turn the paper over. Fold and unfold it in half from side to side.

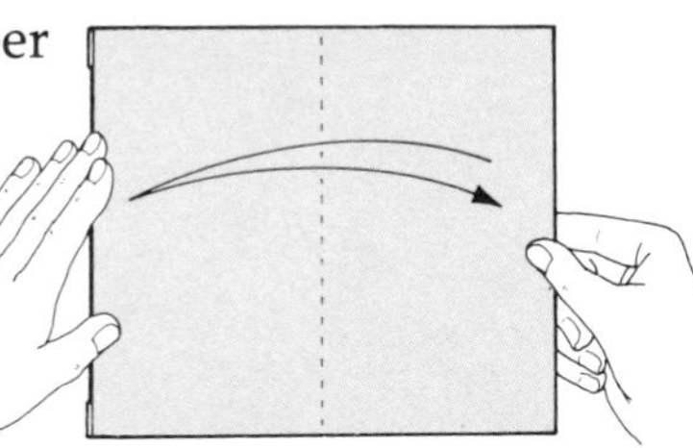

3 Fold the sides in to meet the middle fold-line. Press them flat and unfold.

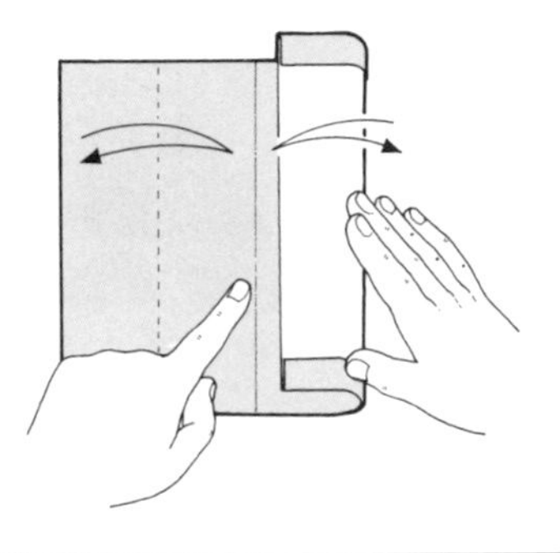

4 Fold the sides back in. Tuck one side inside the other, so making the paper become triangular and three-dimensional.

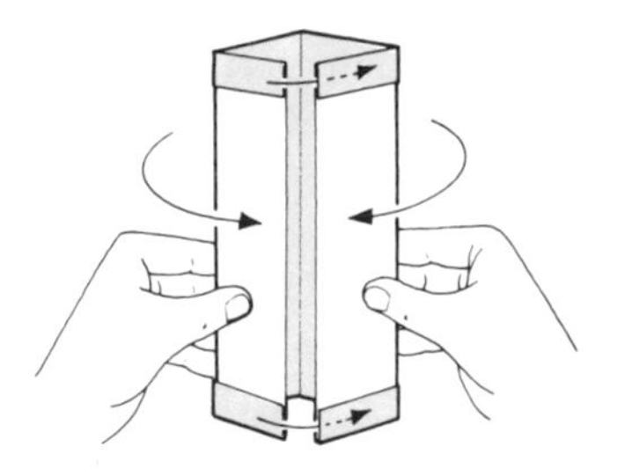

5 Here is a completed skittle. Decorate it by gluing on an animal face.

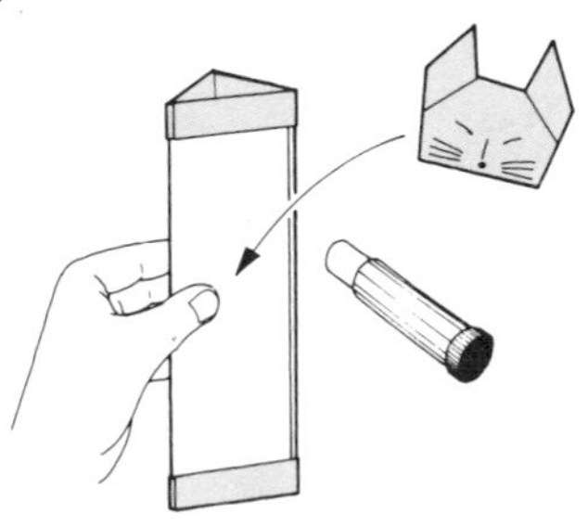

6 Repeat steps 1 to 6 with the remaining nine squares to make a complete set of skittles.

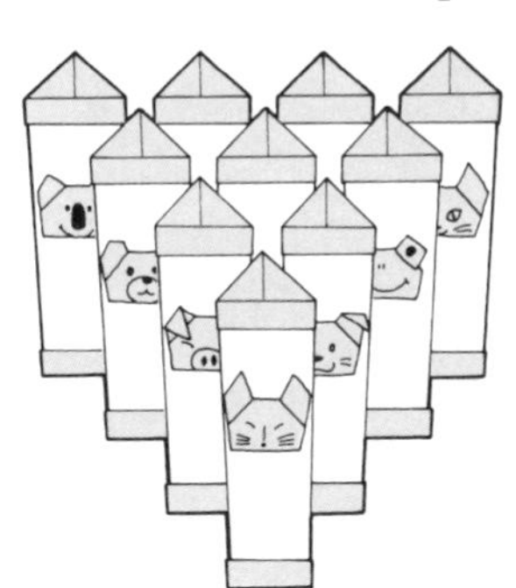

7 Using the rolling ball on page 77, why not have a game of skittles with your friends?

Flapping Bird

Traditional

Who the creator is of this amazing piece of action origami is a mystery. But you will have a lot of fun folding it, as you will learn how to fold two very important origami bases.

> **You will need:**
> Square of paper, coloured on one side and white on the other

1 Turn the square around to look like a diamond, with the white side on top. Fold it in half from top to bottom, so making a triangle.

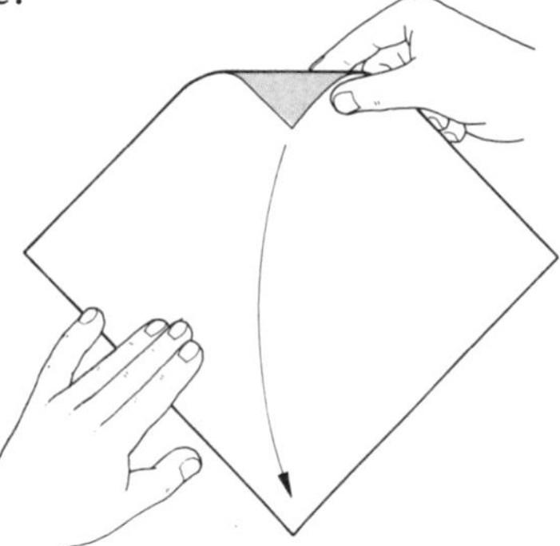

2 Fold the triangle in half from side to side.

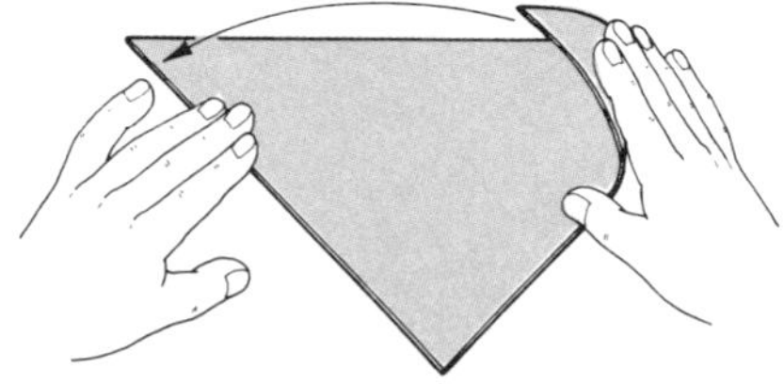

3 Lift the top half up along the middle fold-line. Start to open the paper out . . .

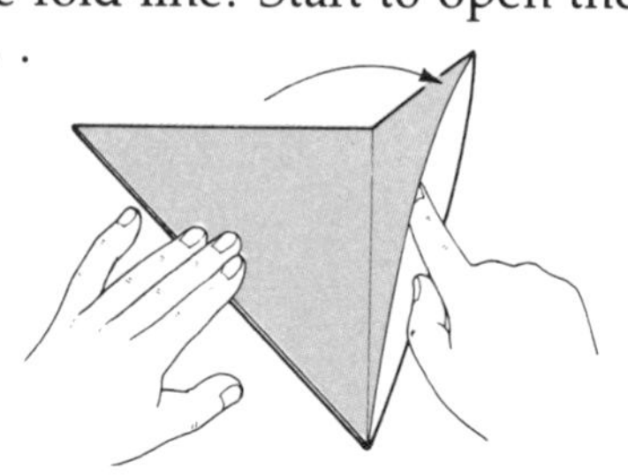

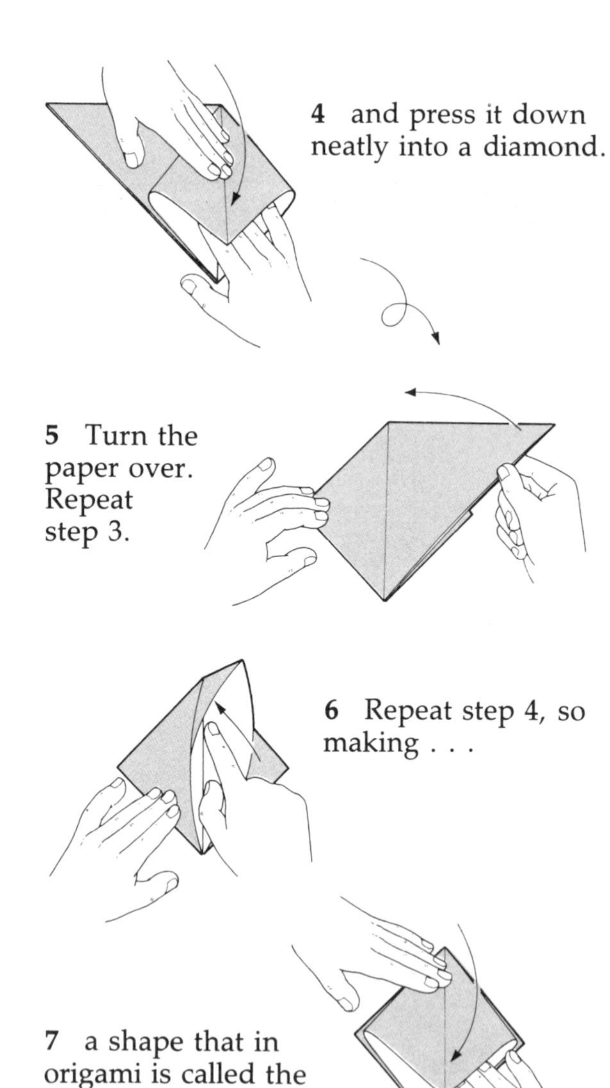

4 and press it down neatly into a diamond.

5 Turn the paper over. Repeat step 3.

6 Repeat step 4, so making . . .

7 a shape that in origami is called the preliminary base.

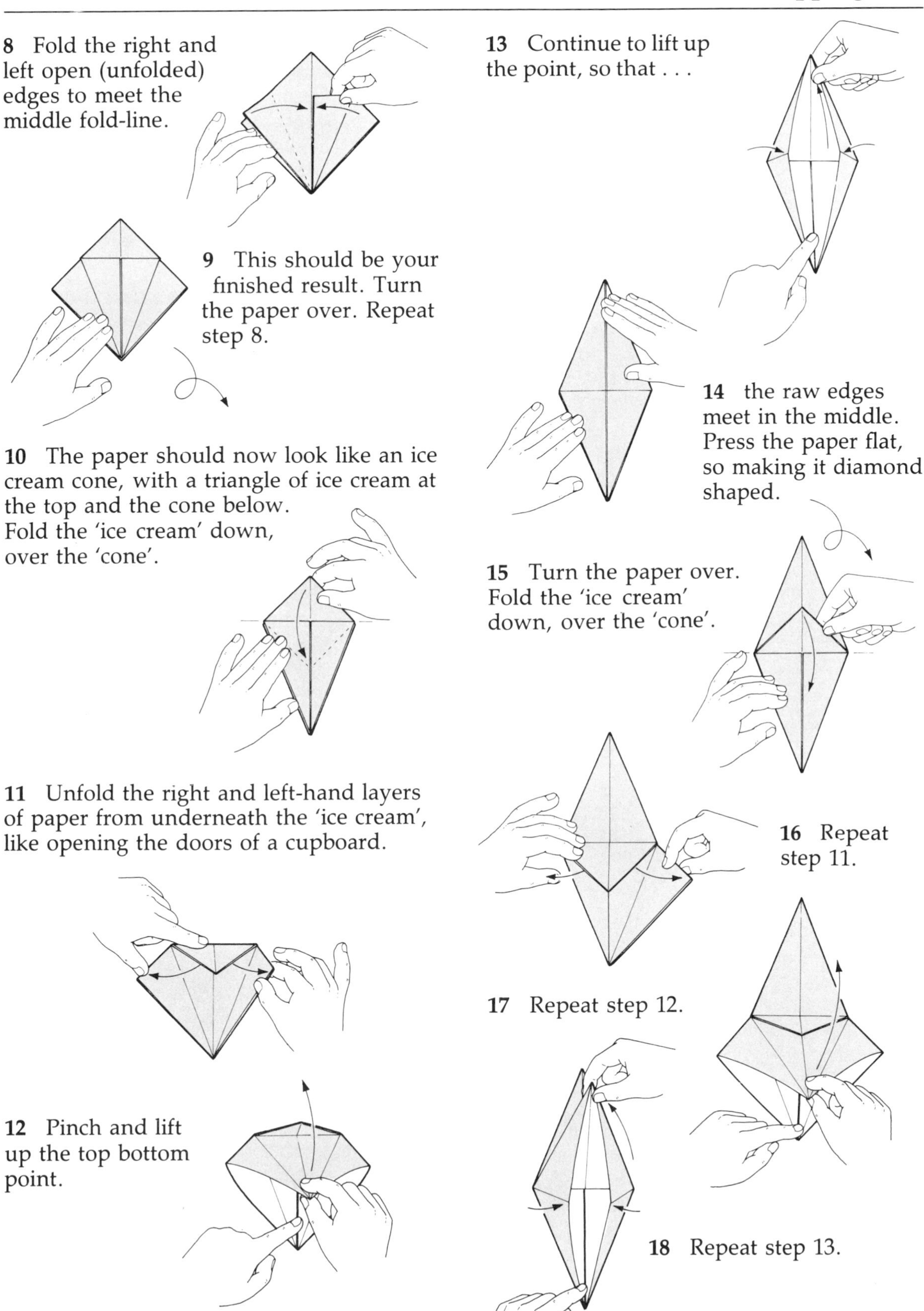

8 Fold the right and left open (unfolded) edges to meet the middle fold-line.

9 This should be your finished result. Turn the paper over. Repeat step 8.

10 The paper should now look like an ice cream cone, with a triangle of ice cream at the top and the cone below. Fold the 'ice cream' down, over the 'cone'.

11 Unfold the right and left-hand layers of paper from underneath the 'ice cream', like opening the doors of a cupboard.

12 Pinch and lift up the top bottom point.

13 Continue to lift up the point, so that . . .

14 the raw edges meet in the middle. Press the paper flat, so making it diamond shaped.

15 Turn the paper over. Fold the 'ice cream' down, over the 'cone'.

16 Repeat step 11.

17 Repeat step 12.

18 Repeat step 13.

Flapping bird

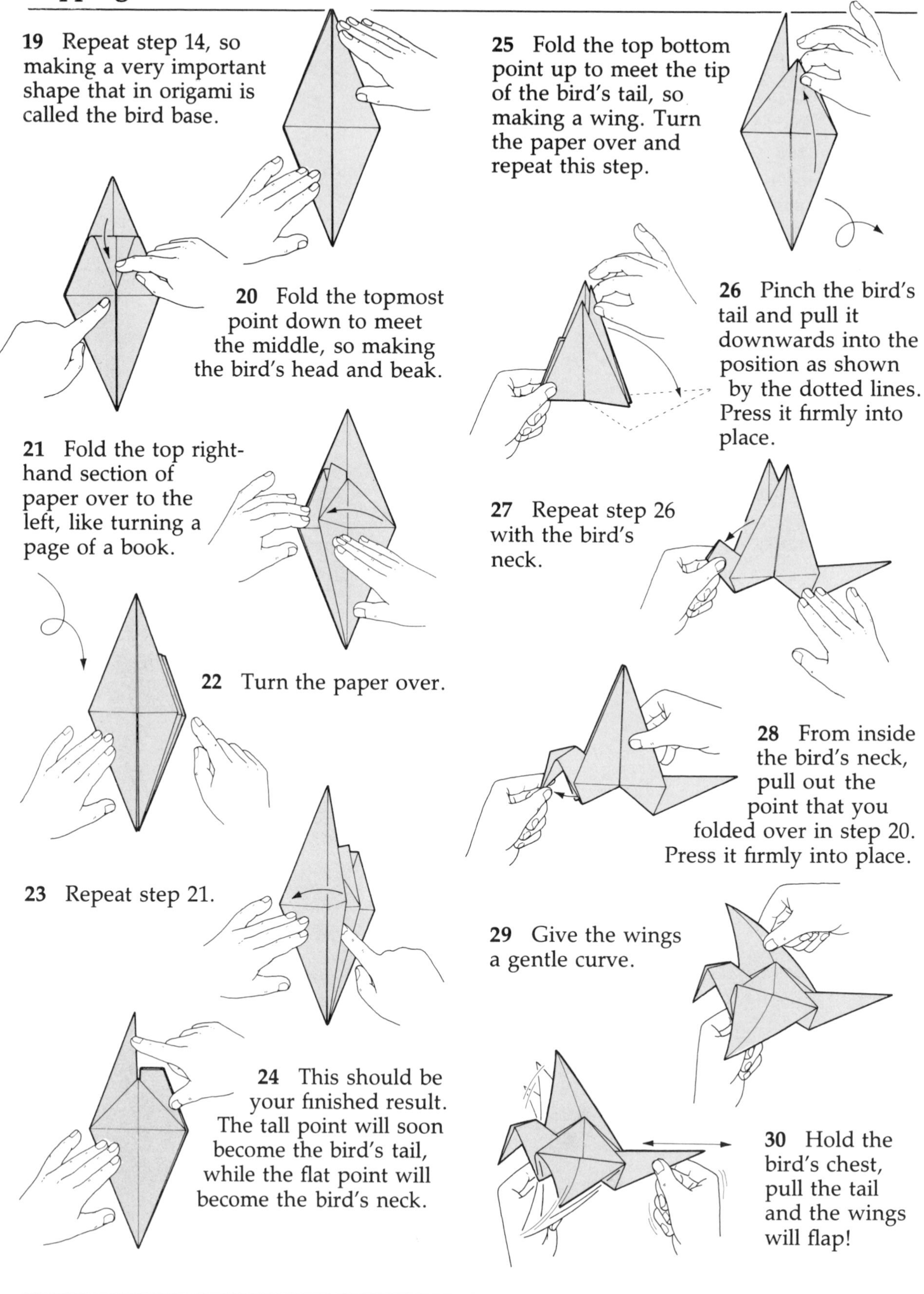

19 Repeat step 14, so making a very important shape that in origami is called the bird base.

20 Fold the topmost point down to meet the middle, so making the bird's head and beak.

21 Fold the top right-hand section of paper over to the left, like turning a page of a book.

22 Turn the paper over.

23 Repeat step 21.

24 This should be your finished result. The tall point will soon become the bird's tail, while the flat point will become the bird's neck.

25 Fold the top bottom point up to meet the tip of the bird's tail, so making a wing. Turn the paper over and repeat this step.

26 Pinch the bird's tail and pull it downwards into the position as shown by the dotted lines. Press it firmly into place.

27 Repeat step 26 with the bird's neck.

28 From inside the bird's neck, pull out the point that you folded over in step 20. Press it firmly into place.

29 Give the wings a gentle curve.

30 Hold the bird's chest, pull the tail and the wings will flap!

Crane

Traditional

This most famous of origami folds is often used throughout the world as a symbol of peace. If you fold a thousand cranes within one year of your life and string them together, it is said that they will bring you long life and good fortune.

You will need:
Square of paper, coloured on one side and white on the other
Miniature coaster (see page 91)
Needle and cotton

1 Start with step 19 of the flapping bird on page 82.

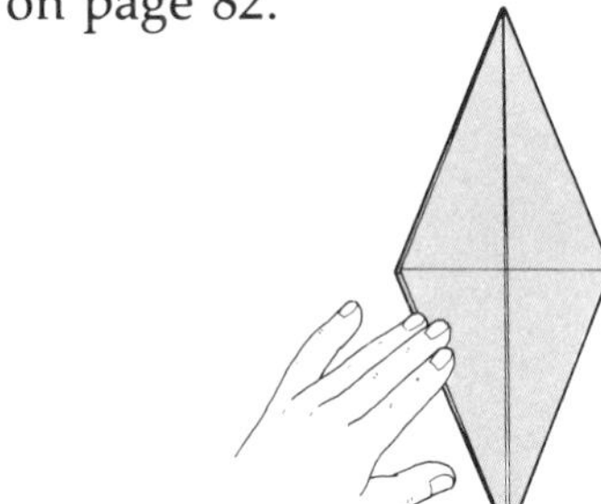

2 Narrow down the lower points by folding the top right and left-hand sloping sides in to lie along the middle.

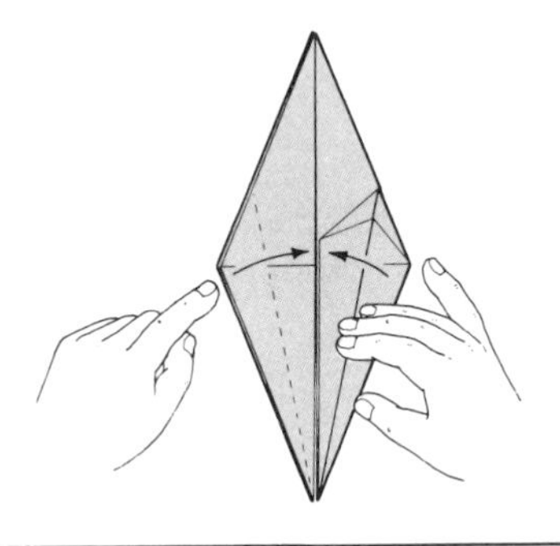

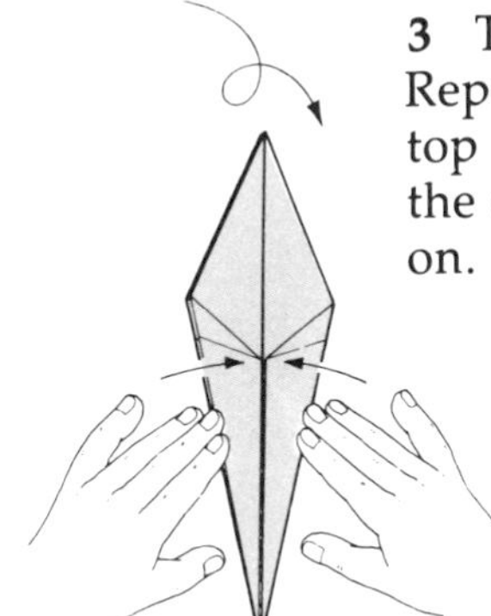

3 Turn the paper over. Repeat step 2. The two top points will become the crane's wings later on.

4 Fold the top right-hand section of paper over to the left, like turning the page of a book.

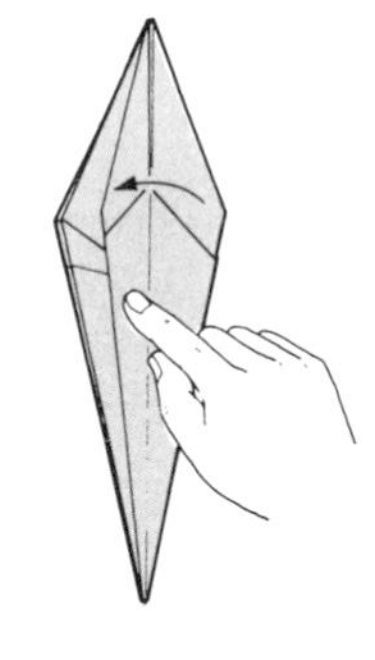

5 Fold the top bottom point up to meet the top of the crane's wings.

6 Fold the top left-hand section of paper over to the right, like turning the page of a book.

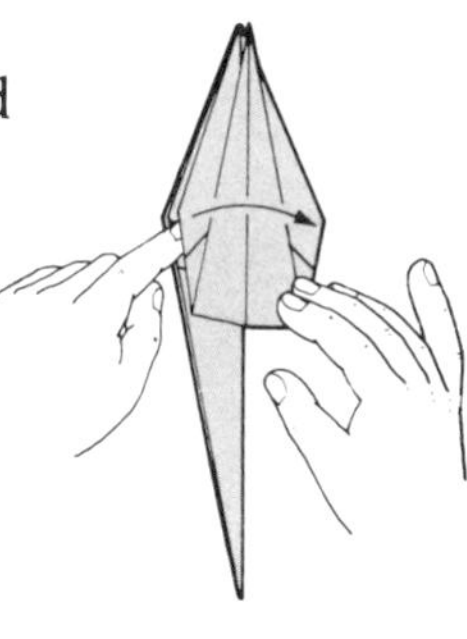

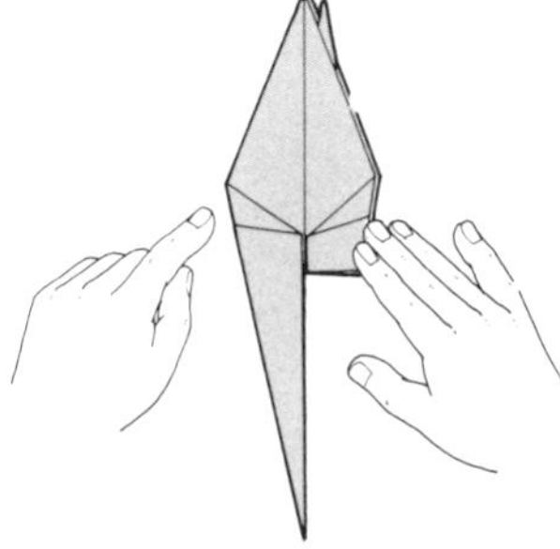

7 This should be your finished result.

8 Repeat step 6.

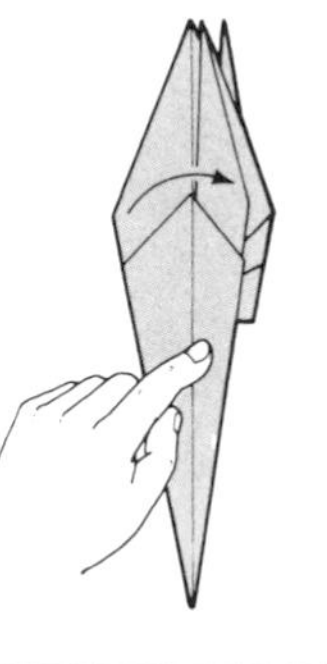

Crane

9 Repeat step 5.

10 Fold the top right-hand section of paper over to the left, like turning the page of a book.

11 Pinch both points and pull them outwards. Press them firmly into place.

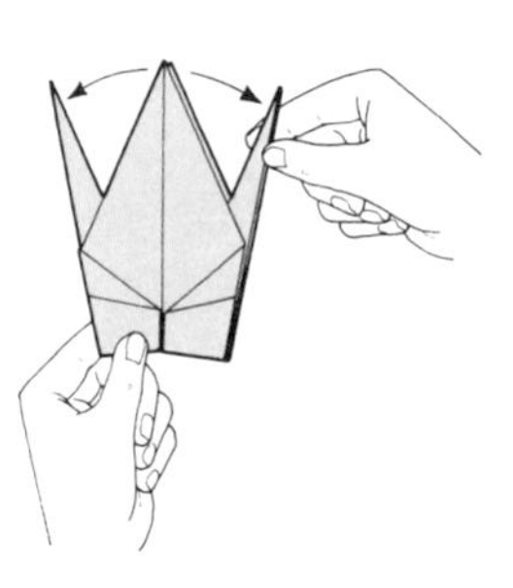

12 Place your thumb into the groove of the right-hand point. With your forefinger on top, pull the point down inside itself, so making the crane's head and beak.

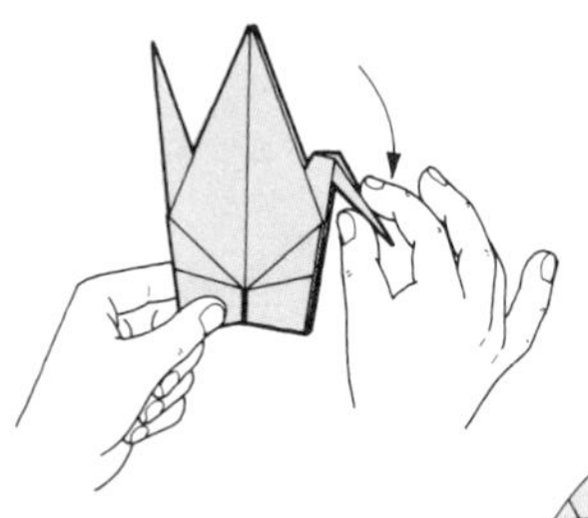

13 This shows you step 12 in more detail.

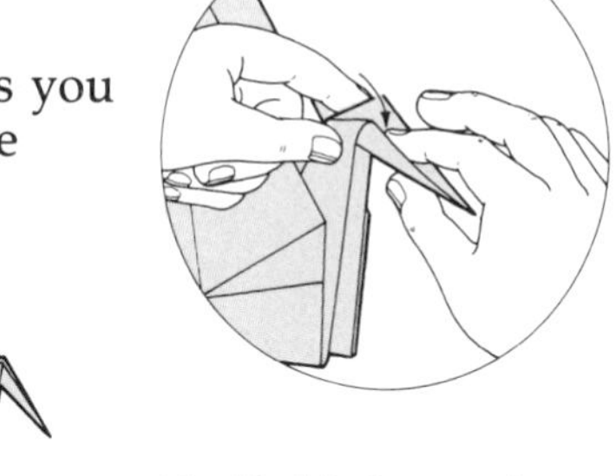

14 Fold down the topmost wing.

15 Turn the paper over. Repeat step 14.

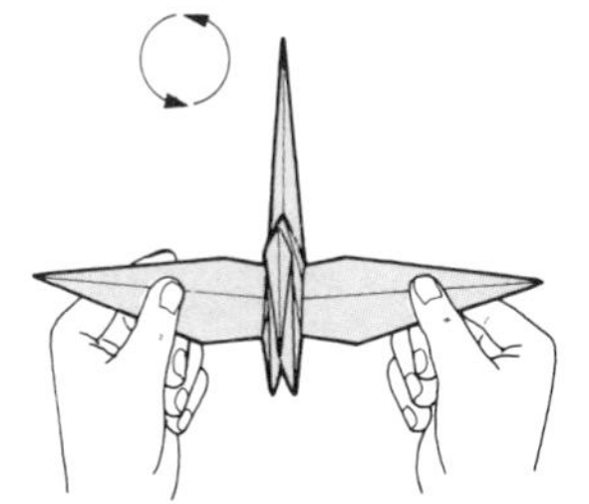

16 Turn the crane around. Take hold of a wing in each hand . . .

17 and gently pull them apart, so flattening out the middle point a little.

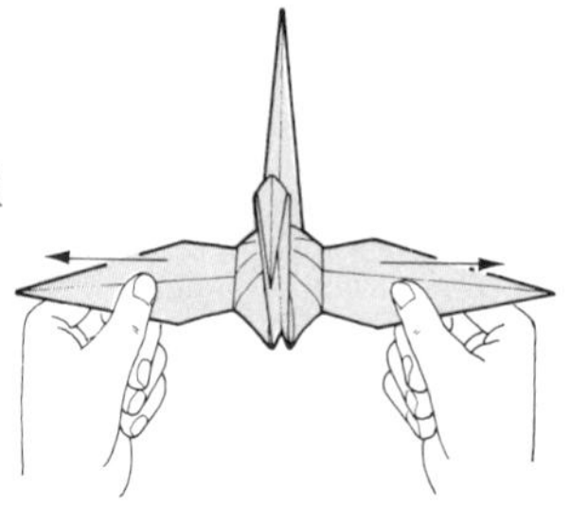

18 Here is the completed crane.

19 Make a few more cranes and thread them together along with the miniature coaster for a very effective decoration.

Pop-up star

Traditional

The beauty of this fold lies in the lines and shadows that are created by the folding. For a very stunning effect, try making the star with a square of paper that is coloured on both sides.

You will need:
Square of paper, coloured on one side and white on the other
Needle and cotton

1 Fold the square in half from bottom to top with the white side on top.

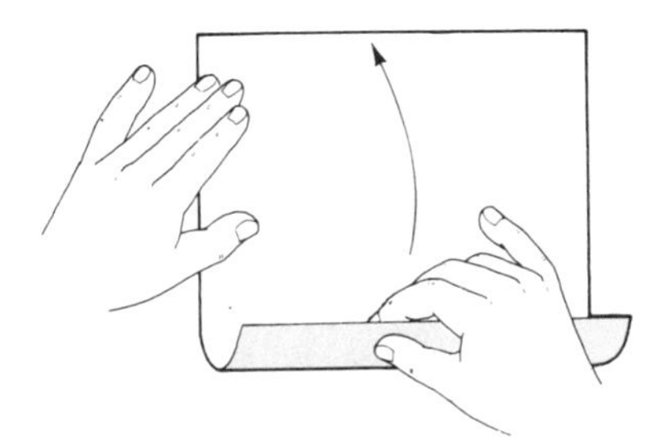

2 Fold it in half from side to side.

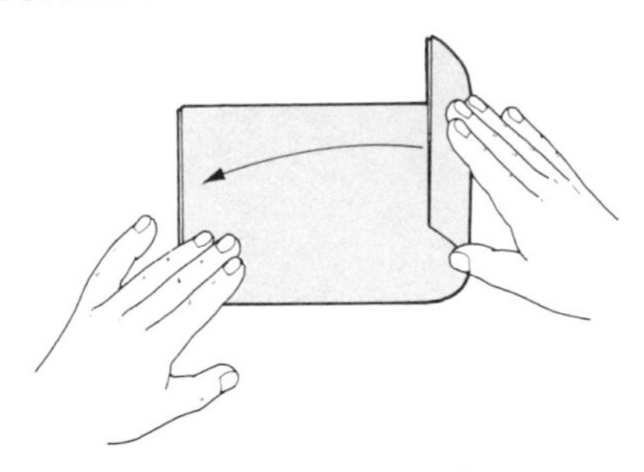

3 Open out the square completely, back to step 1. Fold the corners in to meet the middle, so making the blintz base.

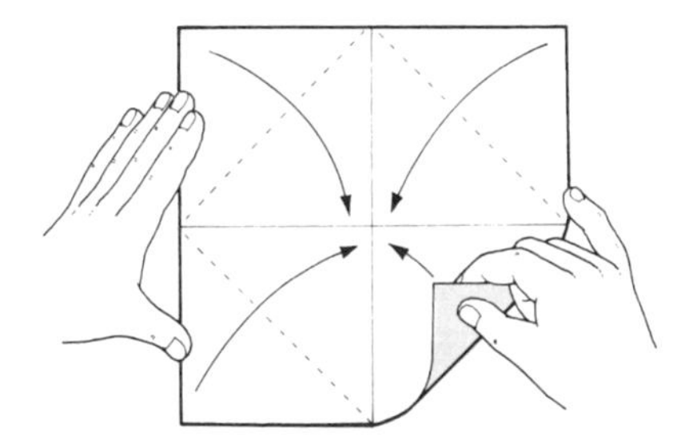

4 Turn the blintz base around to look like a diamond. Fold it in half from top to bottom, so making a triangle..

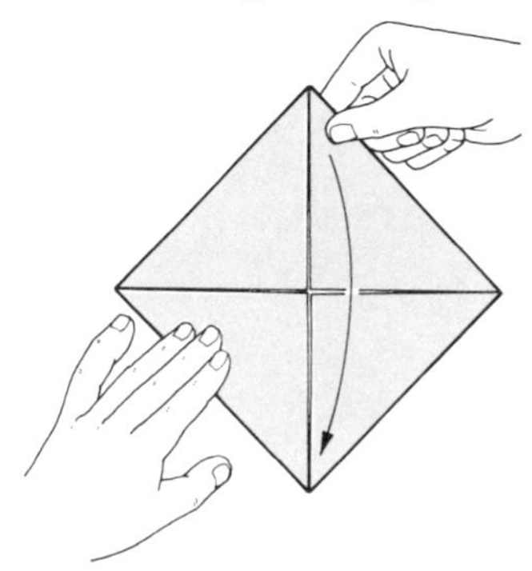

5 Fold the triangle in half from side to side.

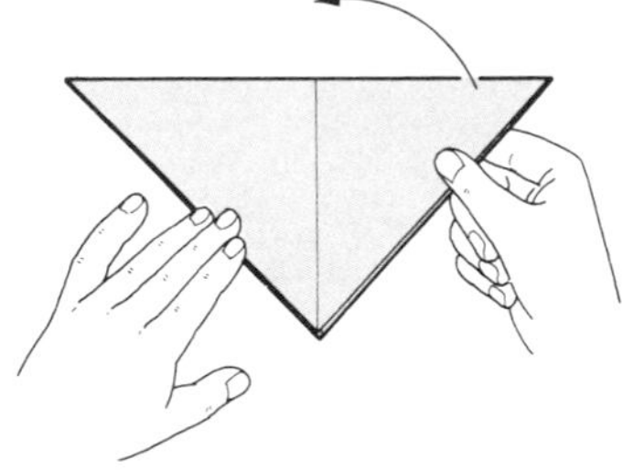

6 Lift the top half up along the middle fold-line, start to open the paper out and . . .

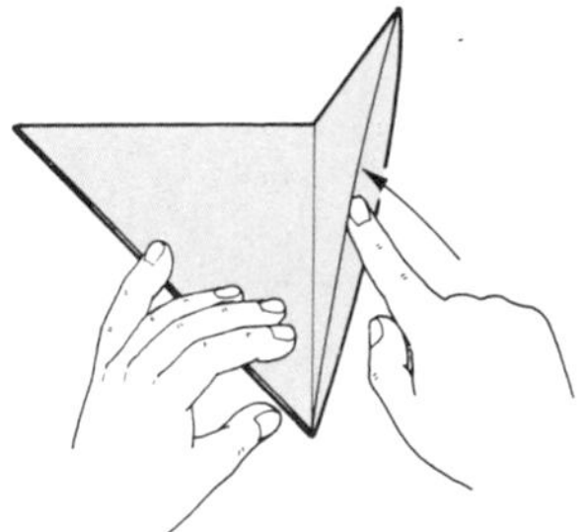

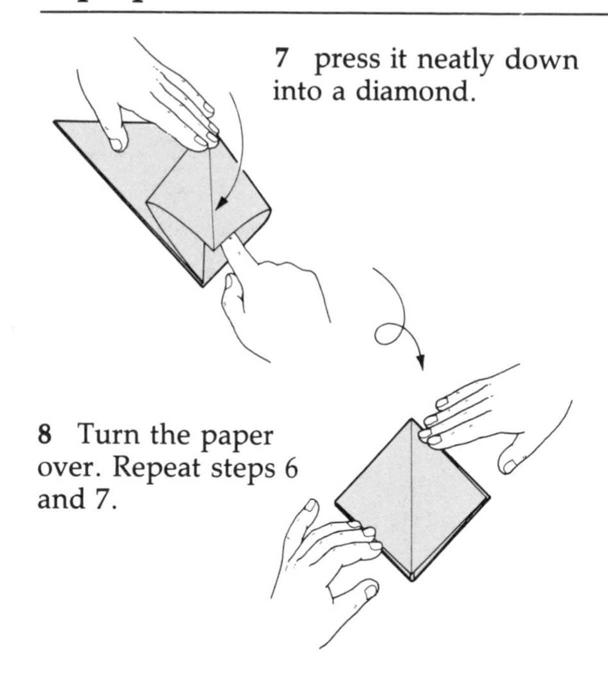

7 press it neatly down into a diamond.

8 Turn the paper over. Repeat steps 6 and 7.

9 Repeat steps 8 to 19 of the flapping bird on page 81.

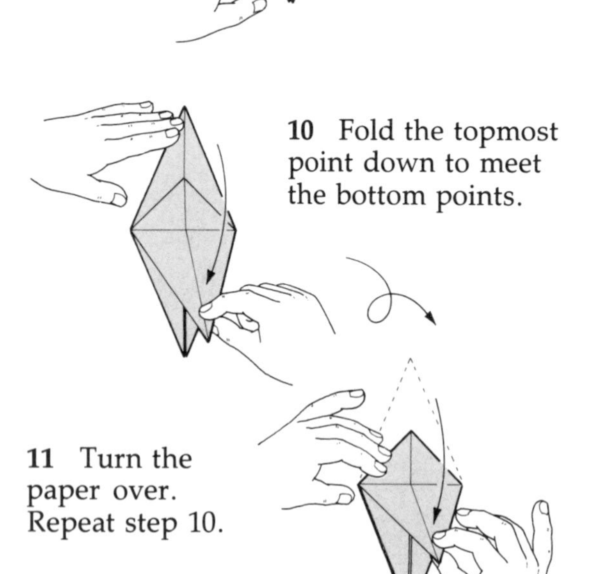

10 Fold the topmost point down to meet the bottom points.

11 Turn the paper over. Repeat step 10.

12 Turn the paper around. Pinch the two inside points and . . .

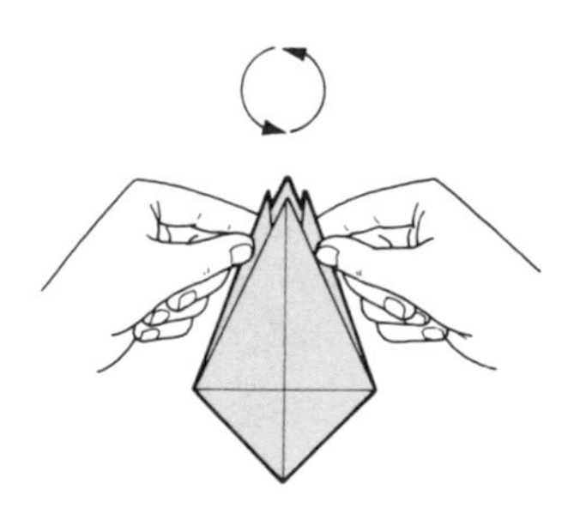

13 pull them apart . . .

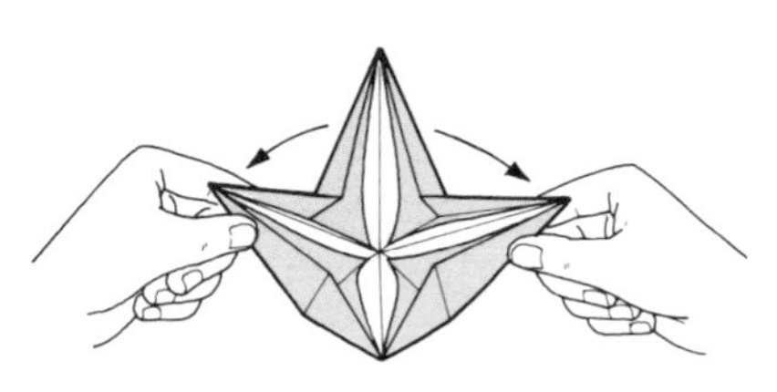

14 until the folds in the middle of the paper vanish with a 'pop'.

15 To complete the star, attach a loop of cotton to one of the points, so that the pop-up star can be hung as a decoration.

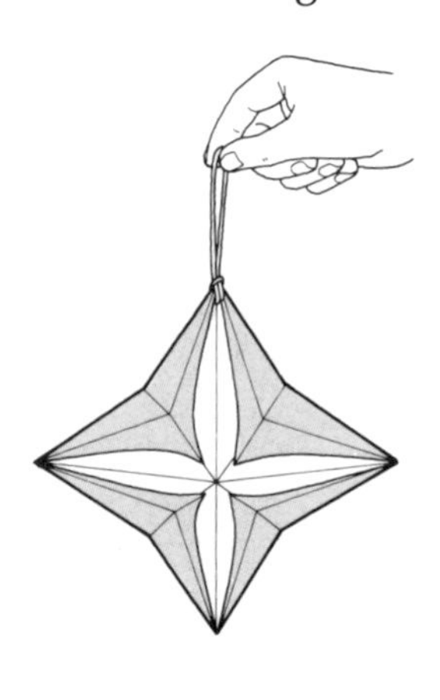

Cat

Toshie Takahama

When two different types of fold are joined together, as with this charming cat, the finished result is called compound origami.

You will need:
2 squares of paper the same size, coloured on one side and white on the other
Scissors
Glue
Felt-tip pen

1 Cut one of the squares into quarters, as you only need a quarter-square for the cat's head. *Body:* Using the larger square, fold steps 1 to 19 of the flapping bird on page 80.

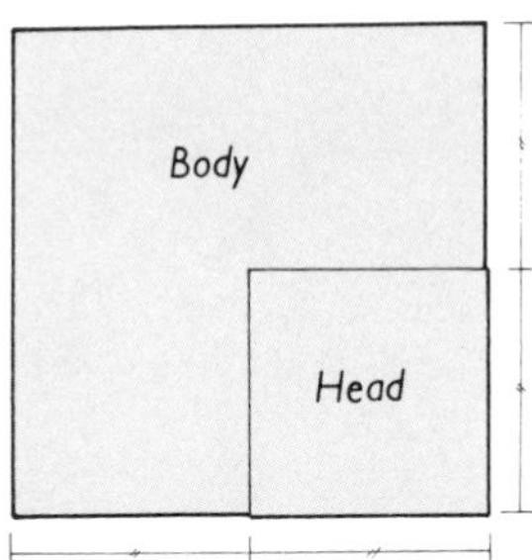

2 Fold the topmost point down one-third of the distance to the middle.

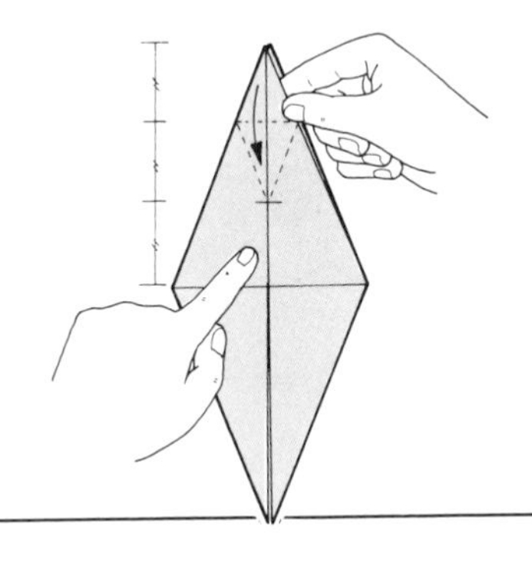

3 Fold it down to meet the middle.

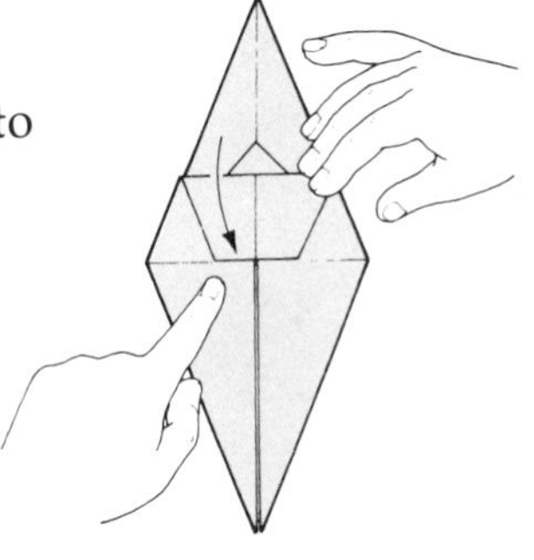

4 Finally fold it down along the middle fold-line.

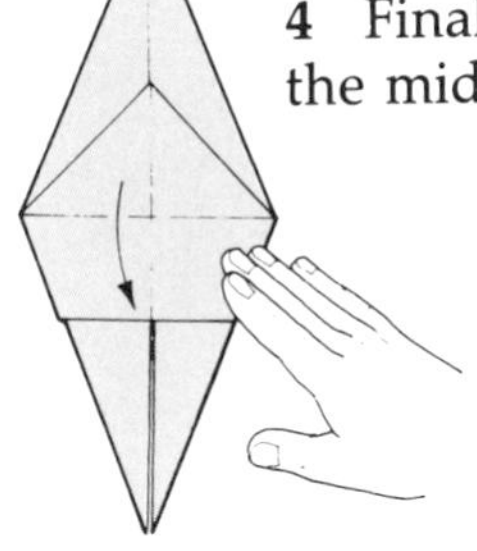

5 Place your forefinger in the groove of the bottom right-hand point, and with your thumb . . .

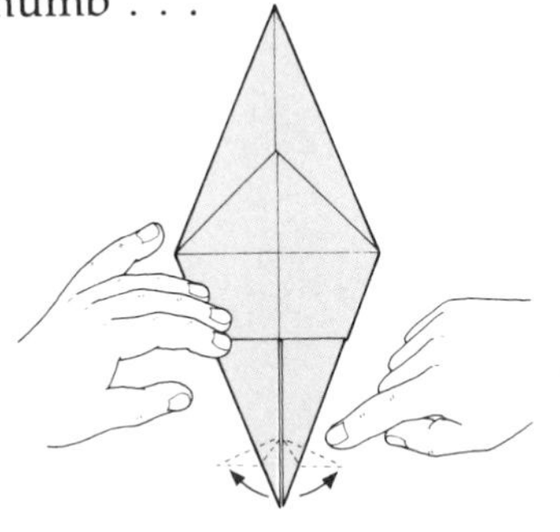

6 pull the point up inside itself.

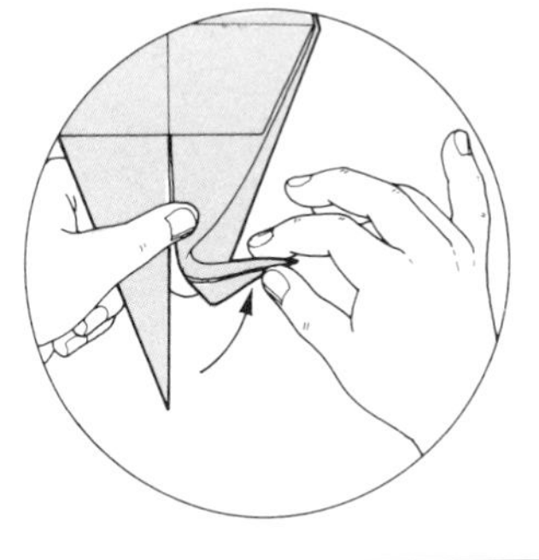

7 Press the paper flat into this position, so making a paw.

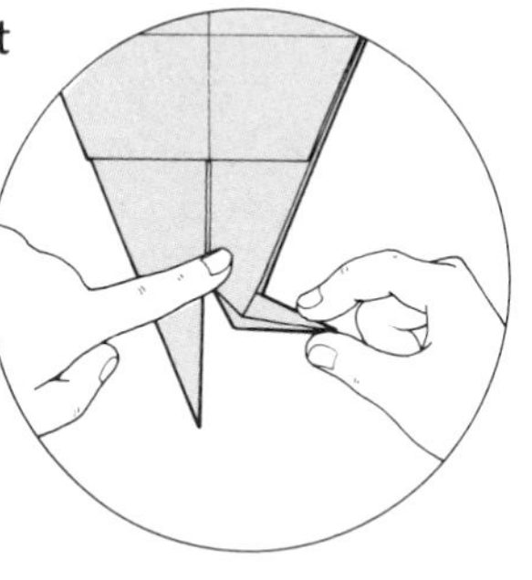

8 Fold a little of the paw back inside itself.

9 Repeat steps 5 to 8 with the bottom left-hand point.

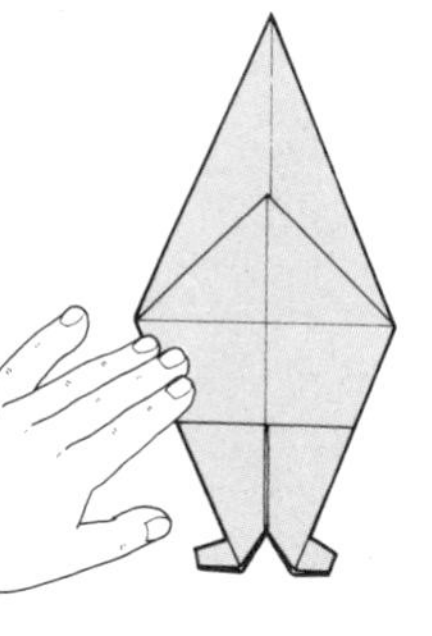

10 Turn the paper over. Narrow down the top point by folding the sloping sides in to lie along the middle.

11 Pinch the top point from behind, so bringing the sides together.

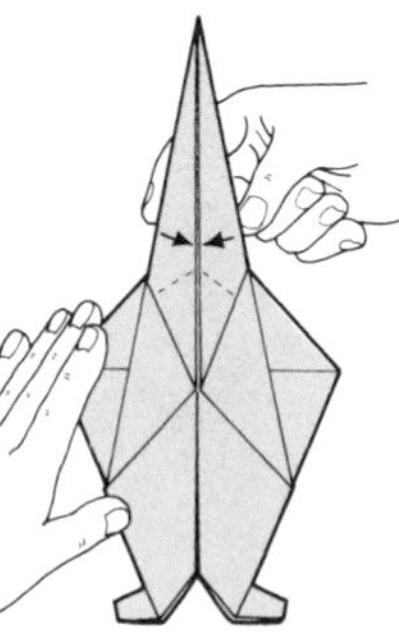

12 Bring the point down towards you and . . .

13 fold it over to the right, so suggesting the cat's tail. Fold the small protruding point down at a slight angle.

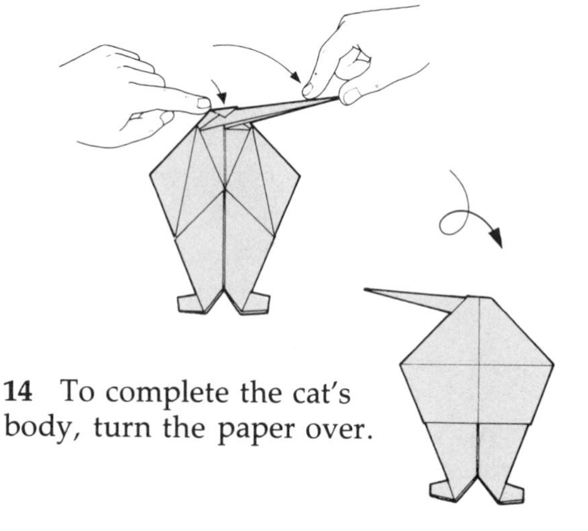

14 To complete the cat's body, turn the paper over.

15 *Head:* Turn the quarter-square around to look like a diamond, with the coloured side on top. Fold and unfold it in half from bottom to top.

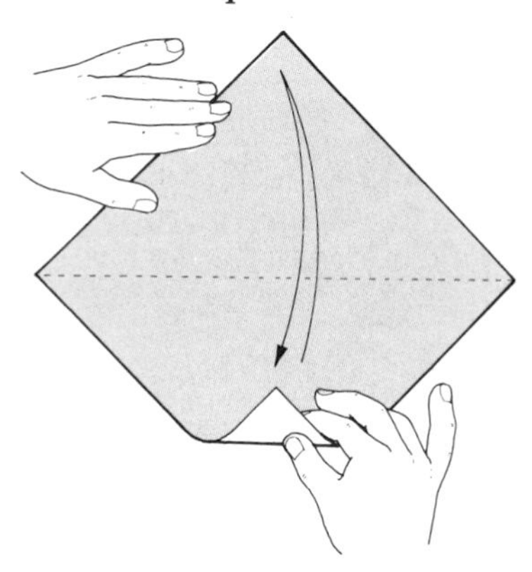

16 Fold it in half from side to side, so making a triangle that points to the left.

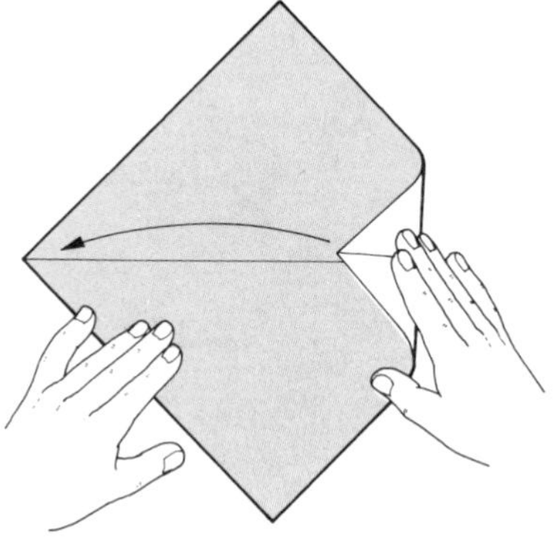

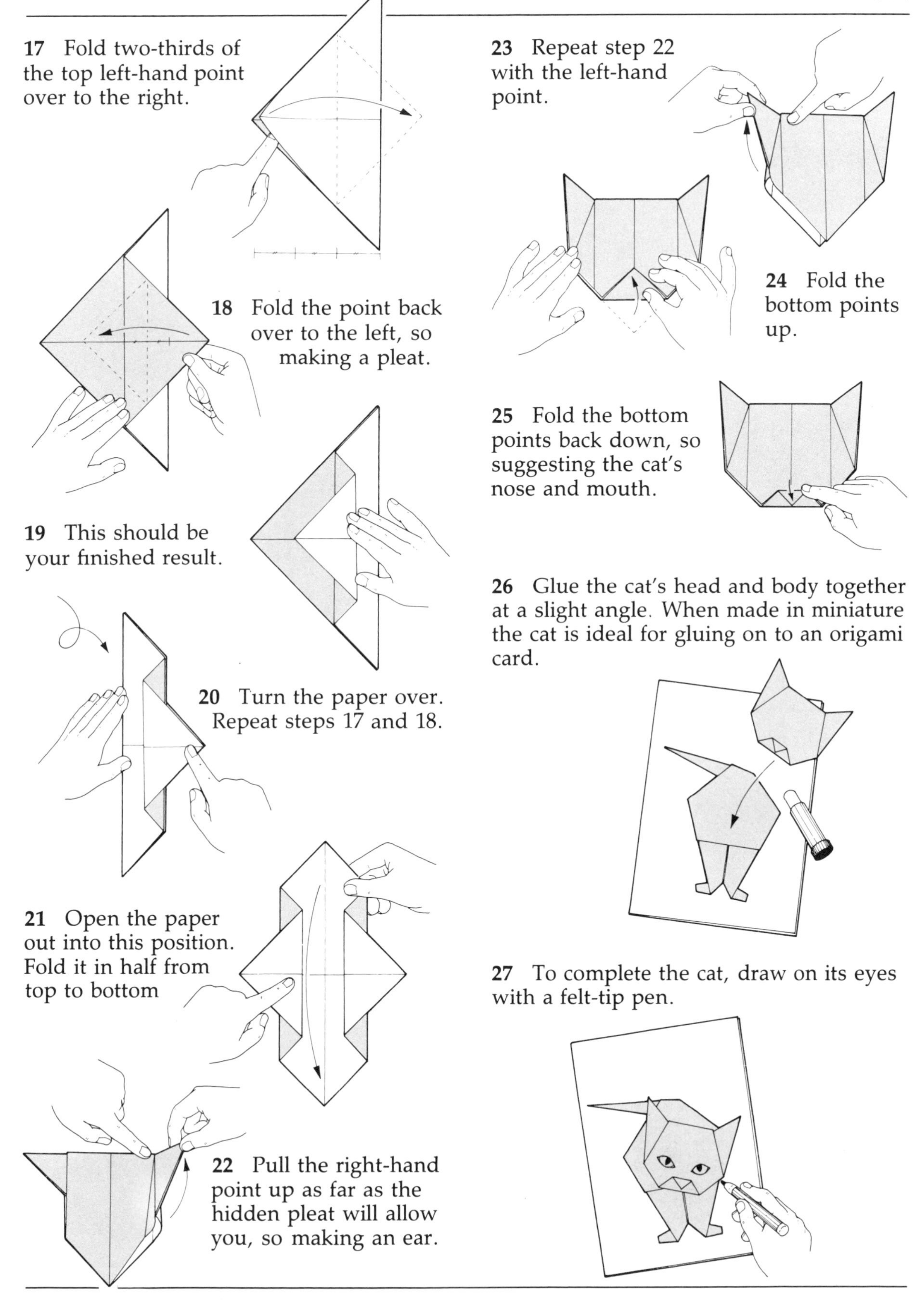

17 Fold two-thirds of the top left-hand point over to the right.

18 Fold the point back over to the left, so making a pleat.

19 This should be your finished result.

20 Turn the paper over. Repeat steps 17 and 18.

21 Open the paper out into this position. Fold it in half from top to bottom

22 Pull the right-hand point up as far as the hidden pleat will allow you, so making an ear.

23 Repeat step 22 with the left-hand point.

24 Fold the bottom points up.

25 Fold the bottom points back down, so suggesting the cat's nose and mouth.

26 Glue the cat's head and body together at a slight angle. When made in miniature the cat is ideal for gluing on to an origami card.

27 To complete the cat, draw on its eyes with a felt-tip pen.

Jewel unit-fold

Toshie Takahama

All of the following folds are based around this very easy unit-fold. Try making them in several different colours to vary their finished appearance.

You will need:
Square of paper, coloured on one side and white on the other

1 Fold and unfold the square in half from side to side, with the white side on top.

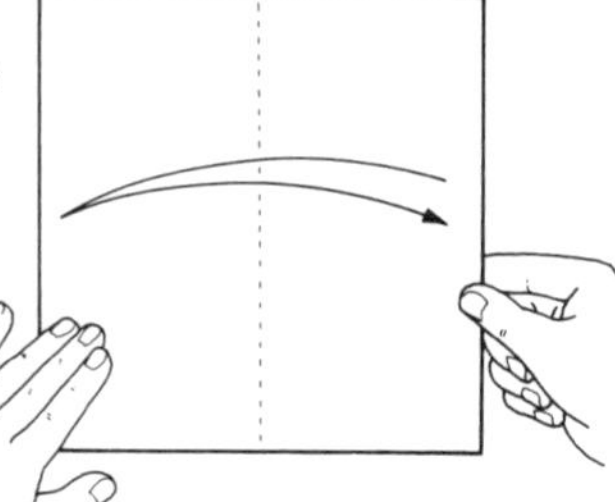

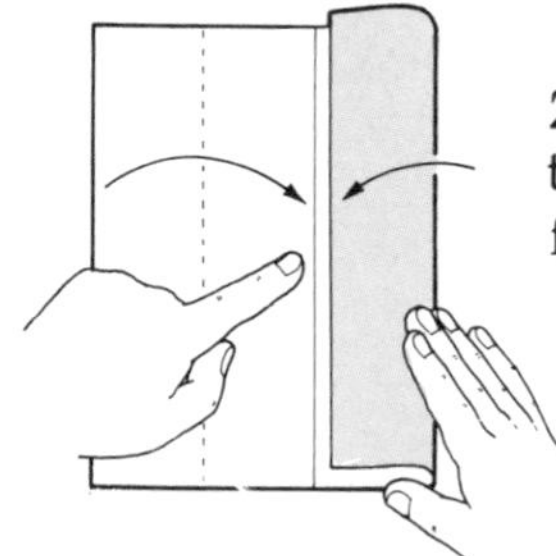

2 Fold the sides in to meet the middle fold-line.

3 Fold the bottom right-hand corner up, so that it lies along the left-hand side. Fold the top left-hand corner down, so that it lies along the right-hand side.

4 Press the paper flat. Unfold the last two folds.

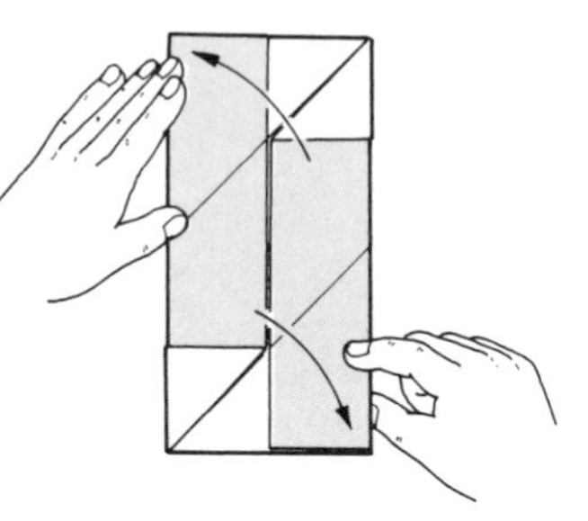

5 Repeat step 3, but tuck the bottom right-hand corner underneath the left-hand layer of paper, and the top left-hand corner underneath the right-hand layer.

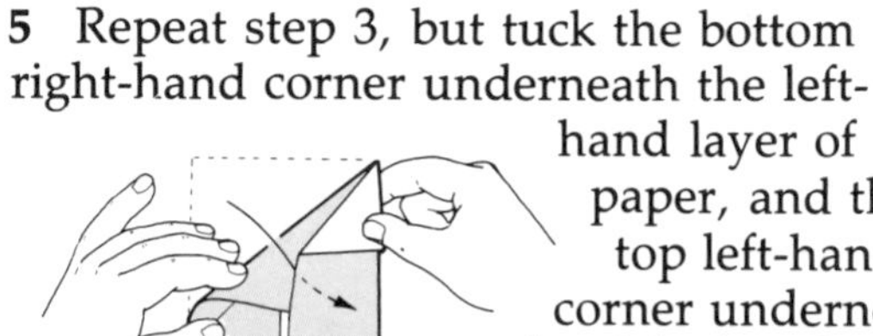

6 Fold the top and bottom flaps back and tuck them inside.

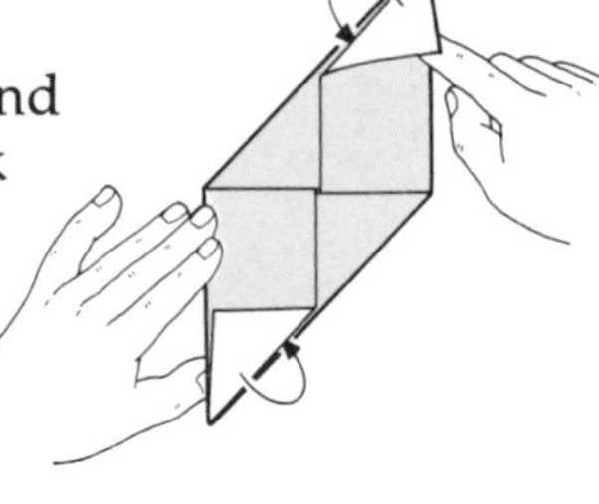

7 Turn the paper over. Fold the top and bottom triangular points in. Press the paper flat.

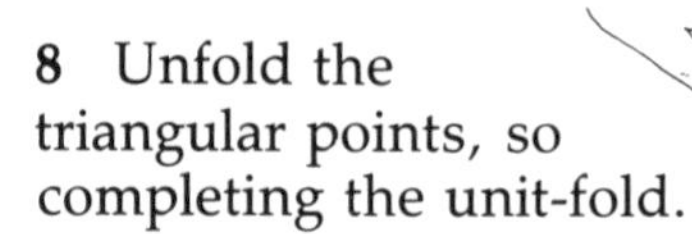

8 Unfold the triangular points, so completing the unit-fold.

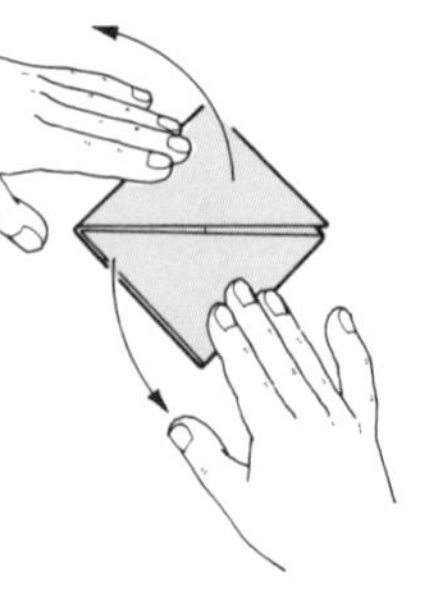

Coaster

Traditional

To help you understand what is happening with this and all the other unit-folds that follow, we have shaded in each new unit as and when it is tucked into place.

You will need:
2 squares of paper the same size, coloured on one side and white on the other
Pencil
Needle and cotton

1 Fold each square into a unit-fold (see page 90). As a help during the assembly, label them A and B, with the pencil. Turn unit B over.

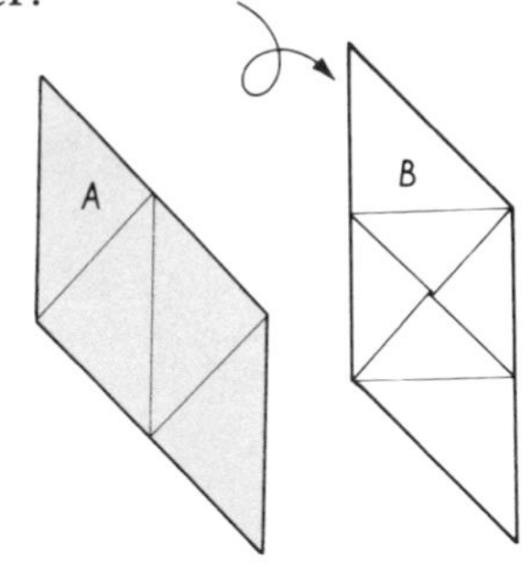

2 Turn unit A around on to its side. Place units A and B back-to-back crossways.

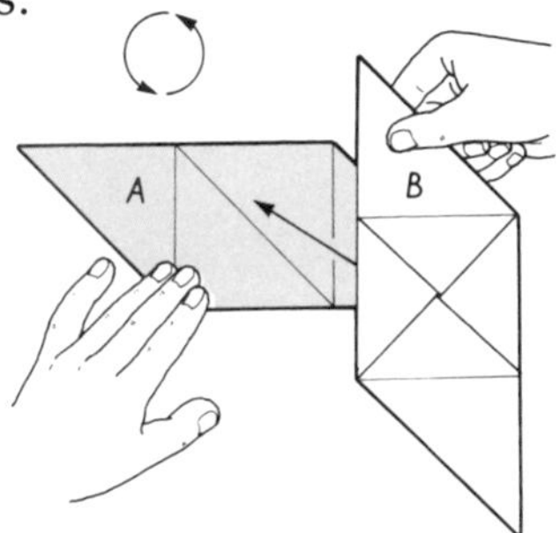

3 Tuck the two triangular points of unit A inside unit B.

4 This should be your finished result.

5 Turn both units over. Tuck the two triangular points of unit B inside unit A.

6 Here is the completed coaster.

7 Make a few more coasters and thread them together to make a very effective mobile.

8 The coaster also makes an ideal place mat.

Decorative cube

Traditional

This is a little more complex than the previous fold. But with a little patience it can be made very easily.

You will need:
6 squares of paper all the same size, coloured on one side and white on the other
Pencil

1 Fold each square into a unit-fold (see page 90). Turn all the units over. As a help during the assembly, label them from A to F, with the pencil. Tuck unit B into unit A from the left-hand side.

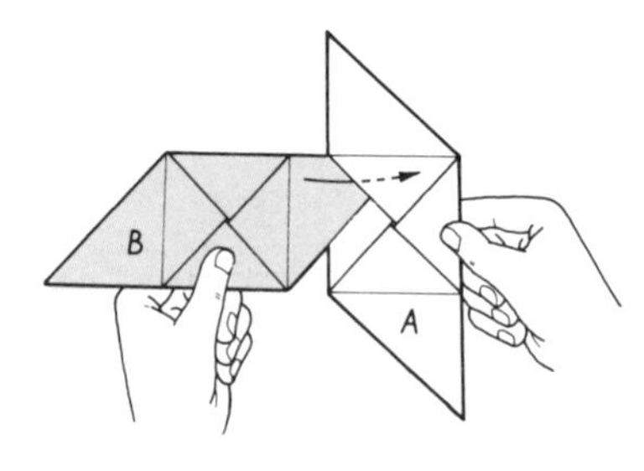

2 Tuck unit C into unit A from the right-hand side.

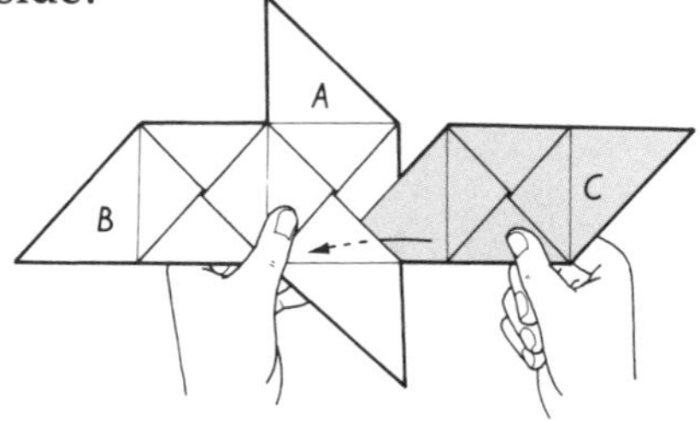

3 Tuck unit A into unit D from below. Tuck unit D into units B and C, so that . . .

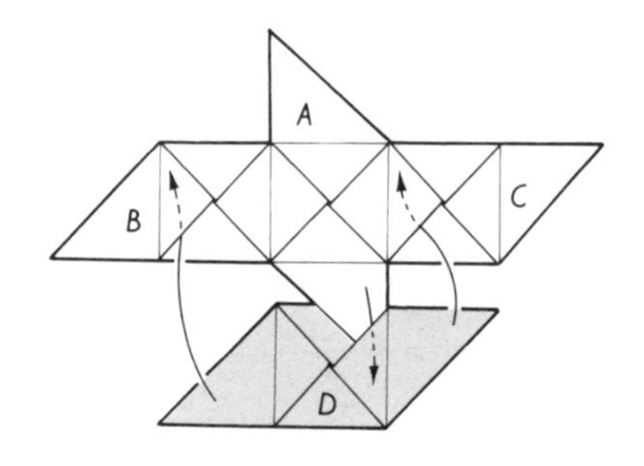

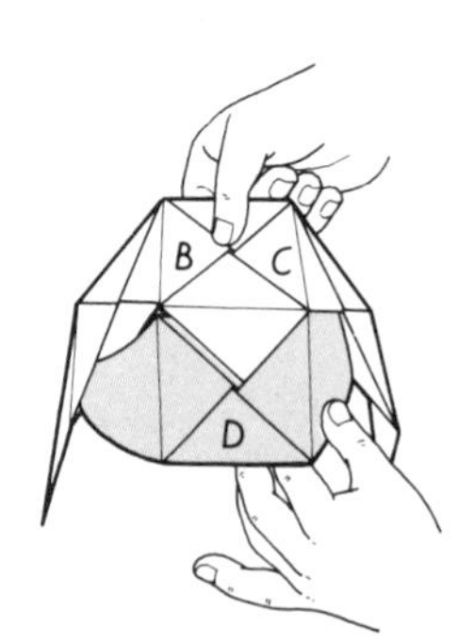

4 the units become three-dimensional.

5 Turn the units around. Tuck unit A into unit E. Tuck unit E into units B and C.

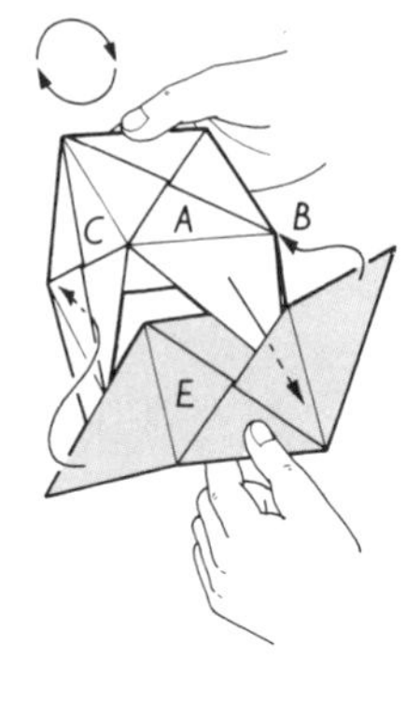

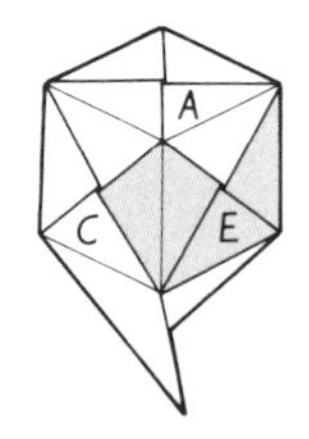

6 Almost there.

7 Turn the units over. Finally tuck units B, C and F into place, so completing . . .

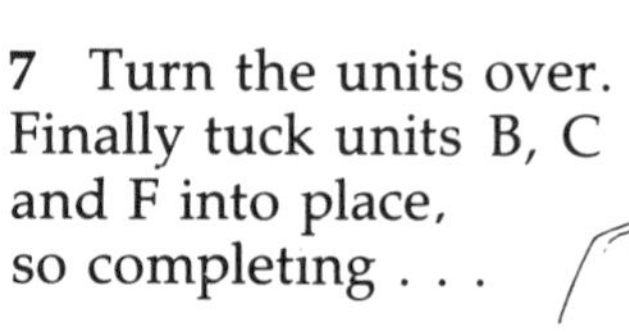

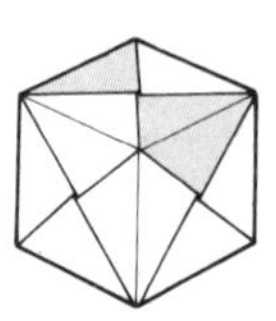

8 the decorative cube.

Pop-up jewel

Toshie Takahama

Just like the decorative cube, this fold is very easy to make and only needs a little patience.

> **You will need:**
> 3 squares of paper all the same size, coloured on one side and white on the other
> Pencil
> Needle and cotton

1 Repeat steps 1 to 7 of the unit-fold on page 90 with each square. Turn all the units over and fold them in half along their diagonals.

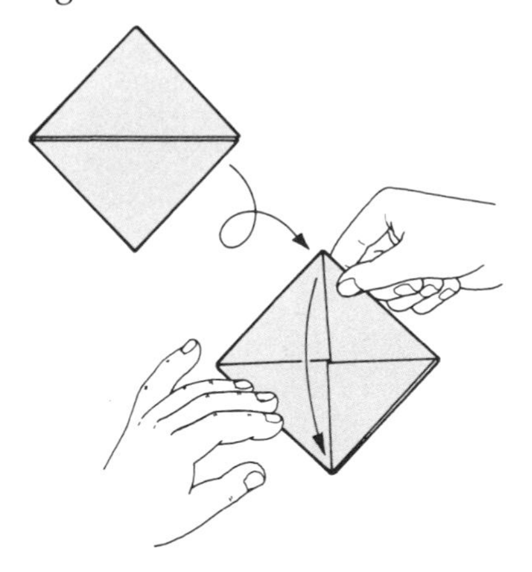

2 Press each unit flat. Allow them to open out a little.

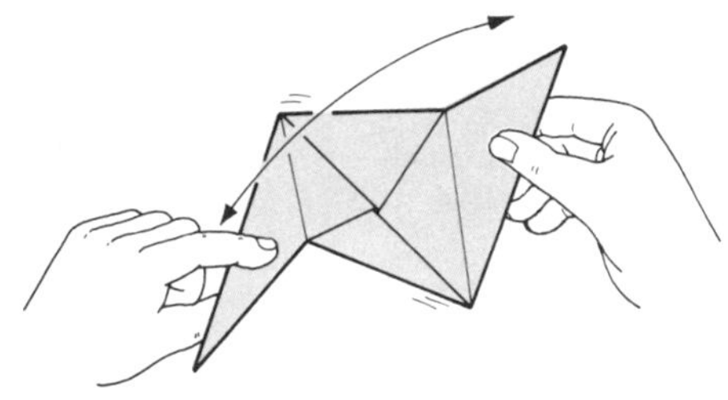

3 As a help during the assembly, label each unit from A to C, with the pencil. Tuck units A and B together

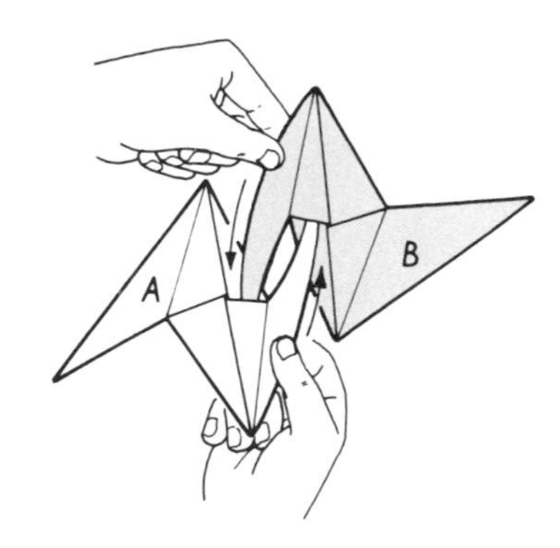

4 Tuck units B and C together.

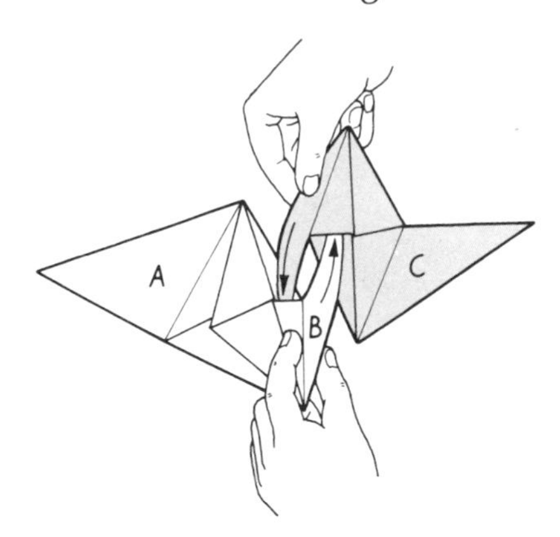

5 Almost there.

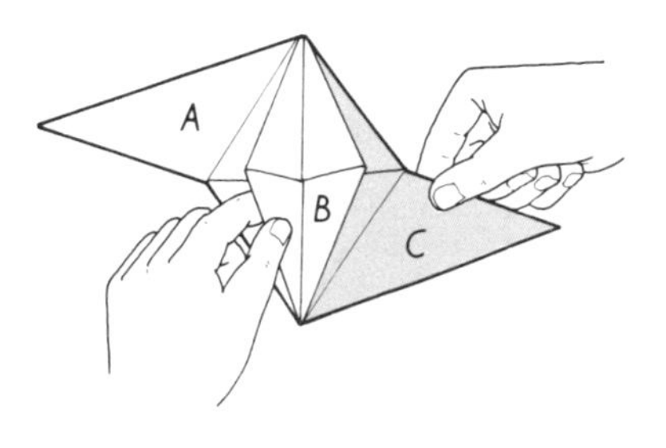

6 Swing the free triangular point of unit A round behind.

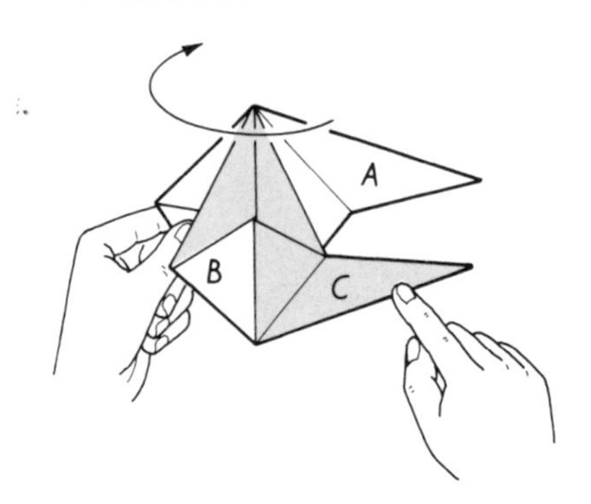

7 Finally, tuck units A and C together, so interlocking all three units.

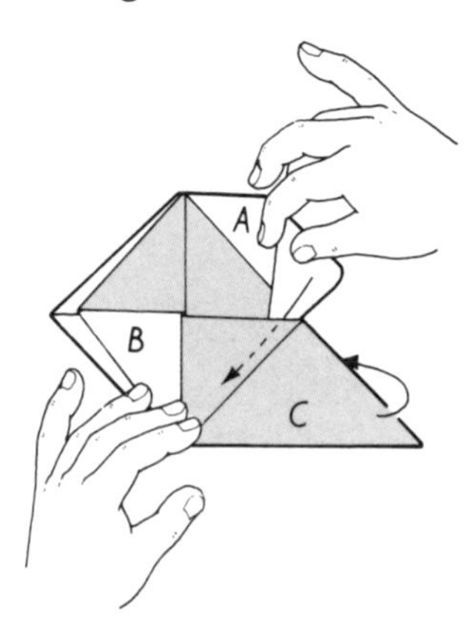

8 Hold the top and bottom points between your palms.

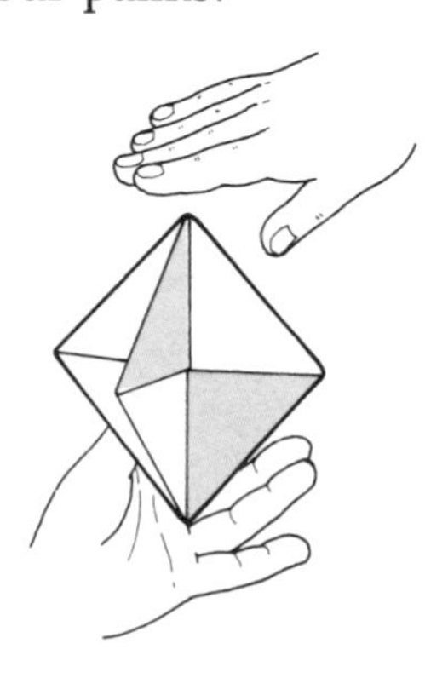

9 Carefully press them towards each other and the jewel will pop into place.

10 Make a few more and thread them together for a very colourful decoration.

Multiplex challenge

Traditional

Please do not attempt this challenging piece of origami until you understand how the previous unit-folds tuck together. As always, follow the illustrations very carefully.

You will need:
12 squares of paper all the same size, coloured on one side and white on the other

1 Repeat steps 1 and 2 of the pop-up jewel on page 93 with each square. Tuck one unit inside another.

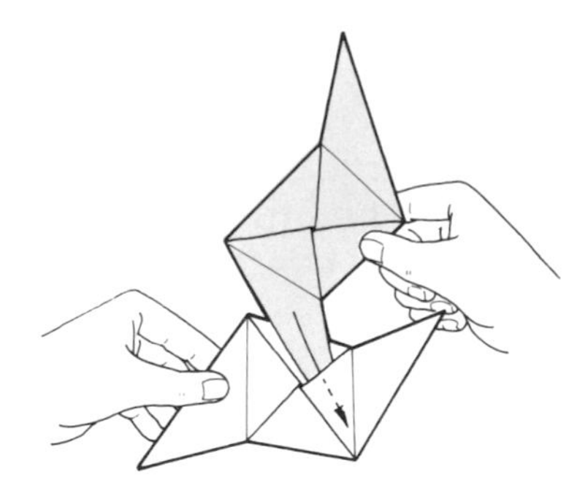

2 Tuck the third unit into place, so making them three-dimensional.

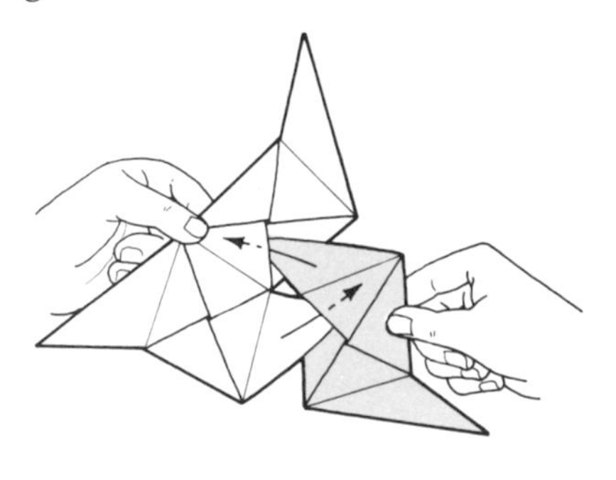

3 Tuck the fourth unit into place. This one is easy.

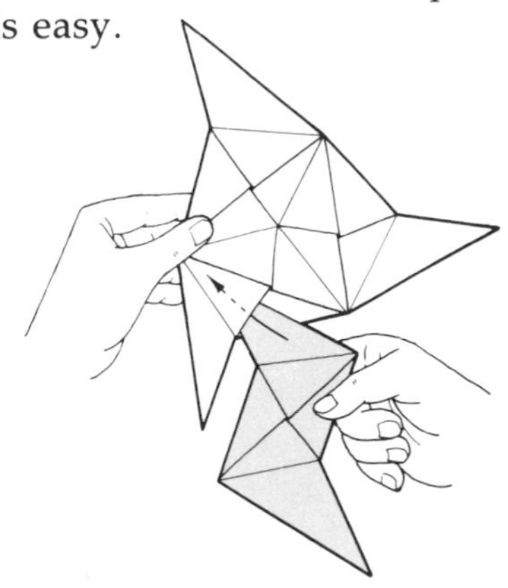

4 Following the illustration, carefully tuck the fifth unit into place.

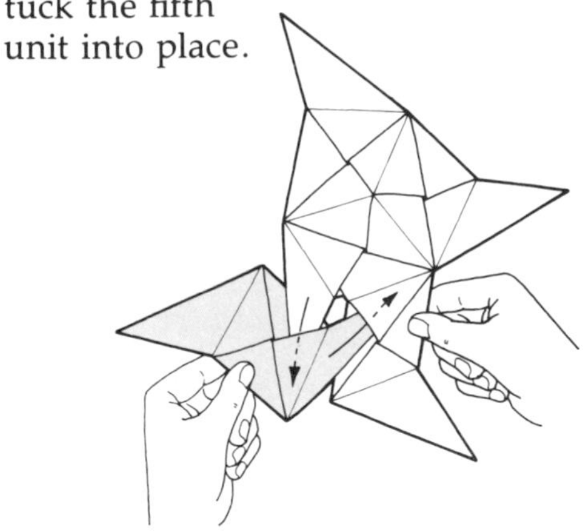

5 Tuck the sixth unit into place. You are now halfway to completion.

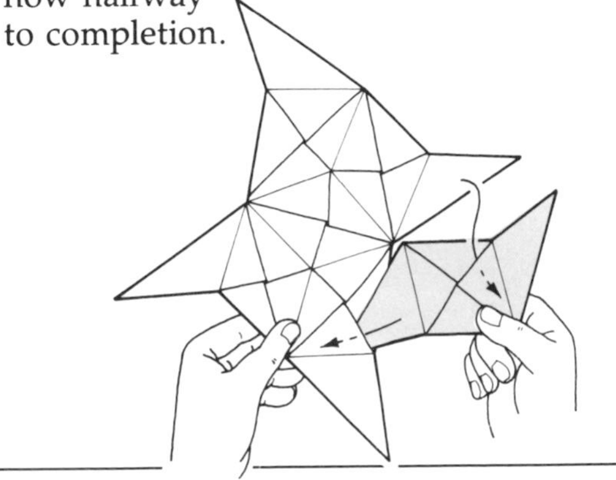

6 With a little patience, tuck the seventh unit into place.

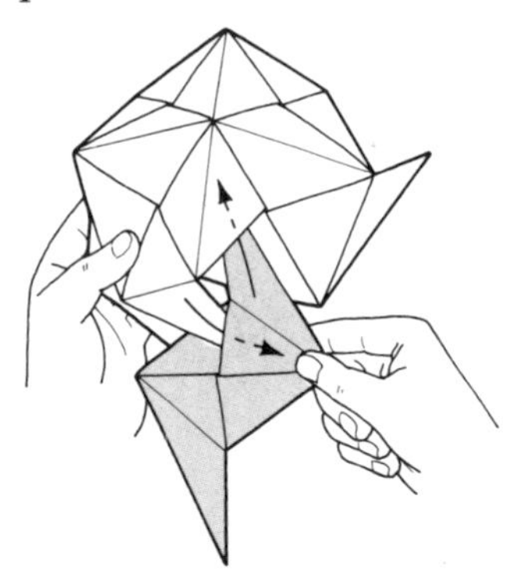

7 Turn the units around. Tuck the eighth unit into place.

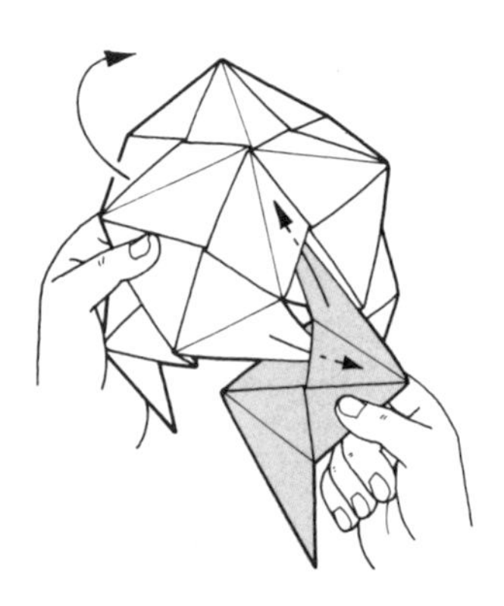

8 Carefully turn the units over. Tuck the ninth unit into place.

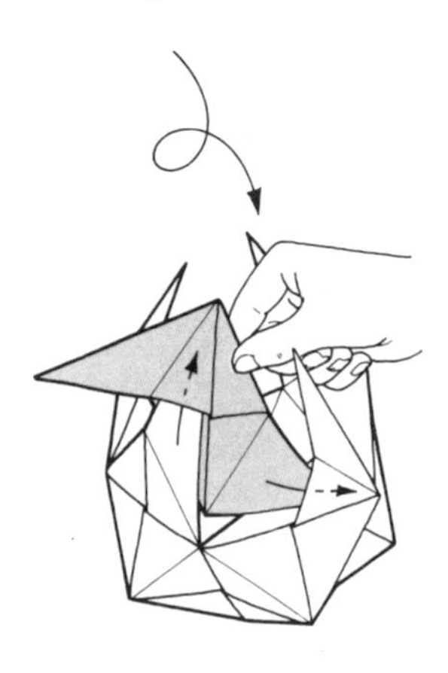

9 Tuck the tenth unit into place. Don't give up – you are nearly there!

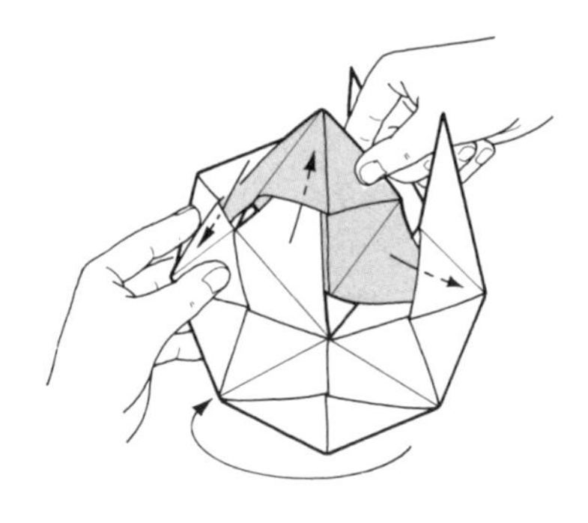

10 Tuck the eleventh unit into place.

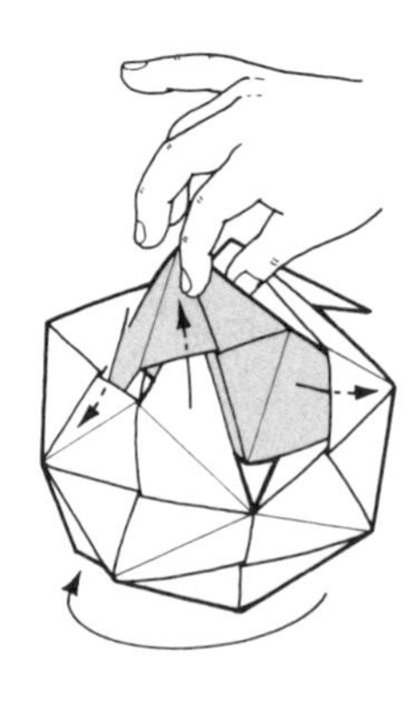

11 Finally, tuck the twelfth unit into place, so completing the multiplex challenge. Did you find this piece of origami a big enough challenge for you?

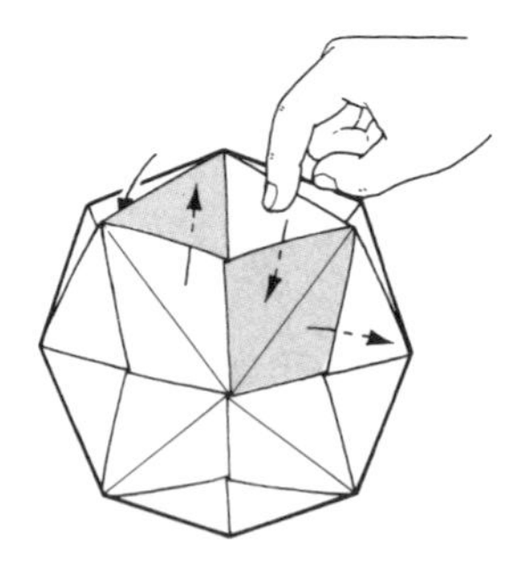

Remember that the real secret of origami lies in the giving and sharing with others. We do hope that you have had a lot of fun and enjoyment with *Amazing Origami for Children*.